Mango Tree Musician

Mango Tree Musician
The Carlos Garnett Autobiography

Carlos Garnett *with*
Jaime J. Ortiz

McFarland & Company, Inc., Publishers
Jefferson, North Carolina

LIBRARY OF CONGRESS CATALOGUING-IN-PUBLICATION DATA

Names: Garnett, Carlos, author. | Ortiz, Jaime J., 1983– author.
Title: Mango Tree Musician : the Carlos Garnett autobiography / Carlos Garnett, with Jaime J. Ortiz.
Description: Jefferson, North Carolina : McFarland & Company, Inc., Publishers, 2024. | Includes index.
Identifiers: LCCN 2024032047 | ISBN 9781476690247 (paperback : acid free paper) ∞
ISBN 9781476655055 (ebook)
Subjects: LCSH: Garnett, Carlos. | Saxophonists—United States—Biography. | Jazz musicians—United States—Biography. | Panamanian Americans—Biography. | LCGFT: Autobiographies.
Classification: LCC ML419.G365 A3 2024 | DDC 788.7/165092 [B]—dc23/eng/20240712
LC record available at https://lccn.loc.gov/2024032047

BRITISH LIBRARY CATALOGUING DATA ARE AVAILABLE

ISBN (print) 978-1-4766-9024-7
ISBN (ebook) 978-1-4766-5505-5

© 2024 Ana Maria Gaskin de Garnett and Jaime J. Ortiz. All rights reserved

No part of this book may be reproduced or transmitted in any form or by any means, electronic or mechanical, including photocopying or recording, or by any information storage and retrieval system, without permission in writing from the publisher.

Front cover image: Carlos Garnett (Photography by Michael Wilderman/jazzvisionsphotos, used with permission)

Printed in the United States of America

McFarland & Company, Inc., Publishers
  Box 611, Jefferson, North Carolina 28640
    www.mcfarlandpub.com

To Ron Warwell, Pisces Soul Brother ·360·

Table of Contents

Preface by Jaime J. Ortiz — 1

PART 1. PANAMA ROOTS

Up from Paraíso	5
The Gay Crooners	14
Black Majesty	19
Isthmus Conquered	24
Up from Panama	25
The Baby Grand	28
Poughkeepsie Swinging	30
Leo Price Is Right	32
Guns of Freeport	38
Coughing Lungs	40
The Drug Dealer's Girlfriend's Sax	43
Willie Bobo and the Blue Coronet	44
Giggin' with Freddie Hubbard	46
Art Blakey and the Jazz Messengers	51
Lifting My Voice with Andrew Hill	53
Messengers in Japan	55
Mingus Times	60
My African Queen	61
Roy Brooks	62
First Return to Panama	64
The Universal Black Force (UBF)	65

Table of Contents

Miles Davis!	74
More with Norman Connors	83
Black Love	85
Journey to Enlightenment	92
Let This Melody Ring On	95
The Tony Silvester Era	99
Cosmos Nucleus: The Big Band Experiment	100
The Girl at the Warehouse	105
Mario Bauzá	106
The Kidney Stone	107
The New Love	109
Roland Alphonso at the Apache Restaurant	113
Downward Spiral	113

Part 2. Life After Life

The Miracle	117
The New York State Division for Youth	122
Black Eagles	123
A Note on Self-Defense	125
No Sax Carlos	126
Slow Cook Back	128
Resurgence	130
Fuego en Mi Alma	133
Much Change	135
Back to Van Gelder's	137
Just Like Kenny G	138
Under Nubian Skies	141
The Trip to Jamaica	142
Jamaican Diabetes	145
"He Said" in Swahili	147
The Motherland via Ghana	148

Table of Contents

Moon Shadow	149
Katy, Texas	150
Mighty Sparrow and Montego Joe	151
Back to Panama, Like Mother Wanted	153
Panama Jazz Festival	155
Who's Got the Key?	157
Tearing Up the Festivals!	159
The Selecter	161
Oh No, Rubén	163
Ana, My Purum	164
Sonny Rollins, My Brother	165
"La Magnolia"	169
Sheila	169
If Joe Lovano Says So…	171
From Continent to Continent	172
A Panama Jazz Festival in My Name	173
Unlimited Creative Imagination	174
An Unforgettable Return to Japan	175
Shekinah's Smile	178
"Derrame Leve" (Mild Stroke)	179
The Salvation Army	182
The Diggers Descendants	185
In the Latter Years…	187
Mr. G at the Anita Villalaz Theater	191
The Autobiography and the Pandemic	193
Let Us Go (To Higher Heights)	195
Index	203

Preface

BY JAIME J. ORTIZ

This is the fascinating saga of "the Mango Tree Musician" as told by him personally.

Carlos Garnett was blind, a frustrating disability he developed and lived with for the last eight years of his life. To get this story to you, I had to take on the responsibility of writing, investigating, transcribing, editing and most importantly motivating my dear friend Carlos to remain positive along this tumultuous journey. This book is the result of thousands of conversations (and often heated discussions) with Carlos. Getting him to trust me with his story was no easy feat.

One of the first things that Carlos came up with as we discussed the possibility of this project was the title. He was keen on naming it "Up From Panama: The Saga of a Mango Tree Musician."

But why?

Carlos liked to refer to himself as "the Mango Tree Musician" and I can certainly draw many parallels between the luxurious tropical fruit and his sweet and sour persona. In Panama, there are mango trees everywhere. He grew up climbing them and eating so much mango people would call him mango belly.

"The Mango Tree Musician" also represents him as a self-taught musician and as someone streetwise. He was very proud of what he achieved professionally, having worked tirelessly to learn music on his own. The title also symbolizes his rebellious personality, as fruit was sometimes illegal to pick from trees in the Panama Canal Zone where he grew up. He didn't care; he went on and climbed the trees anyway.

Preface

Carlos' life stands as a testament of a special part of Panamanian culture. The isthmus of Panama has always been a culturally fertile mixing pot with people from all over the world coming together and creating a unique, complex and culturally rich society. He is the product of a distinctive mixture of heritages from African slaves in the New World and descendants who settled in the West Indies and then migrated to Panama in the tens of thousands. This massive influx was due to the availability of steady jobs in various infrastructure developments toward the end of the 19th century such as the interoceanic railroad in the 1850s and, later on, the development of one the greatest engineering marvels of the world, the Panama Canal.

Panama was certainly an interesting place for Carlos and his family to grow up. The high officials of the Panama Canal Zone strived to create a tropical (white) utopia and prove to the world that they could master the inhospitable tropics and "civilize" the "barbaric people" who inhabited it. The truth is that by the time the United States of America rolled around to build the Canal, Panama was much more developed economically, technologically and culturally than they would have liked to acknowledge.

There can be no denying that Carlos Garnett's family had to raise their children within the boundaries set by the eugenic ideas of those who devised the masterplan for the Panama Canal Zone. Systemic racism was very much present, with highly segregated communities and differentiated social structures in place: "gold roll" salaries and benefits for whites, and a lower "silver roll" status for Carlos and his family.

This apparent discrimination shaped much of Carlos' personality as he always strove to prove wrong those who didn't believe in him, fostering his incredibly high self-esteem. International recognition and stardom was a complete anomaly for a "silver roll" kid from the Panama Canal Zone, but he went on to succeed.

On the afternoon of March 3, 2023, as the files for this book were finally being sent to the publisher, I got the sad news that my dear friend Carlos Alfredo Garnett Watts had passed away. Carlos transitioned at age 84, and he would have been the first person to say to anyone what an amazing achievement it was to live as long as he did considering everything you are about to read in the following pages.

Preface

Carlos was a very bright man, with an incredible memory capable of remembering details that amazed everyone who spoke to him, but even he would have some momentary lapses of reason. To get the most accurate accounts for this book, I had to conduct extensive research on my own to piece together his story and form an accurate timeline of his life's events. My findings always tended to spark a new road to explore inside Carlos' fruitful mind. Looking back, this was one of the most rewarding aspects of our project.

Carlos and especially I must be excused for anybody that we might have missed in this story or for any detail that perhaps fell through the cracks. We both tried to do our best. I certainly did what I could to pick these stories out of Carlos' brain while always trying to stamp his way of talking and thinking into the words you will be reading soon.

Part 1

Panama Roots

Up from Paraíso

I am what was known as a "war baby," as many of us were called—those born just before or during World War II. I was born on December 1, 1938. My grandfather, Alfred Uriah Garnett, was of West Indian heritage, and my father, Alfred Ezekiel Garnett, was born in Panama in a community known as "El Marañon" on June 3, 1907. My mother, Elmozine Albertha Garnett Watts, was conceived in Panama but was delivered to my grandmother, Caroline Watts, in Jamaica on August 18, 1910. When I was born, my sister Doris was 12 years my senior, the result of a previous relationship of my mother's. I was the first born to the union of my father and mother. I was named Carlos Alfredo Garnett. Although both my grandfather and my father were named Alfred, my father chose not to give me his name; he named me Carlos Alfredo so as not to have a junior, he once told me.

My brother Stevens was born two years after me. My sister Beverley arrived two years after Stevens, my brother Marvin two years later, then brother Wendell two years after that, and then my youngest brother Fernando was born two years later. Six years after Fernando's birth, my youngest sister Annesta arrived on the scene. From when I was born until the birth of Fernando, we were all two years apart until Annesta, who people called a late baby for my mother's age.

I was born in what was then the Canal Zone, in a community built for the laborers who worked for the Panama Canal Company, which was owned by the United States. This community was called

Part 1. Panama Roots

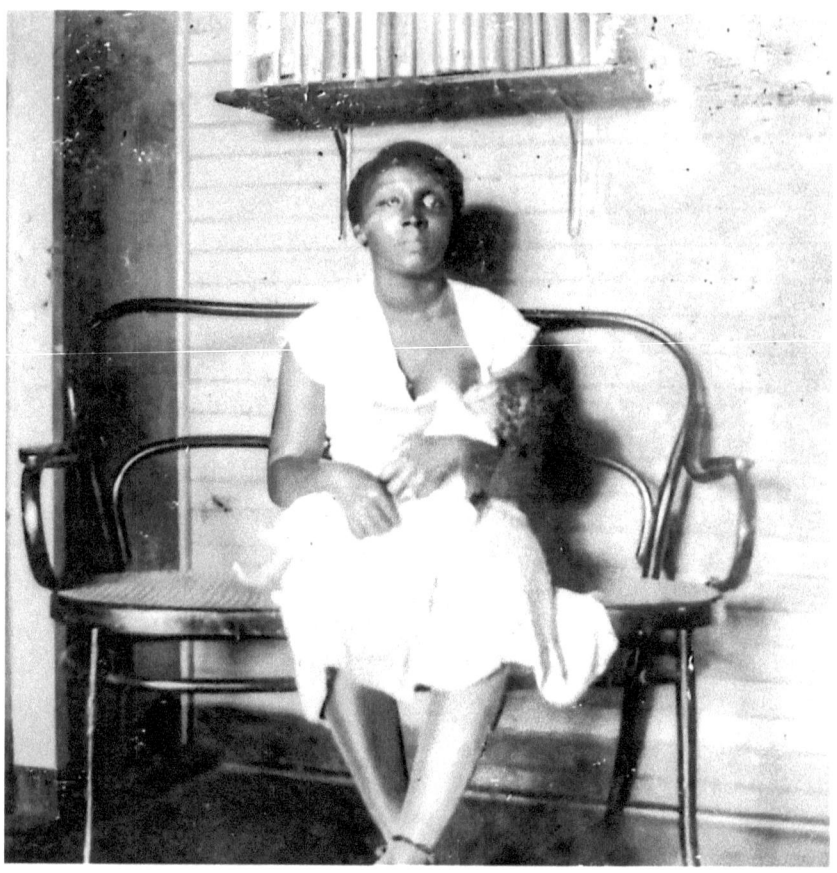

Carlos Garnett with his mother Elmozine in Red Tank, Panama, 1939 (Carlos Garnett personal archive).

Red Tank. My parents' first four children—Stevens, Beverley, Marvin and me—were born there. The others were born in a community called Paraíso. When our parents moved to this new community, I was about six or seven years old. The township of Paraíso is where I grew up and started my musical career. These towns were mostly segregated communities for Black people, or "silver roll" workers. Even though the community was mostly Black, we also had Panamanians from different descents living among us.

My father worked on the Pedro Miguel and Miraflores locks on the Panama canal for 48 years until he retired. You see, the Panama

Up from Paraíso

Canal works with a system of locks that takes boats from sea level up to almost 100 feet above and then back down to sea level. Father was what they called back then a straw boss—that is, a supervisor at the locks for the Panama Canal Company. My mother was a homemaker; she took care of everybody back at the house. She was a great cook. Back then, it was always pot roast and chicken, rice and peas, and stuff like that. A lot of times, when I finished playing, my mother finished cooking and everyone came and ate. When we moved to the town of Paraíso, there were wooden buildings all over, but the Canal Zone kept expanding, so construction workers came to build bigger and better concrete buildings. My mother used to cook, and I would carry the food and distribute it to the workers and collect the money. Everybody loved her food.

My father couldn't whistle a tune, but my mother used to play organ in the Baptist church, and I think that most of my early musical and artistic ideas came from her and from my grandfather, because he used to play guitar and dabbled in photography. Before the age of ten, I was making some form of music. As kids, many of us would wrap wax paper around a large comb and blow air through it so that it would vibrate, making a sound. Many of us had fun with that. Later, we had a toy instrument called a "Gazoo" or "Gazooka." It was shaped like a small submarine. The toy had a hole on the top in which we would place a piece of wax paper into it and blow, and the paper would vibrate, producing a sound. I still remember those toys, which were my first wind instruments.

Around the age of 11–12 years old, a neighbor of mine called Louis Gerald used to hunt deer in the woods. He would bring the deer back and skin it, wash it and hang it to dry, and then stretch it. I used to watch him doing his thing with the deer skin, for we both lived in the same building. When the skin was ready, he would attach it to a barrel of various sizes and make himself a drum we called a "tumba" or conga drum. At this point, he would hold it over a small fire and slowly turn it around to tighten it until he was satisfied with the sound he wanted. I used to watch him all the time, and soon after he would allow me to play the drums he made.

The ukulele was an instrument that the immigrants from Jamaica, Trinidad and Barbados used when they sang calypsos. It

Part 1. Panama Roots

was a favorite instrument in our community, serving as an important part of our culture. In my early teens, I learned how to play it and to sing calypso songs using it as well. My friends playing the ukulele back then were Vincent Ford, Newton Walker and Norton McNally. By watching them play and asking questions, I was soon able to play the instrument proficiently. To this day, I still have a ukulele. I have always had one around throughout my life. As a matter of fact, I wrote quite a few compositions with it that ended up in some of my best-known albums.

My father was an avid health nut and one of the founders of the Red Tank/Paraíso Canal Zone Weight Lifting Club. He was also a mechanic and usually did repairs on his car as soon as he came home from work. He often would call me or my brother Stevens to help him, but I was not interested. We would rather go and play games with our friends. Like most of the youths in our community, I loved to play baseball and basketball and was very good at both.

The name of our community was Paraíso. It is the Spanish word for "paradise," and we surely lived in a paradise because our community was in a beautiful area right by the canal. We had many fruits and vegetables growing naturally all around. Where we lived, there was an abundance of mango trees. I knew where every tree was located and would eat many mangos whenever they were in season. I remember my mother telling me that I ate too many mangos and that I would have a mango belly. Later, as I grew older, my friends called me "mango belly" and "mango king."

As youths, we lived a carefree childhood with school, games, and a lot of fun. I loved my childhood. My father, like most of the men in our community, worked daily to provide for his family, come rain or shine. My parents and their peers were strong Black men and women who suffered from the bigotry of their white racist bosses. With strength and dignity, they did what they had to do to make a good life and education for their children because work and living conditions for whites were very different from the segregated communities where we West Indians lived. Up until 1948, there existed in the Panama Canal Zone a "silver roll" and "gold roll" labor pay system in which segregated workers like my father would earn much less than white workers doing the same jobs. Schools, playgrounds, theaters, bathrooms and even the water fountains were labeled accordingly, so as a kid I couldn't go to the same places and do the same things as the white kids.

The authorities of the U.S. government in the Panama Canal were very strict when it came to plagues and mosquitos, so they routinely sprayed the entire town with DDT, which was later found out to be poisonous. Malaria and yellow fever were not common anymore, but the bosses still made sure their employees didn't get sick by trying to eliminate the dangerous mosquitos altogether. The health officials used special trucks that went all around the neighborhood and released these big clouds of thick smoke. Whenever we would hear the truck coming, all the children in the neighborhood left whatever they were doing, and when the truck passed, everyone ran behind inside the thick cloud of bug spray! I later learned it was DDT in the mosquito spray! When I think back, I can't believe the driver would allow us to do that. Were white kids also doing this crazy thing in their neighborhoods? Don't think so. They were poisoning us, and no one in the community knew about it. I would leave my food on the plate and run behind the truck for fun! I give thanks and praise to Yahweh, because a lot of people I know died from cancer. I think my longevity has to do with the fresh fruit and vegetables we used to get from the Chinese gardens and markets: papaya, tangerine, orange, cane, and much more. We always had good fresh food at our home.

We also played all kinds of games. I remember "La Queda," a game in which, using sticks, you decide who hides, and then the rest of the kids go looking for that person. We also had fun with spinning tops and another game using bottle tops called "platillos." I remember trying to move the spinning top with the power of my mind. My friends and I would go swimming a lot in the canal waters, but mostly we went to a river in Paraíso right across the railroad tracks. You had to walk about two miles to get there. The "Curtina" river, as we called it. We used to go on Saturdays and Sundays when there was no school. Swimming underwater was my thing. I'm sure that helped me with my lung strength and breathing capacity because I practiced holding my breath for long periods, which eventually must

Part 1. Panama Roots

have contributed to making my horn blowing stronger. (Listen to my solo on "Take the Coltrane" recorded live almost 50 years later. It's on YouTube! I blew my ass off for 14 minutes!)

A popular hangout for us kids was at the clubhouse, where we could buy cakes, ice cream cones, sodas, candy, cookies, and so on. The most popular spots for us were the gymnasium and the theater. It was at the theater that I fell in love with the saxophone. I remember seeing many short films with Louis Jordan and his group The Tympany Five. He played the tenor and alto saxophones, but he sang as well. He was a great musician and entertainer. In those days, he was quite famous. When I saw him playing the saxophone, I immediately fell in love with it. Another thing that I still remember very well was that before the movies started, the projector engineer would play a song by James Moody that I loved to listen to. The song was "That's My Desire." That song touched my soul, and I still can hear it in my mind even now. I was so moved by the song that I asked the engineer for the name of the artist and the song to remember it.

Like many of the youths in our community, I hung out at the gym daily, but I also excelled in many sports, including basketball, baseball, track, ping pong, shuffleboard, wrestling, and swimming. In school, I was in the glee club due to my love for music. My homeroom teacher, Mr. Cragwell, was a music teacher and also a musician. He tried teaching us how to do "solfeo," which is reading music by sight without any instruments.

One of my childhood passions was assembling toy planes. I had dreams of being a pilot. When I went to junior high school, I chose the college preparatory track, to learn the essential courses such as algebra, calculus, and so on, which were needed to be a pilot. Then one day, as I was walking through the school lobby, I saw my god-sister, Elma Stewart, walking with a violin, and I asked her how she got the instrument. She said that she was in music class. She told me that I had to take general courses to be able to apply for the music class. I went immediately to the principal, Mr. Ellis Fawcett, and asked for a transfer to general courses.

The music teacher, Mr. Gilberto Perez, was an accomplished violinist and virtuoso who was known all over Latin America. He was

Up from Paraíso

very involved in the local music scene with groups that played mostly traditional Panamanian music. In his class, he wanted me to play the violin; I told him that I wanted to play the saxophone, but he said that they had enough students already assigned for the saxophone. Then he suggested the trombone, and again, I refused. I presume that through my insistence on learning how to play the saxophone, he finally agreed, and I was given a beat-up alto saxophone to use in the school band. That was what I wanted desperately to play, and the rest is history.

I started attending school in the town of La Boca because the Paraíso school was being renovated. When it was my turn to carry the sax home for the weekend, the first song I learned was an old spiritual tune that I heard in church; it was called "Abide with Me." At this time, I was using an old reed and a school mouthpiece, and I made a lot of squeaking sounds. My neighbors and friends used to tease me, saying that I was playing lots of blue notes. Still, I continued to practice every chance I got before going to school or to music class. To practice, I used to go in the bathroom at home and close the door to not bother anyone. When my father came in, he would tell me, "Carlos, take that confounded noise downstairs!" I was upstairs practicing, and I guess the noise was too much, so he would ask me to go under the house and rehearse there. (You see, a lot of houses in the Canal Zone were on stilts and stood above the ground, so they had an open downstairs area.) I was so invested in playing the saxophone that I remember one day skipping school to stay home and practice. Little did I know that people in my classroom could hear me practice because the school was close enough to my home. Ironically, it was the school's instrument too!

I was a very athletic youngster and excelled in many sports like basketball and wrestling, but I was a star at baseball. I was a pitcher and center fielder and swung a good bat. Our team was one of the best in the Canal Zone, and we won many championships. I played for the Twin City Team (so called due to the fact that the team had youths from both the Red Tank and the Paraíso communities).

I remember one game when we were playing for the championship against a rival team from the town of La Boca. The game was on

Part 1. Panama Roots

the line, and we needed some runs to win because we were down by two. I came up to bat with runners on first and second base, and my father shouted from the packed grandstand, "If you don't hit a home run, you will get no rice." Whack! I hit a home run and became the game's hero even though I didn't like rice. They could never find that ball. To this day, some of my friends remember and tease me about that game. My brothers and friends thought I would become a professional baseball player, but I chose music. Good memories!

I was also on the basketball team and could shoot long-range shots from outside the free throw line, and sometimes from half court. Most of my teammates would drive down the middle closer to the basket to score, which I also did for a while until I realized that I got too many blows, so I decided to stop penetrating the defense and became a good free throw shooter. Years later, when I moved to Brooklyn, my mother gave me a certificate that I had won for shooting. I placed seventh out of all the schools in Paraíso, Gamboa, La Boca and Rainbow City. I had forgotten that I had won this prize, but my mother, bless her heart, had saved it for me. I still have it somewhere in the house. When I was in high school, the awards kept coming, and I was voted most likely to succeed, most talented and the best dressed. The confidence in my ability to excel in whatever I wanted was on the rise.

As far as music went, my experience in Mr. Perez's music class was not what it should have been. My impression of him was that he was interested only in the good wages that he earned as an employee of the Canal Zone government. He showed me the basic finger positions and nothing else. It was nothing deliberate from him, I guess, but most likely a product of conformity. He showed us just enough to play the marches and songs for the school programs, and I really did not learn anything else useful from him, though I did make some long-lasting friendships with other students in the music class. There was Sol Atkinson on trumpet and Roberto Martinez on alto sax. There were many others whose names I cannot remember. By then, I knew that I wanted to switch eventually to the tenor sax.

Whenever we had study periods or lunch breaks, some of my friends and I would meet in the study hall and play songs while the other students would sing and dance. Some of the students were not

Up from Paraíso

in the music class but had learned to play their different instruments at home or elsewhere. There was Elma Stewart or Eric "Midget" Townsend on the piano, Herrington "Boza" Thousand on congas, Sol on trumpet, Roberto on alto sax, me on the tenor, Ernest "Prince" Blades on bass, Carlos Prescott on bass drum, and others whom I cannot recall.

We did this jamming thing very often. Soon we were asked to perform at some of the school affairs and dances, where I was chosen as the band leader. I did most of my practicing in our bathroom at home every day and did not want to stop. My father used to tell me to be careful because I would surely burst a vein from so much blowing. Later in my budding career, when I was already one of the most popular saxophonists in Panama, he would proudly tell his friends, "That's my boy."

When I began to sound better on the sax, one of my friends, Vincent Ford, invited me to his house to listen to some jazz. He mostly played jazz from the West Coast, such as Stan Getz, Dave Brubeck with Paul Desmond on alto sax, Shorty Rogers (trumpet), Phil Woods (alto sax), Zoot Sims (tenor sax), the Stan Kenton Big Band and many other musicians from that era. I was hooked on the creative aspect of this music, so every day, after I practiced, I would go to Vincent's home and listen to jazz and read the information that was on the back of the album covers.

Even though I could not write or read music, I created a song for our gang (which we all called the "Down the Road Gang"). The title of the song was "Club Excellos," and it went over big with my group. Some of my friends still remember that song after 50 years. My friend Prince Blades would bring it up when we saw each other! I had forgotten all about it.

There were many great bands and musicians in Panama in that era, and because I love to dance, I frequented many dances not only for dancing but also, and most important, to listen to the music and watch the bands. I used to leave my girlfriend at the table and walk over to the bandstand and watch the sax sections. No matter what band was playing, there I was. When the band took breaks, I would go to the sax players and ask them to show me what all the keys were and what each did exactly. Remember, the music teacher in school did not teach me much—just the finger positions to play certain marches for the different school activities.

One such sax player who took the time to explain and showed me things on the horn was Carlos Francis, who has remained my friend for over 50 years. When I met him, he was playing tenor saxophone. He is a good brother, and I love and respect him to this day. Another young saxophonist from that era who invited me to his home and took time to help me was Reggie Johnson. One time, while chasing my first wife, I was dancing to a big band that included Reggie. I went over to him and introduced myself, telling him I liked some things he was doing on the horn. He then told me to come by his house in the "El Marañon" neighborhood. I did so and paid repeated visits to him for a couple of Sundays. Reggie explained some of the keys, as well as different positions. Twenty years later, when I came back to Panama from the United States for the first time in many years, Reggie came over to me, and this time he was asking all the questions!

Reggie was around my age, but back then he was out there playing with some of the big orchestras of the day. He was already doing what I wanted to do, which was to solo in a band or orchestra. There he was, doing some fantastic work as a young man. I remember so well that I would be dancing with my girlfriend listening to his solos, which I enjoyed very much.

By then my older sister Doris had bought me an old Buescher alto sax. This gift enabled me to stop using the school horn and to start making money in the city as a musician. It was an old instrument that needed a lot of repairs, but I did not mind because I finally had my own horn and continued to progress significantly. She got the sax from this kid, Chino Williams, Jr., who was the son of a famous Panamanian Olympic cyclist with the same name.

The Gay Crooners

The most popular vocal quartet in Panama during these times was called the Gay Crooners. (In those days, circa 1956, the word

The Gay Crooners

"gay" meant happy, merry, and so on.) All of them were from Gamboa, another town by the Canal Zone, but much farther away. My good friend Rudolph "Lefty" Charles was a singer with this group. He knew me and had heard me because his aunt lived behind my house. Lefty recommended me to his bandmates and convinced them to let me join the group. They accepted, and this invitation opened a lot of opportunities for me. We began rehearsing together, and soon enough I had my first shows with them. My abilities as a soloist had improved a lot thanks to all the jazz I was listening to, along with all the information on the instrument I was getting from fellow horn players, not to mention my obsession with rehearsing.

As part of the show, two of the band members of the Gay Crooners would lift me up while I was soloing and throw me to the other two, something the audiences always loved. I wasn't too fond of this routine, but I had no choice. I guess an important part of the show was doing all kinds of crazy acrobatic antics while soloing with my alto sax. I was using rubber bands as springs. I remember playing many times when the G-sharp key would get stuck, and I had to pull it back as fast as I could while playing. With the Crooners, I would play the horn under one leg, under two legs, switching legs and dancing, and other pranks. It was crazy, but, again, the audience loved it! At the same time I joined the group, the Gay Crooners added a female singer called Violet Proverbs. With the addition of Violet and me, the group got even more popular. We performed at all of the best nightclubs in town; eventually, we got to the point that we began to produce our own shows and always packed the theaters. My favorite part was that I was becoming very popular in the process.

Inside the Gay Crooners group, four members were what we called "congolee," which is when Black people press their hair to look like white people. One of the band members was not "congolee." That was Carlos Garnett. I did not go that way. Many were frying their hair to make it straight, but not me. I wore my afro proud.

One of Panama's legendary musicians, Mr. Victor Boa, had a jazz quartet, and I went to see them play all the time. Victor was a great pianist, composer, arranger and orchestra leader. His band had my friend Carlos Francis on tenor sax, Cecil Leacock on bass, and Junior

Part 1. Panama Roots

Walker on drums. They performed every weekend at a club above the "Encanto" theater. This locale had various names: it was also called Club 24, the Elks, and so on. I usually checked them out when I finished performing with the Gay Crooners.

Victor Boa played all kinds of different music, but you could hear the jazz influences within his compositions and arrangements. In those days, most of the orchestras played Latin music for the various popular dances, such as the cha cha cha, mambo, guarachas, calypsos, merengues, boleros, and more. Victor played all of that stuff, but he had a unique ear for incorporating jazz elements into everything he played. I got to eventually play with Victor's group at Club 24. It was here that I first heard a saxophone "laugh." My friend Carlos Francis showed me how to do it and also how to do the flutter tongue. Victor and I never recorded during this period, but we would later. One of the shows I did with the Gay Crooners and Boa's group had a master of ceremonies (or MC) who was a top Panamanian calypsonian who went by the name of Lord Byron. Later, I would become good friends with his daughter Idania, who even got to record with me. Lord Byron was a calypso singer in the "Nueva Alegria Big Band" that also included my friend Reggie Johnson on sax.

By now, I was meeting most of the musicians in town because of my popularity with the vocal group. My friend Vincent Ford (whom I will always thank for getting me into jazz) was now playing guitar. He and I formed a group, the Vincent Ford & Carlos Garnett Combo. Our friend Newton Walker, Jr., played piano, and we had Mr. Slow Jim Turner on bass and Albert McCleary on drums. After Albert left for the United States, we got a singer/drummer named Oscar Reid. Years later, Oscar would record with a Panamanian singer called Leroy Gittens a song of his titled "My Commanding Wife," which turned out to be a hit all over the world.

Our group played jazz but also calypsos, Latin music and some of the popular songs from the radio. I believe that one of our first gigs was at a place called the Golden Gate Club in J Street. Later, we performed at various clubs around town as our popularity grew—places like the Teatro Rio Abajo, Club Maxim and the Golden Key. Eventually we became the house band for a popular club called the Sabeb

The Gay Crooners

Lounge in the city of Colón, which is on the Atlantic side of the Isthmus of Panama. My home and that of all my bandmates was on the Pacific side, so we commuted every weekend to this club. You see, Panama is very unique in that you can be by the Pacific Ocean in the morning, and by lunchtime you could be staring at the Atlantic Ocean in the Caribbean port of Colón.

There was this tenor saxophonist named Chico Thorne from Gamboa who played the fourth tenor in the sax section for the Chachi Macias Ritmo Tropical Orchestra (also known as the Nueva Alegria Big Band). Chico worked for the Canal Zone government and had a new King 500 tenor saxophone. When he could not make the gig with the Chachi Macias Orchestra because of his job, he would lend me his tenor to fill in for him. This was heaven for me! Imagine playing a brand-new saxophone after so much time playing an old, rusty alto sax ... yes, I was in heaven. Here I was, playing with the popular orchestra, mainly Latin tunes, although I had to read some music. I was not a great first sight reader—as a matter of fact, I was a poor reader, but my ears and memory are excellent, especially when it comes to music.

The guys in the sax section for the Chachi Macias Orchestra included Reggie Johnson on alto, Earl Jarvis on baritone and his cousin Raul Jarvis on tenor. They would all help me out by showing me my parts, which I then memorized. I was a very proficient soloist, and Reggie and I had the soloing duties. That was exciting for me—I loved it. Reggie and I were friendly rivals.

Working and making a decent wage for my age meant I had a lot of money for a teenager. Eager to hear more jazz, I would go to a local bar in the city named the Nueva Gloria in San Miguel. In those days, you could play six songs on the jukebox for only 25 cents. This is when my eyes were really opened to the jazz musicians on the East Coast. I began hearing the likes of Sonny Rollins, Johnny Griffin, Jackie McLean, Charlie Parker, Lou Donaldson, Dexter Gordon, Cannonball Adderley, Miles Davis, Dizzy Gillespie, J.J. Johnson, Charles Mingus, Thelonious Monk, Max Roach, Lee Morgan, Horace Silver, Hank Mobley, Wayne Shorter, and Freddie Hubbard, to mention just a few. My knowledge and thirst for jazz music increased a

Part 1. Panama Roots

thousand-fold. As a lover of jazz, I knew that I had to go to the United States to pursue my dreams of becoming a great jazz musician.

Eventually, I was kicked out of school. My graduation was supposed to be in 1958 with all of the guys and girls who came up with me from kindergarten all the way to twelfth grade. But then I started playing with the Gay Crooners and would arrive home from the shows at 7:00 or 8:00 in the morning. My classmates were going to school, and I was going home to sleep. So I was kicked out and had to graduate a year later in 1959. I was almost kicked out earlier that same year when my first wife Melvina got pregnant. In those days, the school expelled any man who got a lady pregnant from the same school, but Melvina's mother intervened and told the principal that it was not my baby. She knew it was, everyone knew it was, but because Melvina's mom said it wasn't, they did not kick me out. Now, they did go after me because of my busy musical career, and understandably so, as I was missing class most of the time. On October 25, 1958, Melvina gave birth to my first child, Chela.

I was now out of school and had to wait until the next year to finish, so I was performing regularly. My father used to take me, Vincent and Newton up to Colón, have a drink or two, sleep in his car, and wait until we finished the show to drive us back. He supported me all the way, giving me a lot of motivation, which helped me focus on my instrument. I could never thank him enough for all the sacrifices he made for me.

Back in those days, I constantly took the train to Colón to go dancing. I danced at the Station Bar, at the Tropical Club, for the carnival celebrations, for independence day. I was always dancing, and if I wasn't, then I was certainly playing music. One time, I saw Stanley Turrentine and Shirley Scott at the Esquire Club, about a block and a half away from the Sabeb Lounge where I was working. I'd go and watch them, and they came to see me! They were the biggest musicians from the United States whom I met playing locally at the Esquire Club. It was rumored that they fell in love while in Panama. I was told that Sonny Stitt had also come to Panama and performed. I never met him or saw him perform until later in New York City at the Club Barron when I was with Art Blakey. Numerous great jazz artists from the United States came to Panama to play for many years. The local scene was something else.

While performing in Colón with the Vincent Ford & Carlos Garnett Combo, I met a pianist named Roy Prescott who invited me to play with a white rock 'n' roll band called Johnny and the Hot Rods. The group was mainly young white boys whose families were stationed on military bases or worked for the Panama Canal Zone government. We played many songs from the United States that were popular at that time, like Bill Doggett's "Honky Tonk." Another hot U.S. group that had a big hit on the radio stations was Bill Haley and the Comets with "Rock Around the Clock." I knew the songs and played them with my group. They were favorites with the soldiers stationed in Panama.

Thousands of young military personnel passed through Panama at some point, and they were a big part of the success of the nightlife and clubs. I was once told that famous saxophonist Joe Henderson was stationed in Panama during that time. There was also Peter Duchin, the son of famous pianist Eddie Duchin. Peter was not a great jazz player, but many times we allowed him to sit in with us in the jam sessions as a courtesy because of his father's popularity and name. Later, when he returned to the United States, he rode on his father's fame and was doing big shows on Broadway in New York and at clubs in Las Vegas.

Black Majesty

On one of Panama's big holidays, I was at the Sabeb Lounge in Colón working with the Vincent Ford & Carlos Garnett Combo. We would play every Friday, Saturday and Sunday, and sometimes they had a guest band come perform at the club with us. This time, they brought in a popular calypso group that had some big hits on the radio stations; it was Black Majesty and the Mighty Bamboo Band. I had heard their music on the radio many times. They were from the neighborhood of "El Chorrillo," the same community where my girlfriend and first wife Melvina lived. I knew this guy, Flaco, who played the tumba drum in Black Majesty's band. Flaco suggested that Claude Morant (Majesty's real name) let me sit in and play with the band, to which Majesty agreed.

Part 1. Panama Roots

This plan was right up my alley, as I grew up singing calypso and played the ukulele all the time in Paraíso. I can't remember the songs we played, but I do know they were all familiar to me. This must have been 1958 or 1959. So, I played with Majesty, and he said to me, "Carlos, man, I like that!" I think it was the first time he heard me play. I used to hear him practice in "El Chorrillo," but I never got my horn out. Melvina lived in the same neighborhood as Anacleto, the ukulele player in Majesty's band. I used to hear them rehearse underneath Melvina's sister's place.

So, that night at the Sabeb, Majesty loved my performance alongside him so much that he said to me, "We are gonna record in two or three days, I think on Tuesday or Wednesday; you wanna record with us?" I agreed instantly. The rest is calypso history. Before I came into the group, the Mighty Bamboo Band had a clarinet player whom I had heard on the radio years earlier, but he was not with them anymore. I think we did a rehearsal before recording, but I can't recall. The recording was done at the H.O.G. Radio Station Studios near a club called "Lo Que el Viento se Llevó," not too far from the Windsor Lounge (also known as Club W).

The day of the session, they had one microphone in the middle of the room for the whole band. We would all play our instruments, dancing and singing around the mic, and I would step in closer to it for my solos. One thing that Majesty wanted from me was to come up with an intro for his tunes. Most of their music started with a guitar or ukulele introduction, but they asked me to do the intro on two of the songs, and those lines are still remembered to this day. The songs were "Mon Cherie" and "Pony," both similar and on the same key in G. Both tunes became smash hits in Panama, so every day and every night, all year round, it was the Majesty sound.

My involvement with Black Majesty led me to record another couple of singles with his Mighty Bamboo Band. One was for the Grecha label, where we did "Last Day of Carnival" and "The Good Advice." The other single we cut was for the Tropelco label, another of Panama's popular labels at the time. For Tropelco, we recorded "Miriam" (dedicated to Majesty's wife) and another song called "Black Majesty." All these compositions were by Black Majesty

"Mon Cherie" by Black Majesty and the Mighty Bamboo Band (Jaime "Jota" Ortiz personal archive, copyright Grecha Records).

himself, and they serve as proof that he was one of the most original calypso artists from Panama and in the world.

For those recordings, I had some fantastic solos mixed with jazz elements, and they became some of the most listened-to songs in those days. When I listen to those solos now, I am amazed at what I was doing then, despite not knowing any chords. I was playing by ear, feelings and heart. To this day, I remember what my friend Vincent Ford had told me when I started listening to jazz, which was to always keep the melody in your head when improvising.

Back in those days, Black music was popular. It was played on

Part 1. Panama Roots

every radio station in Panama. Grecha Records and Tropelco paid for and produced the records, and Majesty was upset that he didn't make more money. His anger and disappointment meant he wouldn't record anymore. Many years later, after I had already left for New York, I came back to Panama and wanted to see some of the guys from the old calypso scene. I ran into a couple of musician friends, including Black Majesty. I begged him a bunch of times to return to the stage. We were around the same age.

One Sunday, I remember I went to Majesty's conga player's house and Majesty was there, so I started talking to him, telling him to calm down and think about coming back because a lot of people wanted to hear him sing again, but he said, "Naw, man, Grecha and Tropelco stole my money, and I don't want to record, I don't want to perform." I told him he could own his own music, but he didn't care. At this time, his wife Miriam was ill, and, unfortunately, he never played anymore. It was a real shame because Majesty could write really good calypsos, some of the best ever.

I knew all the calypsonians in Panama and enjoyed that music very much: Lord Delicious, Lord Kontiki, Sir Jablonski, Two Gun Smokey, Lord Wymba, Swing Papa, Lord Cobra and Lord Panama, to mention a few. Calypso was big in Panama back then, and I was very happy to be making calypso history with Black Majesty.

I was the most popular saxophonist in Panama at that time, and I found myself performing with five different groups at the same time. By then, I had many girlfriends on both sides of the Isthmus, in Panama City and in Colón. No matter what, though, Melvina Butcher Francis was still my woman and the mother of my first child, Gisela "Chela" Garnett. When I met Melvina, I remember she lived in "El Chorrillo," West 25th Street. She was adopted and could go to school in the Canal Zone because of her adoptive parents' status. At one time, the Paraíso school was shut down because they were doing renovations, so that year I had to go to school in the town of La Boca. I remember looking out the window and I saw her walking, and I told my friend Saye Lashley, who was good friends with Melvina, "You know, I like her; I like her a lot." She was what I call "petit," tiny and cute, with a nice shape. I told my friend to talk to her for me, and he did. One time, we had a school party in La Boca, and Melvina came. I cornered her up and started talking to her, and after that she became my girlfriend.

When I started going out with Melvina, she had ended a relationship with this big muscle guy named Eddie, whose twin brother Franky was also a big muscle guy. I used to go daily from Paraíso all the way to the "El Chorrillo" neighborhood where Melvina lived. Every time I got to the street limits coming in, these two bully twins would come over and start telling me to get out of there and that I couldn't be messing with Eddie's girlfriend. I didn't care and kept going, because I had to go rehearse with the Black Majesty group, but I must admit I was scared!

Those muscle guys didn't know, but Melvina was friends with everyone in "El Chorrillo." Popular guys like Sorolo (who would go on to international fame thanks to Puerto Rican singer Ismael Rivera), Alfredo Payne, and, of course, the great Panamanian boxer Melvin Bourne. Melvina was good friends with both of Melvin Bourne's sisters. I knew him, too, because we rehearsed right under the steps to his house in "El Chorrillo." According to the story I heard back then, Melvin the boxer went over to the muscle twins and told them that he had heard they were threatening me and warned them, "Don't mess with that sax buay Carlos from Paraíso!" That kept those muscle brains off my ass! Afterward, they would see me on the right side of the street and would go to the left side to avoid me. Just like that, no more problems walking through "El Chorrillo" with my alto sax.

I remember one day, on the way to a rehearsal, I ran into this old man with one leg who used to play the black stick (which is what I like to call the clarinet) with Black Majesty's group. He had played in the group right before I joined. I had always seen him with some other old men sitting under the Standard Building playing checkers, so I went over to see what he wanted. He asked me whether I was the young man who played jazz solos with Majesty's calypso group. I informed him that indeed it was me. He said that he liked what I was doing, but he continued giving this advice to me: "Young man, do not let these few things get in the way of your music career: alcohol, drugs, women and ego." That was over 50 years ago, and I still remember his advice to this day. I have fought against those demons all my life.

Isthmus Conquered

In those days, there were many saxophonists in town, but none could solo like I did. I played with many jazz groups then and was always getting better on my horn. As a youth, I remember quite a few horn players who caught my attention and whom I still remember. There was a character named Bepo Dudley, a tenor sax player. He was a very short man, but I remember him soloing at dances and outings for different events. Many times he would solo using just one or two notes; he played them in various ways and had the crowd jumping. It was amazing what he could do with one or two notes. He was an exciting sax player! There was another top-notch jazz saxophonist named Gladstone "Bat" Gordon; he played alto sax. He was a great soloist of the Charlie Parker mold, a player whom I listened to and made friends with. He was about 10 years my senior. I would go and see his group with the talented trumpet player Gene White performing at the Esquire jazz club in Colón, and he would check me out playing at the Sabeb Lounge, which was not too far from where he worked. He retired from music much later. Bat Gordon and I remained friends until his passing.

Then there was Mauricio Smith, a musical scholar. He played flute, alto and tenor saxophones, and the vibraphone. His father was a professor of music and taught him very well from a young age. Mauricio was a first sight reader. For some reason, I had the impression that he did not like me. He studied all those years, and I couldn't read shit, but I was the most popular guy! I played with Black Majesty, the Gay Crooners and the most popular jazz groups. He never held a conversation with me like the other musicians did even though we worked at the same club for years. I worked at Club W (Windsor) with the Gay Crooners, and his group was the house band. Club W also had another regular group, I think it was Marcos Wilson's band. He was Alonso Wilson's big brother. Alonso Wilson was an established figure in Panama, who made quite original music mixing calypso and jazz. (His son, Santi Debriano, would go on to become a very good bass player working in and around the New York scene. Santi and I played together a few times as well. Of course, that was much later in my life.)

So there I was at the Windsor performing with the Gay Crooners, doing my antics and acrobatics, which the audience loved. Maybe that was another reason why Mauricio Smith did not like me. I knew little about reading music or theory, but I was getting a lot of praise for my playing and performances. I was always audacious and courageous even though I knew very little about reading music and yet received so much attention from the public. Years later, Mauricio and I became good friends in Brooklyn. One time in Panama, he invited me to play with Danilo Perez on piano when he was just a little guy coming up, and he was very excited to play with me. Mauricio also invited me to perform with him one time on Marcus Garvey Day, but that was also later in my life. Mauricio would go on to become a key part of my musical career, as he was part of the group that recorded my first album *Black Love* in New York City for Joe Fields' Muse Records.

During my time as an up-and-coming musician in the 1950s in Panama, most of the top jazz musicians and groups were of African, Jamaican or West Indian descent. Why the change now? That is a good question that I am trying to resolve. We had a pianist who sounded like Thelonious Monk; his name was Professor Bright. Other artists included the Pearce cousins, Terry on piano and Jerry on drums, and Ray Cox on the organ. There was also "Rubber Legs" McKindo on trumpet and many others. Later came a guy everyone called Zaggy, who was part of a tap-dancing team, "Ziggy & Zaggy." He played the drums pretty well.

Up from Panama

My great popularity as a saxophonist in Panama led to a desire to go to the United States of America to play with the greats and seek

Part 1. Panama Roots

fame and fortune. I was still a very busy man, playing with the number #1 vocal group the Gay Crooners, the number #1 calypso group Black Majesty and the Mighty Bamboo Band, and the number #1 jazz group with the legendary Victor Boa while also running my own group, the Vincent Ford & Carlos Garnett Combo.

I was a pretty boy back in my days in Paraíso. I liked using a lot of gold. I had a gold tooth, a gold chain, and a Leontine that said "Carlos Garnett" in gold letters, along with a gold buckle that also said "Carlos Garnett." On my belt there was a luke, which had "Carlos Garnett" on it with a saxophone design in the middle and then "Carlos Garnett" again in all gold letters, a gold sax and then a gold chain that went into my pocket. That was my style, and many tried to copy it, to no avail. Panamanians liked to wear a lot of gold jewelry.

There I was, getting praise from a lot of established musicians and groups. My musical career was rising. There was this guy called Roberto Mariette who would write about me as a great up-and-coming musician in Panama. Roberto was a big-time banker in the Canal Zone, and his wife was a professor. He would also later write for the *Tribune* newspaper and *The Time* about me going and making my career in the United States. People in Panama like Roberto were now really starting to pay attention to what I was doing with my career, which was destined to continue in New York. My older sister Doris had already moved to New York, so she and my mother worked out a plan for me to go there.

One time, I was playing at Club Maxim, a middle- to high-class club where you had to have real money just to be there. I was performing with the Gay Crooners, and the guys in the group came up to me and told me that they were leaving for some shows in Colombia, and then from there they would go to Mexico on a tour. They all wanted me to join them on this great tour, but I had other plans, so I told them no immediately. I could hardly wait for the time to go to New York. I wasn't going on any tour with the Gay Crooners! My desire was to go to the United States and play jazz, which was always in my mind because I loved to create, pushing my boundaries.

Before going to the United States, I pawned everything and left Panama without my gold tooth, or gold luke, or gold chain. I didn't even bring my saxophone! I wanted to arrive in New York with some money in my pockets and buy a new instrument over there. I even pawned my Florsheim shoes, black and white (also brown and white). They were expensive back then! I expected to make a lot of money playing music, so I figured I would get all that back.

Finally, everything was set for me to leave. My mother went with me to the airport, and on the way there I promised her that one day I would return to live in Panama. I boarded my flight to New York on January 31, 1962. The first stop was Florida, and I had to spend some time in Miami because there were no jet planes back then; it was a propeller plane. I arrived in New York on February 2, 1962. I will always remember that cold winter night. Snow was all over the ground, and as the car was going up Eastern Parkway, I saw what I thought was smoke coming out of the middle of the street but was informed that it was the vapor coming out of the subway vents that ran under the street. It was exciting—my first night in Brooklyn, New York.

My mom and sister had gotten my ticket from these special discount travel agencies. When they gave my mother the ticket, it came with a token that looked like a dime. She gave it to me and said that when I got to the States, I had two weeks to go down to the Selective Service Board. They made it very clear that it was important that I do so. I had no clue what this place was, but I decided to wait a few days after arriving to figure it all out.

A couple of days after my arrival, some friends of mine from Panama, now living in New York, picked me up and took me up to Harlem and showed me around. I remember being scared as they sped up Harlem River Drive. Quite a few of my friends knew that I was coming to the Big Apple and made contact with me as soon as I landed. One such friend from my community in Paraíso was Raphael "Ralphy" Paddyfoot. We spoke on the phone as soon as I got there.

When I arrived at my aunt Etta's place, she made it clear that I could not stay in her home and eat under her roof if I did not work. In my first week, I had to go out looking for a job. Fortunately, I was able to find one working for some Orthodox Jews who lived not too far from us. While working with the Orthodox Jews, I met my first

Part 1. Panama Roots

American friend, Lorenzo Reid. He showed me the ropes on the job, and we became very good friends. We hung out after work and used to get nice on rotgut wine such as Peppermint Twist or Thunderbird.

The Baby Grand

Ralphy Paddyfoot and I were hanging out one day, and I informed him that I wanted to go to a jazz club. He took me to a club called the Baby Grand on Fulton Street in Brooklyn. There was a quartet jamming there, and I was excited watching these guys play. It was on a Monday night, and, as it turned out, they jammed every Monday night, so I told myself I needed to get back there quickly.

While working with Lorenzo, I told him to take me to the Selective Service Board. It had now been almost two weeks since I got to New York. I had to explain to him how I got this token from the travel agency through my mother and how I had to go to the Selective Service Board office no later than two weeks after my arrival. I had two days left. I didn't want any trouble, especially not at the start of my journey. Lorenzo asked me whether I knew what going to the SS board meant. I had no clue. He yelled at me that if I showed up there, it meant going into the military! Going to the SS board meant you were going to volunteer to be drafted in the army. I told him that Panama was not at war, and so I did not go.

All I had in my mind was playing music and getting on stage for those jam sessions at the Baby Grand. I bothered my friend Ralphy every Monday to take me there, as I was new in town and did not know my way around yet. Since it was a jam session, many musicians came there to have fun but also to test themselves against other musicians and learn. Soon I made friends with the band members and others who came to jam. There was a tenor player named Yaya, Richard Rafique Williams on piano, William Bennett on bass, and Rashied Ali on drums, who would later go on and play with John Coltrane. It was a cooking quartet. I wanted to sit in on the jam, but I had pawned my horn and jewels in Panama before I left to have some pocket money in this new country. I needed to buy or get a new sax as soon as I could. Lo and behold, Ralphy had an alto sax that he was

The Baby Grand

not playing, and he told me that I could use it. Finally at the jam session one day, I worked up the nerve to ask them whether I could sit in, and they let me. Since I could not read well and didn't know much about chords, I asked to play songs that I already knew from my days in Panama playing by ear.

There I was every Monday night, sitting in with the guys and getting more courage and feeling comfortable in my playing as the weeks went by. It was not too long afterward that the usual tenor sax player in the band moved to Washington, D.C. To my surprise, the guys all asked me to take his spot. We were playing a lot of standards that I already knew, and if I didn't, I would listen to the records and memorize them. I was still playing with Ralphy's sax because I did not have the cash to buy one yet. I was living with my older sister Doris over at my aunt Etta's (my mother's younger sister).

Lorenzo, some of his friends and I would get nice on wine and hang out on the corners singing doo wop songs, harmonizing, and having a good time. Lorenzo lived in Canarsie in East New York, and that is where I met my first girlfriend in New York, Jeanette Bowles. They were neighbors, and he introduced me to her. When I met her, she was studying to be a doctor in Westchester County, upstate New York. She was beautiful and intelligent, as well as a lover of jazz, and we had a great relationship.

Meanwhile, I was still playing on Monday nights at the Baby Grand club, getting better and more confident the more I played. While gigging there, I met a lot of saxophone players who came around and sat in. There was Johnny Toussaint, Jimmy Heyward, Hugh Brodie and others I cannot recall at this time. Later, I met Roland Alexander, who became a very good friend of mine for many years until he passed away. Roland was one of the guys I met playing under the Bridge Street Subway, where people would gather and jam. He and Joe Henderson were tight, and Roland used to sub for Joe many times.

Across the street from the Baby Grand was a club called the Arlington Inn. One weekend my friend Lorenzo and I went there to hang out. There was a rock group called Wee Rockin' Willie and His Band. The place was rocking and jumping and filled with beautiful girls. Jeanette was getting busier at college and had no time to go out with me as her studies advanced. As usual, I was eager to play with the group, so Willie let me sit in, and I fit right into the groove, for I played rock'n'roll coming up in Panama. The group was popular, and the club was jam-packed every weekend. From the stage, I would look for a girl who I liked and set my eyes on her. On the breaks, I would seek out the girl I liked, and that's how I met Betty W., later to be the mother of three of my beautiful daughters: Lisa, Myra and Naima. (Naima was the name I later gave her because of John Coltrane's song.)

Around this time, I left another job I had at a book-binding factory but never ceased to work at other jobs. One of them was at a hydrogen peroxide plant, covering the bottles. This job did not last too long, because the chemicals were eating my fingertips away. Next, I worked for a luggage and pocketbook store, which was not bad at all. I also worked for another Jewish man and his father, and they treated me well. While working there, I was able to save enough money to send for my wife Melvina and our daughter Gisela "Chela" to come to New York.

Poughkeepsie Swinging

While sitting in with Rockin' Willie, I met an organist named Bill Scott, and he asked me to play with him in upstate New York at a township called Poughkeepsie. Since he was playing jazz and it was a three-night a week gig, I jumped at the opportunity because it meant better money. It was an organ trio playing jazz, which served as my first opportunity to play in this format. I enjoyed the gig, as it allowed me to be the lead instrument playing the melodies and soloing, doing what I loved to do. Up there in Poughkeepsie I bought my first car, a 1959 Chevrolet, with green wings in the back. Before that, I used to take a train from Grand Central Station in the center of Manhattan to upstate New York, going along the Hudson River and enjoying the view of the countryside. With my new car, though, there were no more trains to Poughkeepsie. The car was about three or four years old when my sister helped me buy it with a little loan. I remember going to the used car lot in the outskirts of Poughkeepsie and picking it basically just because I could afford it.

My older sister Doris got herself her own apartment, so my younger sister Beverley, my wife Melvina, our daughter and I moved in with Doris at her new place in Brooklyn on Sutter Avenue, East New York. Bill Scott had rented a house in Poughkeepsie, and I would often stay there while working in town with him. I have some fond memories of that town. I was well liked and respected, and folks would always invite me over to their house for dinner.

By then I had met a sweet young girl who worked as a babysitter for Bill's wife. Her name was Cecilia W., and soon she became my lover. She used to keep my bed warm, since it was very cold in upstate New York during the winter months. I also had a couple of other lady friends who dug me and treated me especially nice. In those days, I was crazy, and on some weekends I would drive back to Brooklyn after work just to party. While I was enjoying myself to the max, Bill stopped playing and moved back to Brooklyn and became a minister in a church. Before this change in his life, Bill was doing all kinds of crazy stuff. I remember one day trying something he called "peppermint bush," which was a marihuana cigarette with embalming fluid. Man, that was too much!

During the gigs with Bill, I met another organist/singer named Paul Monday. He worked across the Hudson River in a town called Newburgh. He asked me to work with him, and I accepted. I was a very happy camper, doing what I loved the most and having beautiful women chasing after me. They said that they liked my Panamanian accent, and if that is what it was, I had no problem at all.

Once I had a close call, though. One of my sexy lady friends took me to her apartment to make out and do some music of our own. This night, as we were "improvising in bed" after the gig, there was a loud banging on the door. She told me not to worry because it was her ex-husband and he did not have a key. However, the ex continued to bang on the door harder, and with each knock he got louder, shouting, "I know you are in there with somebody." By this time, I began sitting up and feeling for my big knife that was under the pillow. I always had it with me, which was a habit that I had since Panama

Part 1. Panama Roots

because I was usually going home alone late at night and had to be prepared. The guy finally kicked the door in and entered, but by then I was sitting down on the bed with my clothes on. Wisely, he said to me, "I do not have any problem with you, but I want to talk with my ex-wife alone, so please leave." He did not have to say that twice, and in a flash I was gone and thanking the Almighty Creator for protecting me, for had he attacked me, one of us would have probably died. That was the last time I slept there.

I was making a little money and was able to buy my first sax, a tenor sax out of the pawn shop. It was a Quinon, a brand that I had never heard of, but I didn't care because now I had my own horn purchased with my own money. With my new horn in hand, I finally returned the borrowed alto sax to my friend Ralphy. I had been using it for a long time, more than a year, and was very grateful to him, but I was now happy and proud to have my own. I had started to practice daily for hours (regardless of the complaints of the neighbors) and became a frequent musician at the Bridge Street jam sessions, where I met many other musicians. My next step was to play as much as I could and strengthen my technique to build my own sound on this new tenor.

Leo Price Is Right

As a youngster in Panama, I always loved women and dancing. I still love to dance even to this day. My friend Lorenzo and I would go to clubs that had live music and beautiful women. At one such place, I met a guy called Leo Price, who turned out to have a rock band. Leo was the younger brother of the famous singer Lloyd Price from New Orleans, Louisiana. Lloyd was known all over the world because of hits like "Stagger Lee," which I remember listening and dancing to many times back in Panama.

Not long after Leo and I met, I became a steady member of his band and eventually the musical director. We played at the top Chitlin' Circuit clubs, those in the southeastern states and on the East Coast that catered to the Black R&B artists who were not allowed to perform in the racist white clubs or theaters of the time. Playing in

Leo Price Is Right

the Chitlin' Circuit was a good gig for me. I was making $25 a night, playing Thursdays, Fridays, Saturdays and Sundays. Back in those days, that was a lot of money. I wasn't paying taxes then, but I did have a steady income. I had no other job and no schedule; therefore, I could devote myself to practicing all day. It was common for me to practice from 9:00 in the morning until 9:00 at night, stopping only for some water, juice and a sandwich. I was shedding mostly Coltrane at this point, making sure not to copy his licks or phrases. I was into his direction mostly, using his complex musicality to devise my own ideas.

Leo's claim to fame (according to him) was that he co-wrote a couple of hits with Little Richard, songs such as "Lucille" and "The Girl Can't Help It," but nobody knew whether that was true. Leo's older brother Lloyd had some big hits in those days, so he was well connected. I also learned that his family were gangsters in Nassau County, Long Island (this fact would come into play in my story later).

We were playing constantly in a place called the Celebrity Club, the most popular club on Long Island. It was always packed. Popular R&B, soul and rock'n'roll artists performed there every weekend, such as Gladys Knight and the Pips, Wilson Pickett, Rufus and Irma Thomas, Bobby "Blue" Bland, Theola Kilgore, Jimmy Reed, and many more whose names I cannot remember now. Later, we performed behind Diana Ross and the Supremes, Jackie Wilson and Marvin Gaye. Here I was, the Mango Tree Musician, playing behind many of the rock'n'roll and R&B stars whom I had listened to as a young man in Panama.

The Celebrity Club was an oasis for the young women who came up from many southern states to work as live-in nannies for the white folks in Long Island. The only form of release for most of them was going to this club for fun and relaxation, so it was full every Thursday to Sunday night. Any place where there are a lot of women, the men will surely be there as well. I was having the time of my life then, playing music with a popular band every weekend and enjoying a lot of women. As the band director, I always sought the opportunity to take sax solos whenever I could. Even though I was working with a rock band, my solos were always jazz oriented and funky sometimes.

Part 1. Panama Roots

While all of this was happening, I still hung around jazz clubs and among many musicians in Brooklyn. I would go to their houses or apartments and talk about music with them. I remember this Trinidadian multi-reed musician named Trevor Laurence. He had a piccolo, flute, bass flute, soprano sax, alto sax, C melody sax, tenor sax, baritone sax, and all of the clarinets; he was also a great reader. I was amazed at all of the instruments he had and his musical knowledge. One day he invited me to go to a club with him on Utica Avenue called the Fantasy Lounge, to hear him with a jazz group. The leader of the group was a drummer called Gus Johnson. Gus saw me with my sax and asked me whether I wanted to sit in; I told him sure. He asked what song I would like to play, and I told him that I would love to play "Bye Bye Blackbird." Even though I could not read music and knew very little about chords, I had played that song many times before in Panama and at the jam sessions in Brooklyn, playing by ear and memory. When I finished my solo, I received a standing ovation. My friend sarcastically asked me whether I knew what chords I was playing; he knew very well that I did not. I replied, "No, but the people liked what I did." From that very moment, I told myself that I would really get to know what I was doing musically, digging even deeper, since I had to be ready whenever the opportunity came for me to play with a top jazz group.

I began by writing down the C major scale and memorizing it and the intervals to each note relative to the other notes. Every free minute that I had, I was studying the scales. In the bathroom, in the subways, everywhere, all day long. I also bought some musical books. I was studying and practicing daily. I never thought of going to a music school, as I could not afford it. Somehow, someway, I met and made friends with a trumpet player named Mike Ridley. I was able to get Mike in the rock'n'roll group that I played with, and we became very good friends. Mike was studying with trumpet player Kenny Dorham and began showing me the lessons that he received from Kenny. I was immediately drawn to his lessons and was soon practicing with Mike every chance we could. Can you imagine that? I was one person away from Kenny Dorham now and almost learning directly from him. A direct line of communication to someone like

Leo Price Is Right

Kenny Dorham was now possible for a person like me. That made me practice harder and harder.

One of the many women I had in Long Island moved to Brooklyn to live with me. She was Lucille C., a sweet and good woman who loved me very much and who would soon carry a child for me, a daughter we called Sheila.

The place where Lucille and I lived in Brooklyn was around the corner from another musician who became my friend, a tenor sax player by the name of Claude Bartee. I think he told me that he was from Texas or something. He was a beautiful brother, and he could blow his ass off, so we became very good friends in no time. I met Claude through trumpet player Mike Ridley, and can you believe it? Mike's brother, Larry Ridley, was the bass player in Freddie Hubbard's quintet! So suddenly I was a couple of guys away from another jazz trumpet great like Freddie. He even turned out to live right up the street from Claude and a few blocks from me! In retrospect, I was placed in an environment that would have a positive effect on my musical career, considering that Claude was also a good friend of Freddie Hubbard.

Sometime thereafter, another horn player in Leo Price's rock band, called Philpott, moved to another state, and that is when I was able to get Mike Ridley in the group. Mike was still studying music with trumpet player Kenny Dorham, who was already considered a jazz great, with recording credits with the top jazz groups of that period.

While working and traveling with Leo's band, I was the only one in the band who did not get high on marihuana or anything else, other than some brandy or beers occasionally. I would tease them that they were a bunch of potheads. Mike would bring some music sheets over to my crib and show me what he was studying, and I would make copies for myself. I began to learn music little by little with Mike. By then, I was becoming an ardent follower of John Coltrane. I bought all of his albums and listened to him all day long in my apartment. I believe that I already had my own kitchenette apartment somewhere in Brooklyn. I moved around a lot, though.

We used to dress up for our gigs with Leo Price, wearing red,

Part 1. Panama Roots

green or blue sequined jackets with black lapels and black pants. We used to do dance routines while we played; I hated doing that, but a gig was a gig and the girls liked it. On any given night, I had six to nine girlfriends in the club. I had to become an accomplished liar, telling different things to each one and remembering what lies I told each of them. Madness for sure!

During the weekdays, Mike and I were always shedding. I began to buy books and records and did everything I could to learn music well. Since it did not enter my mind to go to a private teacher, I was always learning by myself. I recalled the process of how I was taught in school as a young boy: the teacher would write the assignments on the blackboard; we would then copy it, take it home, study and memorize it to answer questions the next day in school. I followed that system and was soon memorizing all that I studied. I would be watching football games, and at the commercial breaks I would look at my notes to memorize and practice them all day while also listening to John Coltrane and other saxophonists.

The *Thesaurus of Scales and Melodic Patterns* by Nicolas Slonimsky was another tool I used a lot to learn new techniques and practice them. New patterns were emerging in my head constantly thanks to what I was getting from the book. Coltrane and other greats used to study Slonimsky's *Thesaurus*. Oliver Nelson was one of them. So was Eddie Harris, who wrote the famous tune "Freedom Jazz Dance."

Back in Panama, I had listened to many sax players like Johnny Griffin, Sonny Rollins, Hank Mobley, Harold Land, Gene Ammons, Dexter Gordon, Ben Webster, Lester Young and many others. I was more into the laid-back Coleman Hawkins kind of flavor—also Lou Donaldson and Cannonball Adderley, but preferably tenor sax players. I think I heard Wayne Shorter with Art Blakey too. I dug Jackie McLean; people always told me Jackie played slightly out of tune, but I thought he sounded great. I liked Charlie Parker, but I never played any of his songs. He wasn't that big of an influence on me for some reason I do not know.

Brooklyn was the home base for many jazz musicians, and I was always jamming, practicing and learning new stuff on my own

Leo Price Is Right

as well as from other great musicians. Sam Brown, a trumpet player and excellent arranger, showed me a lot about music. There was also Roland Alexander, a tenor sax player I became very good friends with. I used to go to his apartment to talk about music and practice for hours. There were also people like trombonist and euphonium player Kiane Zawadi, Ed Stoute the pianist, and Daniel Mixon, another young pianist who was about 17 or 18 years old then. Another good friend was saxophonist Johnny Toussaint. Then there were Maurice Brown and George Hicks, both drummers. With Maurice a few years later, I would go around town doing LSD and peyote too. We would walk the Brooklyn Bridge on hallucinogens. Maurice was a good guy, and it was sad when I heard he jumped off a building. Someone told me once that it happened because he was tripping on LSD and walking around a rooftop and jumped because he thought he was Superman or something crazy like that. God bless his soul.

There were many musicians for me to practice with, so I engaged with as many of them as I could. There were drummer Al Hicks; Skip Crumby and Hakim Jami, both bassists; Jimmy Hayward and Scott Brodie, both tenor saxophonists; Gerald Hayes on alto sax; Wes Anderson the drummer; and many others.

I was having the time of my life: a steady weekend gig with Leo Price that paid good money, practicing almost daily with Mike, buying and listening to many jazz records, reading the liner notes on the back of the albums, meeting and hanging out with many musicians at the jam sessions, practicing and developing my technique and getting better on my horn. Yes! Those were the good ol' days.

There was an incident around this time that could have changed all that was going good for me. One day, I was on the Atlantic Avenue bridge, and this other car started to race me. I must admit, we were both going way too fast. We were already on the bridge, and I could see the cross street going east and another one going north to New York. The light was green, so I pushed on the pedal and went even faster, beating the other car by some distance. But when I was in the middle of the street, the light changed to red! The car on the cross street started moving forward, and I made a right turn, missing him by inches. Halleluyah! I stopped by the side of the road, got out of the car crying, and thanked Jesus (I was into Jesus those days) for allowing me to live another day.

Guns of Freeport

As if almost dying in a car accident weren't enough, I had a situation very soon that I wasn't particularly proud of over in Freeport, Long Island. I said before that Leo Price's Nassau County gangster connections would be helpful to me and here is how.

I used to go out with a very pretty girl; she had a little alligator skin but was very cute. Trelessa was her name, and she was one of my many girlfriends in those days. At the club back in the day I had around seven or eight of them. Was it the accent? My bushy hair? Or my blowing? I guess all of them. I really don't know how I managed to lie to all my girls like that. As a matter of fact, Trelessa and I split because of all the girls I had.

Leo Price had what I called a "go for" guy named Ernie. A "go for" guy was like, you know, someone who Leo sent to go for this and go for that—one of his "yes men." Ernie was going out with Trelessa's sister, but Trelessa and I were separated and she already had a new boyfriend. One day we were at the bandstand playing over in Freeport, and Ernie came in bleeding and yelling that some guys had ganged up on him outside and beat him up. Everyone started to get angry at the situation, so people started to bust out their weapons. It was normal back then that everybody in the band had a gun except for me.

We all started to ask what happened and who did it, and Ernie told us it was Trelessa's sister's boyfriend as well as Trelessa's new boyfriend. I told everyone that I was going outside with Ernie to try to help in some way. Leo didn't wait one second before giving me a gun. As soon as we walked out of the club, Ernie started to go straight to the guys across the street. Next thing I knew, this big guy came running aggressively toward me, so I got the gun and aimed for his feet. I wanted to only injure him, but I missed, and he kept coming at me. Soon enough, POW! I shot one more time, but this time it hit him an inch or less from his heart. The man in question turned out to be Trelessa's new boyfriend, so I got out of there quickly. That same night, Leo put me in contact with a guy called Friedman, who was a lawyer who represented him and his gangster connections. After this incident, I kept working with Leo, but I was all day worrying whether anything was going to happen to me. After asking many times, I heard the guy had survived, but I was still concerned.

Three months later, two burly detectives came by the entrance to the club where I was playing with Leo. They wanted to come onto the dance floor, but in those days, everyone had a gun; Jimmy Kesler the MC had a gun, and so did everyone in the band but me. The guys from the band wouldn't allow the police detectives in the place to get me, as they demanded we finish playing first, and the police agreed to that.

After the show, the detectives came to me and told me I had to go with them to the station, but before I left, Leo told me not to worry about anything. It turns out, in the interim between the shooting and that very day, Leo Price went to the home of the guy I had shot and warned him not to tell anything about what had happened, as they knew he was a wanted man in North Carolina. Leo and his gangsters used that information to threaten him and keep him silent! I kid you not! This stuff was like something out of a movie.

When I got to the police station, I was told they were waiting for Trelessa's boyfriend to come. They sat me down, and I kept hearing the phone ringing over and over. The police finally answered, and I could hear them say, "Yes, Mr. Friedman; yes, Mr. Friedman," and they passed the phone to another one who said the same: "Oh, we understand, Mr. Friedman." They passed the phone to me, and the mighty Friedman told me not to say anything! Not a word! So, I did the same thing as the police: "Yes, Mr. Friedman; okay, Mr. Friedman; sure thing, Mr. Friedman." Friedman was the top criminal lawyer in Long Island.

Finally, Trelessa's boyfriend came to the station. He was told to identify me by looking through the glass square on the door, but he said right away it wasn't me. He didn't rat me out because he probably would've died at the hands of the Nassau County gangsters.

I was a lucky man back then and still am. I owe all of that to the

Part 1. Panama Roots

Almighty Creator. The near miss on the Atlantic Avenue bridge and the shooting in Freeport, Long Island—two things I was lucky to get away with. Not only that, but I also remember drug dealers in my building getting killed and busted all the time in those days. It was such a common thing, especially in the Black communities, but when I was selling drugs later in life, nothing ever happened to me.

Coughing Lungs

I had another lovely girlfriend back then called Rose, whom I had met through my longtime friend Timmy Olton, who was seeing Rose's sister. Sometime thereafter, Rose's sister dumped Timmy and got herself a new boyfriend. This new fella sold pot and was always offering me a bag, which I continually refused. I told my friend Mike Ridley about this new hookup, and he urged me to get the bags for him to smoke. One day, I finally accepted the marihuana and gave it to Mike. While studying, working and hanging out together, Mike kept urging me to try the reefer. I didn't want to because I remembered this one time during my young days with the "Down the Road Gang" of Paraíso around 1957, when one of my friends and I were sitting on some steps and my friend told me to take a drag of his marihuana. I did so, coughing my lungs out, and I didn't like it one bit. That day with Mike, though, I finally gave in and tried it. I began coughing my lungs out once again, and my head felt like exploding until tears began coming out of my eyes. Very soon I became paranoid, and my heart began beating very fast.

My horn was close to me, but it took me what seemed forever to actually walk over there and grab it. I began practicing hard and long on my horn, hoping this bizarre episode would end. Soon thereafter, I mellowed out and began to feel a nice buzz. When we stopped laughing about my new experience, we had some beers. While we sipped our beer, I heard a melody in my head and began blowing it over and over, and thus I wrote my first song, which I named "Bedroom Eyes." This was around 1964/1965. After that came many other songs: "Crystal Mist," "Bedroom Waltz" and others. I remember one I titled "Zepia." Needless to say, I was a pothead after that day. In

Coughing Lungs

Panama, all I had was a lot of liquor, especially "Licor Fundador" and Hennessy. I got too drunk sometimes, and was now enjoying marijuana more after that day with Mike.

As I was now writing many new songs, all I wanted was to hear them played by some musicians. Mike by now had gotten married to a schoolteacher and could not hang out with me like before, so I started to get some musicians together and eventually formed my own group. This enabled me to hear how my compositions sounded. My first group had Danny Mixon on piano, Skip Crumby on bass and Ron Warwell on drums. Ron was later replaced by Al Hicks.

We played at many small clubs around Brooklyn and were getting popular. I was looking for every possible gig that I could find. Soon we landed a Sunday matinee gig at a famous jazz club called the Blue Coronet on Fulton Street owned by some guys back then who I think were the Kardashian brothers, but I'm not really sure. The group was very fond of the Sunday schedule, because we could do some other gigs during the week and still do our Sunday matinee. The Blue Coronet was a great place to earn notoriety, for every week a different famous jazz artist performed there. Some of those were Miles Davis, Art Blakey, Sonny Rollins, Sonny Stitt, Thelonious Monk, Freddie Hubbard, Max Roach, Horace Silver, Lee Morgan, and the list goes on and on. Miles Davis once got shot coming out of the Blue Coronet, supposedly because he was getting booked by white promoters in Brooklyn and some of the Black brothers in the business were not too happy about it.

I was now smoking pot regularly and writing many new songs every single day, playing my tenor constantly, trying to get better and better. One thing that held me back was that I didn't play jazz with many other people apart from my quartet because I still couldn't read music very well. My strategy was to go ahead and write every pattern that I created in my head instead of learning perfect reading techniques by studying the standard methods. I kept writing more and more and started to incorporate my tunes into the gigs because before all I was playing were jazz standards.

One friend would always tell me about writing my own stuff, and that person was Stanley Wright. I met Stanley when I had just formed

Part 1. Panama Roots

my first group because he was a good bass player in and around the scene. There was some gig I had to do in Brooklyn, and I called together a "pick a side" with him in it. He used to sell incense, and I remember his wife was a teacher. They had a house that I frequented a couple of times. He later changed his name to Suleiman-Marim Wright and tried to get me to change mine, but I refused to change to an Islamic name. His life sadly had a tragic ending (which I will tell later). Even though I was already writing my own music, Stanley (or Suleiman) was constantly encouraging me to work on my own material. I was playing stuff like "Somewhere Over the Rainbow," "There's No Greater Love," "Impressions," and "Softly as in the Morning Sunrise," and Suleiman kept telling me, "Garnett, you gotta write your own shit to get the money!"

The other musicians liked my songs, which motivated me to continue writing. I wasn't doing my thing with the Leo Price band anymore. By then, I had begun to realize what my real potential was, because musically I had evolved a lot, and to make matters even better, I met a very important figure in my life through Mike Ridley and my friend Claude Bartee. That person was none other than the great Freddie Hubbard. We would hang out at Freddie's home, which was around the corner from where Lucille and I lived. Claude Bartee also lived close by. Around this time, Lucille was pregnant with Sheila, and my other girlfriend Rose was pregnant with Kecia; as if that weren't enough, Betty was carrying our second daughter, Myra. I was a busy yet crazy musician. Cocaine was now introduced into my life by Claude. At that time, I was only interested in music and the ladies. I had three women pregnant and all conceived in 1965. Later, Lucille and Rose both disappeared from my life. I cannot say that I blame them. All that I cared about back then was playing my horn and getting lots of women. Melvina and I were still married but separated.

I was playing all around Brooklyn with my group and with other groups as well. To keep some cash in my pockets and the horn in my mouth, I was also a regular with the Bartlett Contemporaries Band, a very popular band at the time. The leaders were two brothers; Charles played trumpet and the younger Carl played tenor sax. They had a lot of gigs around New York.

The Drug Dealer's Girlfriend's Sax

A few years earlier, when I first moved to Brooklyn, I had met a nice young lady who, unlike most of my other women, loved jazz; her name was Crystal D. We had a long on-and-off relationship. There were times when we had not seen each other for a long time and we had lost contact, but we easily connected as soon as we saw each other again. One night she showed up at the Blue Coronet, and we rekindled our romance. She informed me that she was now living with a big-time drug dealer, so we saw each other again only when we could. Here I was, hanging with my sweet lady who was supplying me with some of the best cocaine, hashish and reefer around Brooklyn.

One night she asked me which was the best tenor sax around, and I told her that it was the Selmer Mark VI saxophone. She told me to meet her the next day, and she took me to the Sam Ash music store and bought me a new tenor saxophone. My first brand-new horn! In those days, the Selmer sax cost $300 or $350. You could not hold me back then; I had not only a new horn but also the very best. This meant the end for my Quinon sax. I wailed with that horn! Crystal D. had now given me something that would inspire me more than any drug or any woman I ever had, and that was the beautiful new Selmer saxophone.

Sometime in 1966, I met this singer from Trinidad by the name of Roderick George. He asked my friend Mike Ridley and I whether we wanted to go perform his music in a few different countries on a Caribbean tour. We both gladly agreed. At first, we went straight to Trinidad and met a rich promoter named Choy Aming who owned a club named the Penthouse. Choy was one of Trinidad's top orchestra leaders in the 1950s and 1960s, so he knew about great music and, of course, calypso, which I love dearly. We talked about some of the great Panamanian performers and their Trinidadian counterparts. Great calypsonians (calypso singers) from Trinidad always had Panama as one of their favorite stops.

Choy Aming had some pretty ladies at his club too. These ladies were probably prostitutes, but I got it for free. The women worked for Choy and, since he brought us all the way from the United States, we pretty much had everything covered, including a room for myself. Choy's place was bumping all the time, for sure. Choy knew how to host a good party. One night after we had a concert, I went out partying. The next day, I was still sleeping with one of the ladies when somebody started banging on the door. The band had a sound check, and they were trying to find me because everyone else was there already. They finally tracked me down and sent a car for me.

While with Roderick's group, I went to multiple islands in a month or less: St. Thomas, St. John, St. Croix, Antigua and, of course, Trinidad and Tobago. I was blowing my brand-new Selmer tenor on the tour and found myself liking the sound I got out of it more and more. We played a mixture of Trinidad calypso, soca and rock'n'roll, but I always found a way to include my own patterns that I regularly used in jazz while stretching the basic harmonies of Roderick's repertoire.

Willie Bobo and the Blue Coronet

Back in Brooklyn, I was getting high and kept writing more and more songs. Composing and arranging now came easily for me. The guys in the group and the audience liked my songs, which gave me a lot of encouragement. In retrospect, I believe that the fact that I always made up my own arrangements for every song that I heard on the radio (or danced to) helped me develop into a great composer and arranger. Composing all these new songs helped me to write and read music better, for my melodies were complex and I had to learn how to break them down and write them out piece by piece.

Playing around was making me very popular among musicians. Somewhere along the line, I met this guy Mike Martin from Trinidad. I used to go to his home and blow my horn with him, just sax and drums. I used to do the same thing with George Hicks, Ron Warwell, and, much later, Shingo Okudaira. Mike Martin used to mainline (a crazy habit of shooting heroin in the blood). Since arriving in New York, I had heard a lot about heroin, but I didn't want to do that. With Mike, I tried to skin pop (that is, inject under the skin) and didn't like it. I never intended to shoot with a needle. I didn't want no air bubble going to my heart!

Willie Bobo and the Blue Coronet

One afternoon, while performing a matinee at the Blue Coronet jazz club, Willie Bobo, the great percussionist and band leader, came to me to ask me to work with his Latin jazz group. Willie was a few years older than me, but he was already recognized all over the world. He even had a contract with Verve Records in place at the time. He was one of the top Latin jazz musicians in the scene and had many gigs. He had a band with Mongo Santamaria! Willie asked me right then and there whether I played the flute, and I told him that I did not; I then told him about another Panamanian on the scene who played flute and led him to my friend Felix Wilkins, who not long after got the gig. I could have just said yes and gotten that gig, but I decided not to. In Panama, I had played a lot of Latin jazz and Caribbean rhythms, so I wanted to do something different and play deeper, more improvised music. On top of that, the opportunity felt like a good fit for my friend Felix, who needed something to kickstart his career in New York.

Felix had studied with me at one time in Paraíso—well, not really study; he would come just to ask me questions. I was very popular from my work with Black Majesty and the Gay Crooners back then, and Felix was trying to play alto sax. When he came to New York, I was already pretty popular, and so I helped him establish himself. Later in life, I even got him to play with me on a show representing Panama at a time when I had just cleaned up from snorting. I told Felix then that he had to stop doing coke. I told him I had stopped, but he continued. He stayed involved in that stuff, and when I came back to Panama much, much later in my life, I heard he wasn't in very good shape. In Panama, you can get very good cocaine easily, which can be a problem for someone trying to quit. He is now doing well, from what I have heard more recently, which is great!

My friends and fans all kept telling me to go across the bridge to Manhattan to perform, so the jazz audiences and musicians over there could hear what I was all about, but I never did. I do not know why. It might have been a lack of confidence, or maybe fear, or simply lack of time—I was gigging all around Brooklyn at the Blue Coronet, the Gig, the Kingston Lounge, the Keg, Gaithers, the Happy Landing, the Baby Grand, the Brevoort Theatre, the Up and Over Jazz Club, the Fantasy Lounge, and more.

Part 1. Panama Roots

Many things happened during this time in my life. Everything was moving fast and changing right before my eyes. I had left the Leo Price rock band after working with him for about two to three years. My hands were full when it came to women, with Betty, Lucille, Rose, Crystal, and many others in between (I'm not proud of my lifestyle from back then, but it is a fact and part of my history).

That year, 1968, on April 4, the Reverend Martin Luther King, Jr., was assassinated. I remember writing a few songs inspired by the unfortunate events surrounding his death, one of them called "Black Sunday." I never recorded it, but it did spark in my head for the first time the idea about the Universal Black Force that would come later. There were all these laws being created for the police, and at the same time brothers were robbing and killing each other, so I felt this fire starting to burn inside me. I was a Black man from Panama, fighting against the odds of society as a minority within a minority in the 1960s. My perseverance got me to where I was, but it took a lot of me to carry on. Some people with rich families, or perhaps just by being white, had a much easier time. It was necessary to show them everything was possible and, most of all, to love oneself no matter what! Music was a great way to take the message to everyone who wanted to listen.

Fortunately, the gigs kept coming all around Brooklyn with my quartet, and my major break would come later that same year.

Giggin' with Freddie Hubbard

Through Mike Ridley, I had met alto saxophonist Gerald Hayes, Louis Hayes' younger brother. Louis was playing drums with Freddie Hubbard's quintet, and they both lived in the same apartment building. As I mentioned before, through Claude Bartee and Mike Ridley, I was an insider with Freddie's clique. I lived on Bergen Street and had Nostrand Avenue to the left and New York Avenue to the right going up to St. Marks. Claude Bartee lived around there, and I used to walk to his place all the time. On the next block was where Freddie Hubbard lived.

My quartet was still the mainstay at the Blue Coronet jazz club matinee on Sunday afternoons. One of those afternoons, Freddie

Giggin' with Freddie Hubbard

came in and, after the gig, asked me whether I would like to work with his group. By now, I believed that I was ready for the next level, but one still tends to be nervous. We talked, and I agreed to join right away, but then I was surprised when he said that we were leaving the next day for Philadelphia! I asked whether there was going to be a rehearsal, and he just replied, "Don't worry, Carlos; you can handle it." Freddie had more confidence in me than I had in myself! All the pressure prior to this big moment, together with my lack of complete confidence, turned out to be a great thing, as it made me work hard every day. Years earlier I had told myself that I was going to be ready when the big break came for me. The occasion I longed for came via Freddie Hubbard, and I was even more ready than I thought.

Freddie informed me that we were going to do six nights at the popular jazz club named the Savoy Lounge in Philadelphia. Blue Mitchell's group was playing too. Needless to say, I was excited and nervous, because there were no rehearsals! On the drive down, I reviewed the charts thoroughly and blew some lines in the dressing room. Freddie had some tough charts. With my heart in my mouth, I played all of the songs with no problems and was amazed at the response I got after my solos. My confidence grew, and I was able to relax and blow with more focus for the second set. We played "Red Clay," "The Intrepid Fox," "Lil' Sunflower" and many of the new songs Freddie was planning to record in just a few months. By the fourth and fifth nights, I was cooking, and the audience response was overwhelming. I knew right then that I was ready for the big leagues. The Mango Tree Musician was on the move!

Now everyone on the scene wanted to know more about me. I was a happy camper, excited and very happy with all of the attention. Woody Shaw came and introduced himself to me. He told me how much he enjoyed my playing and style. He asked me where I was from, so I told him that I was from Panama, now living in Brooklyn, and we exchanged numbers.

Freddie had a tight group: Kenny Barron on piano, Juni Booth on bass and Louis Hayes on drums. I was on the tenor sax, with Freddie on trumpet and flugelhorn. One of our next gigs was at Club La Boheme in New York City. We were playing at all of the popular jazz

Part 1. Panama Roots

clubs in New York City—Le Baron, Bird Land, the Five Spot, the Blue Note, the Village Vanguard and Slugs, to name a few. Before these new musical adventures, I had never crossed the bridge for gigs. Now I was all over the place, and at each gig, I began to meet many musicians interested in my sound.

While playing with Freddie, I also met Joe Henderson, the tenor player. The two of them used to play a lot together. I was looking for somebody to teach me some stuff on the sax because I was hungry for new musical concepts. I thought of going to Joe, as he was an established musician who had recorded with the top jazz guys. One day, while hanging out with him and Freddie, I asked Joe whether he would teach me some stuff. He agreed and invited me to his house.

When I got to Joe's house, I took out my horn, and he sat at his piano. He told me to play alone so he could just listen to me for a bit, and when I was done, he said, "You cool, man; you need nothing from me." That's it—that's all he said! We hung out for a few minutes more, and then I left. I figured he didn't want to teach no rival, and in the end, I guess I didn't need anything from him either. It was still a great experience because Joe Henderson was one of the top players in the world, with many acclaimed albums as a leader for the best jazz labels. Just being at his house and having him say I needed nothing from him was the best lesson he could have given me.

After all those years tearing up the Brooklyn scene, I was now all over New York City, meeting and hanging out with many well-known, respected jazz artists. We are talking about guys whom I knew from seeing their names and photos behind album covers! One of the musicians I met while working with Freddie was Lee Morgan. Lee was a musical genius. His sound on the trumpet was unrivaled. Lee was born the same year as me, but I was just getting started in the Panama scene when he was already recording for big labels with the best musicians in jazz. Meeting him meant a lot to me, and I wish I could have played with him.

Back in those days, I was selling cocaine from time to time, and when I went to the gigs, all the guys were buying from me because they wanted to taste my stuff. Usually, I had a little packet that I shared with the musicians. One night after a show at Slugs, we were doing some coke, passing it around, and when it got to Lee Morgan's hands, guess what? I didn't get nothing back! After this incident, I had a special extra packet for the big nose guys.

Many musicians, including myself, had problems with drugs. I guess the struggle to be someone in the music business while facing racism, criticism and economic hardships contributed to that. Everyone was young and trying to have a good time, so sometimes bad decisions were made. Anyway, we were all getting high in those days, and since I had my special lady friend supplying me with the best stuff, the guys would always be glad when they saw me, for I always had top stuff.

I will always be grateful to Freddie Hubbard because one day he told me I should write my own songs, which I was already doing, but I wanted to join BMI Publishing House in the United States to protect my music. To join BMI, you must have two songs recorded. I talked to Freddie about it, and he told me to write two songs for him. Next thing I knew, he wanted to use the songs for his album *A Soul Experiment*. My two compositions for that album were "No Time to Lose" and "Hang 'Em Up," which allowed me to create my own publishing company. That's when I started Caragar Music (short for Carlos Alfredo Garnett Music). My first two songs published through Caragar were thanks to Freddie Hubbard. I remember going to the A & R studio with Freddie sometime in late 1968 or early 1969. It was my first experience at a professional studio, and I felt right at home. All my hard work allowed me to have great confidence in myself even if there were some top musicians in the session like Kenny Barron on piano, Eric Gale on guitar and Bernard Purdie on drums.

Freddie had a reputation for having a big ego, and he loved fine women. On many occasions, he would leave the bandstand to go after any fine woman who caught his eye. He would tell me to play a ballad while he went after his love quest. On such occasions, I would play one of my favorite ballads, "Lover Man." How appropriate!

I remember this particular night while performing at the East, a Black-owned cultural, educational and entertainment center of the Black Diaspora located in Brooklyn (which would go on to become a huge part of my life). Freddie saw a lovely lady and went right to

Part 1. Panama Roots

A Soul Experiment **album by Freddie Hubbard (copyright Atlantic Records).**

her as soon as we finished the song. As usual, I played "Lover Man." When I finished, everyone gave me a thunderous standing ovation. The crowd clapped and shouted for more. They wouldn't stop! I was slightly embarrassed, for they continued even after Freddie had returned to the stand. For me, it was embarrassing getting that kind of response as a side man; it was bitter and sweet. The next night was even worse. The wife of one of the East's owners requested the same song; I informed her that it was not my group and that she would have to ask Freddie. She went to him, and so we played "Lover Man" again, and this time the audience screamed and hollered louder than ever. When I was done, I walked to the corner in the back of the bandstand, trying not to be noticed.

That night after the show, Freddie drove me home in his car. As we were approaching my stop, he told me that I should form my own group. It came as a shock initially, but it felt kind of good when I really started to think about it, as it meant he believed deep down in what I was capable of. One thing was a shame, though, and that was that I had rehearsed all of the songs Freddie planned to record in a couple of weeks for his *Red Clay* album. Before that opportunity came about, I was fired. He said that he was going to use Junior Cook again but ended up using Joe Henderson.

Art Blakey and the Jazz Messengers

About two or three weeks later, I received a call from Woody Shaw informing me that Art Blakey was looking for a saxophonist and that he had recommended me. Around the same time, I learned that I had received a scholarship from the New England Conservatory of Music. So now I had to make a big career choice, and of course I decided to go with Art Blakey and the Jazz Messengers! There I was, the Mango Tree Musician up from Panama, now a "Jazz Messenger" playing with a real jazz legend. I could not believe it.

In my early days in Panama, I had listened to Blakey on many records, and I could only dream of being a part of his group, which by this time included Woody Shaw on trumpet, George Cables on piano, Mickey Bass or Scotty Holt on bass, Art on drums, and me. The group sometimes changed, and in would come Jan Arnet or Skip Crumby on bass, John Hicks on piano and Randy Brecker on trumpet. No matter who was playing, it was always a strong, young group, and Art allowed us to write some of the music besides playing some of his hits and favorites. Even the great Curtis Fuller joined the group on trombone for a gig at the legendary Newport Jazz Festival of 1969. That edition of the festival had big names like Miles Davis, Dave Brubeck, Frank Zappa and Sly Stone on the same day as us!

I did more traveling out of state with the Jazz Messengers than I had with Freddie's group, going all through the Midwest and beyond. I remember one time in New Jersey, we did a live recording in a big theater in Newark where I played a burning solo on "Night in Tunisia." The crowd went crazy. We also toured through Chicago,

Part 1. Panama Roots

Cleveland, Columbus, West Virginia, Pittsburgh and Philadelphia. Art Blakey's Jazz Messengers always played to packed venues.

On this tour, there was a situation that had me worried and concerned. I believe that we were traveling through the backwoods of West Virginia. We stopped to get some refreshments and use the bathroom. I got out of the car and headed for the front door, when these guys grabbed me and told me that we had to use the back entrance. That was the first time such a thing had happened to me, I guess because I was always in the Black neighborhoods in New York City. All of a sudden, these racist guys began talking out loud about how they hoped that the car did not break down on one of the back roads we were taking. They noticed I was listening and said even louder while looking over at me that if one of those redneck sheriff cars pulled us over, we would be in deep shit! I had never been in a situation like that before even though I played all over Long Island, upstate New York, Poughkeepsie, Newburgh and Buffalo. This was my first experience dealing with this kind of racist behavior and segregation in the United States, so I was very glad when we got back into Philadelphia.

With Art Blakey we traveled all over the East Coast too. I remember well that once we were playing at this place called Marvelous Marv in Boston for several nights. One of those nights, a guy looking like a street junkie walked in the club and asked me whether I was interested in an alto saxophone, so I told him to show it to me. He pulled out a Selmer alto sax, saying that he was Bunky Green's brother. I knew who Bunky Green was; I had heard him on some albums from Chicago. He asked for $80! Knowing that he was a junkie, I acted like I had no money. After haggling for a while, he sold me the horn for $60. It was in superb condition! It was in a green army-type bag, with no case, but I did not care, as I had myself a new alto sax. My guess is that it used to belong to his brother Bunky, but it got sold to me for drug money.

Art's band was playing daily all over the United States with a fast-paced lifestyle involving alcohol, drugs and women. One time, we were performing at Le Barron's Club on 135th Street in Harlem, sharing the stage with the Sonny Stitt group (I considered Sonny a terrific musician and technician, and I enjoyed listening to him a lot). During our break after the second set, some guys and I were all getting high in the dressing room or bathroom. There was a lot of cocaine going around. I pulled out some of my good stuff and passed it around as well. This had been going on for some time when a package was handed to me, and I took two big hits. I was sorry immediately, for it was heroin, something I never liked. I was sick immediately and started vomiting and was very nauseous. I could not do the third set, I was so wasted. I sat in a corner trying to get myself together. It was a good thing that my girl Crystal D. was there and took care of me, as I was totally out of it. I learned to check all packages that came my way after that!

Working with the Jazz Messengers was a dream come true. Now I was known as a fiery tenor sax player everywhere. Woody Shaw and I became close friends, and he was also regarded as a fierce trumpet player, which I must say he was. When Art was not working, Woody and I formed a quintet and played all over New York City, with George Cables on piano, Juni Booth on bass and Lenny White on drums. Woody and I were writing most of the material, and we also played some of Art's repertoire. This all happened in 1969 and 1970. Woody and I were hot at that time. We used to play at a club called the New World, owned by Panamanians; Hugh Masekela would play there too. In those days I recorded everything myself, using a portable tape recorder that I carried with me everywhere. But since I've moved so many times, I don't know where I left all the tapes. What a shame.

Lifting My Voice with Andrew Hill

I recall that in 1969, Woody and I were called for a recording session at Blue Note Records with pianist Andrew Hill for his album titled *Lift Every Voice*. Woody had recommended me to Andrew. There was Woody on trumpet, Andrew on piano, Richard Davis on bass, and Freddie Waits on drums, with myself on tenor. What a fantastic lineup! I did not want to record with Andrew Hill initially, but Woody convinced me to play this difficult music. He had a lot of

Part 1. Panama Roots

confidence in my abilities. You know, I would have rather played with other groups, but I took a chance. The music was very different, but with the encouragement from Woody, I made it. Before I did my first session with Andrew, he was using top tenor players like Joe Farrell and Booker Ervin, so doing gigs with him meant a lot to me, for I was among the best.

For *Lift Every Voice*, we recorded with a seven-piece vocal group doing all these crazy harmonies. I had never heard anything like it. Andrew Hill's music was something else. His whole sense of composition was unlike any I had come across in the past. That resonated with me because I understood the importance of taking risks in music. The recording session went really well; how could it not when

Lift Every Voice **album by Andrew Hill (copyright Blue Note Records).**

you had all these great jazz musicians creating new sounds? To top it all off, the album was recorded by Rudy Van Gelder at his legendary studio in New Jersey.

Andrew must have liked me, because he called me back into the studio a month later to record as the only horn player, without my friend Woody Shaw. It was a surprise to me, as Woody had been the one who originally brought me to him. For that particular session, Andrew used a string quartet and the same rhythm section as *Lift Every Voice*, which included Richard Davis and Freddie Waits. We did three of Andrew's compositions, and two of them actually got released almost 40 years later. One was titled "Monkash" and the other "Mahogany." On "Mahogany," you can hear me play tenor at first and then switch to soprano sax—a first for my career, I believe! This session was also recorded at Van Gelder Studio.

At the beginning of 1971, less than a year after *Lift Every Voice* was released, Andrew called me up to accompany him on a live TV presentation for the show *Live! On Soul* airing on WNET. It was a great experience that allowed me to play with the great drummer Roy Haynes. The band also featured Victor Sproles, a very good bass player who had played with Clifford Jordan and Sun Ra's group. Sadly, this live TV recording has never been released as far as I know. Ideally, someone will get hold of those tapes and share them with the world before I die because they feature an interesting live performance of Andrew Hill's compositions with some intricate solos by yours truly.

Messengers in Japan

A new year arrived, 1970, and the first thing on the list for Art Blakey and the Jazz Messengers was a tour of Japan. I couldn't believe it. I do not recall what happened or why, but Woody, George Cables and Juni Booth did not make the cut; however, I didn't care because I was very excited to go to Japan with Art. In the end, it was a quartet with Joanne Brackeen on piano and a bass player from Czechoslovakia, Jan Arnet. Blakey informed me that after the first month, trumpet player Bill Hardman would join the band, but I was the main

Part 1. Panama Roots

soloist for most of the tour. This arrangement meant that my responsibility was much bigger than what I had thought initially. The group played dozens of shows, traveling everywhere, and all the while, I had to blow my ass off every night. That was not a problem at the time, for I was in top shape and so kept burning stages down one by one.

Art was well loved and respected in Japan, and they treated us like royalty. The tour had us performing in 32 cities. Tailors came to the fine Nakamura Hotel and measured us for some custom-made suits. This kind of treatment was all brand new to me, and I loved the special attention we received. We did a big TV show on the largest and most popular station in Japan. Someone must have some of those pictures of me looking sharp with my new, custom-tailored suit!

There I was, on stage with Art Blakey, playing all over Japan. At our first performance, I met famous Japanese trumpeter Terumasa Hino in our dressing room together with his brother Motohiko, a drummer "a la Elvin Jones." Terumasa was considered Japan's Miles Davis and was very popular and well known all over his country. After that initial performance, the Japanese had a fancy dinner arranged for the group. We feasted, and then some of us went to a jam session at the Blue Note Jazz Club in Tokyo. I played with a lot of guys from the local scene, including Terumasa and Motohiko Hino. The Japanese love their jazz, and the club was packed.

I was always a long-winded player and used to take long solos. Sometimes, while performing, Blakey would take all of the musicians and leave me alone on the stage while they went to the back to have a drink of sake, the famous Japanese rice wine. Sometimes we drank it along with some Hennessy brandy. The Japanese government did not tolerate any drugs in their country, so heroin and cocaine were out of the question. Curtis Fuller and Freddie Hubbard had carried drugs before when they were with Blakey on previous tours and were arrested. When I went, it was already in the news that you just didn't do drugs in Japan. It was all on the TV; people were getting shot or hanged. All we did was drink sake and Hennessy. Art was into heroin, but, knowing the situation, he must have cleaned up before the tour.

Messengers in Japan

My guide had informed me about a famous Japanese folk song; I used to add it into my solos, and the audience would go wild. I wish I could remember its name. That Japanese theme was incorporated into my patterns and automatically became part of my solos during the entire tour. After every show, the audience would present us with flowers and throw many more on the stage. Everyone wanted to take us home for dinner too. This was great, as our hosts were very hospitable and mindful of my diet, which mainly consisted of fish and vegetables.

After about four weeks of blowing like a madman on every single show of the tour, Bill Hardman and Etta Jones came to the rescue. My head was going to explode from blowing for so long alone! Sometimes I thought that Blakey had forgotten about me on the stage, because he and the others would take so long to come back out. Etta Jones didn't perform in all of the remaining shows, but Bill Hardman did. We went to 32 cities in about two months. I think that we saw more of Japan than most Japanese. We traveled by plane, bus and train. Once we were on a bus up in the mountains with a kamikaze driver speeding on a road with a steep drop; from my window seat I could see the cliffs below and the tires barely on the road. I insisted that the driver slow down or let me off, even though I did not know where we were. Finally, Art told him to slow down. It was mad.

There was another time that made me very scared. We were taking off in a plane from one of those small islands with a tiny runway. When the plane took off, we hit some turbulence or an air pocket, and I thought that we were going to crash because the wing tip was about two feet from the ocean. Scary stuff! The good part was that in every city after our shows, there were always big feasts, which started off with Kirin beers and sake. We were given Yashica cameras as gifts; I do not think they make them anymore. We stayed at the Karamuchi Hotel in a nice neighborhood in Tokyo.

As I had not bought a case for the alto sax yet, I asked my interpreter to take me to a music store to get one, along with reeds and other things. We took a taxi in front of our hotel with a very polite driver. When we got to the store, I realized that I had left my horn in the taxi! Our guide kept telling me not to worry, for Japanese people

Part 1. Panama Roots

are very honest, but I insisted on hurrying back to see whether the hotel manager could locate the taxi company. The interpreter told me again not to worry, that Japanese do not steal. At my insistence, we hurried back to the hotel, and lo and behold, the man at the front desk told me that the taxi driver had found my horn and returned it to the hotel. That made me a believer of Japanese honesty for the rest of my life. (Many years later in Panama, after I had moved back, I was going from the Magnolia bar to a place called the Johnny B, and once again I left my horn in the taxi! My friend waited for hours with me to see whether the driver would come back. He never did. But in Japan, the driver brought my horn back to me right away.)

Jazz Messengers '70 **album by Art Blakey and the Jazz Messengers (copyright Catalyst Records).**

Messengers in Japan

After we had been on tour for a while, Art told the interpreter, whom he knew from prior tours, to take the bass player (Jan Arnet) and me to see some geisha women. I was excited, for it had been a long time since I went over a month without a woman. We went to a club full of geisha women, and they sang and danced, always smiling at us, so I thought that I would get a woman that night. Right at the stroke of midnight, all of the women left slowly while some guy talked with us, drawing our attention from the women. I looked around, and suddenly all of the women were gone! I was very upset and told the interpreter that I had to have a woman that night. We went to several whorehouses trying to get us some women, but at each place we were told that they would do the white man but my manhood was too big! All of them girls picked the white guy (sigh). I had to go to four or five places. None of the Japanese ladies wanted anything to do with the Black guy. Finally, we found one who accommodated my desires, and I was able to relieve my hunger and concentrate on the music again.

My recollections of that great tour are endless. There was another incident at the Shinjuku train station in Tokyo. We were waiting for our train to arrive, and these Japanese porters were trying to help Art take his drums up to the third platform, but they could not carry the drums. As we realized that our train was approaching, Art picked up pretty much his entire drum set (complete with cymbals), carrying them up the three flights with no problem. That short man was strong! I said to myself, "Garnett, never mess with him!" Those Japanese men couldn't carry shit! Blakey was stronger than the three of them combined!

About three weeks before we returned to the United States, we recorded an album at the Victor Studio 1 in Tokyo. It was the first album Art Blakey recorded in Japan even though he had been there many times before. We did some of Benny Golson's tunes, a Bill Hardman tune, I believe another from Harold Mabern, and two songs of mine. One of those original compositions of mine was "What the World Needs Now Is Peace and Love," which we played all over Japan, so it ended up on the record. It must have been my first jazz song released, because the previous ones had been soul oriented.

Part 1. Panama Roots

"Taurus Woman" was another of my compositions that we played for every show during the tour, but for some reason it didn't make the final cut. The title of the album was *The Jazz Messengers '70*. There is some great blowing of mine in there.

Mingus Times

Once the tour in Japan ended, we headed to New York. From what I can recall, Art got sick and we did not do any more gigs together. Everything got canceled, and the band fell apart quickly. Coincidentally, at around the same time, I got a call to play for none other than the great Charles Mingus. That was an interesting gig, and a lot of fun too. The band had Tommy Turrentine on trumpet, Charles McPherson on alto sax, Jaki Byard on piano, Danny Richmond on drums, Charles on bass, and me on tenor and soprano sax.

We had a regular stint at the Village Gate for some time, playing several nights a week. We played only Mingus songs. He wrote some different and strange compositions, but the folks loved it. Working weekly at one location enabled me to study and practice the music. I worked with Mingus for a couple of months. By this time, my name was well established among the jazz community. I am disappointed, though, that he did not record anything while I worked with him. Mingus was another one of those artists whom I knew well from back in Panama, and I was aware of his great influence in music around the world. He always had some top musicians in his groups, so for me not to record with him was a bit of bad luck.

One thing I witnessed that worried me was Mingus' obesity. Before the first set, he would eat a five-course meal, and then he ate the same thing after the next two sets, always with a gallon of wine hidden behind the bass. That scared me. He ate too much! One time at the Village Gate, I saw this huge, tall guy come and talk to Mingus. I looked at him, and it was Kareem Abdul-Jabbar. The guy was a basketball star in those days, and everyone recognized him because of his stature. After the show, we went to his hotel room to hang out, and there I got a good look at how tall this guy was!

With Charles Mingus, I was just another member of his group.

We didn't have any real discussions about the music or anything else. At this juncture, I was interested only in forming my own group. I believe that around this time, I was living alone in a one-room kitchenette somewhere in Brooklyn in the Bedford–Stuyvesant area.

My African Queen

One night, after hanging out with one of my friends, on the way home he mentioned that there was a new jazz club named the Lincoln Terrace and suggested we stop there for a nightcap. Once in the club, we saw some lovely ladies sitting by themselves. We introduced ourselves and sat with them and had some drinks and conversed. We talked for quite a while until the place was closing. The woman I liked drew my attention with her long, shapely legs, wide hips, short afro hairstyle and the face of a regal African queen. We hit it off immediately and began dating; soon thereafter, she became my woman. After a month or so, we were living together and spending a lot of time with each other. She was a beautiful Afrocentric woman who loved jazz. Her name was Evelyn Jenkins; later during our relationship, I gave her the African name "Ayodele"—henceforth everyone called her Ayodele (or Ayo). Our relationship lasted many years, and during that time of change and upheaval in my life, she was very supportive of my music. I had already decided to write music of inspiration for my people.

When we met, I had already stopped eating meat, so my diet consisted of fruits, vegetables, nuts and grains. She used to make very delicious vegetarian meals for us. She was a great, creative cook. Ayodele even affected my music, because my compositions reflected this new change, and I was learning more about my Black heritage and culture too. An excellent seamstress, she made many different "dashiki" shirts for me and dresses for herself. What a blessing she was.

With Ayodele, the period began in which I was writing songs that had messages for the Black communities. My intention was not to focus on "baby, baby, I love you" or anything like that; I wanted to do music with a message that was positive—music to spread love

Part 1. Panama Roots

to my Black American friends. My first composition about the Black experience was written in 1968, after the death of Martin Luther King, but it wasn't until 1970 that I was able to perform and record this music that focused on the beauty of all Blacks.

All over America in the Black neighborhoods, Black-on-Black crimes were rampant. The youths were stealing and killing their own people. I deemed it necessary to write positive messages in my music and incorporated Black consciousness into the lyrics to make a change. This intense feeling of responsibility to my Black brothers and sisters really took off around the time I was with Mingus. I was to utilize all of the rhythms of the Black experience from around the world, including Panama. The Universal Black Force, or UBF, was finally born.

I left behind the quartet/quintet concept to form a larger ensemble with a trumpet, two saxes, a trombone, a piano, two basses, two percussionists, a drummer and four female vocalists to express Black pride and unity. I started to put together this group on my own and was very successful, as I was now well known in the jazz world, especially since I had worked with Freddie Hubbard, Art Blakey and Charles Mingus.

Roy Brooks

I always appreciated the opportunities I got playing along with my friend Woody Shaw. Our esteem for each other was mutual, as I knew he really enjoyed my style and I appreciated his. He could really blow the shit out of that trumpet. My close relationship with Woody led me to perform with some great musicians like Richard Davis and Andrew Hill, as mentioned before. Another important musician I got to share the stage with thanks to Woody was drummer Roy Brooks.

Roy was my age, but he became a well-respected and established musician long before I did, having played with guys like Sonny Stitt, Horace Silver and Yusef Lateef. Roy wanted to put together a group for a show at the Left Bank Jazz Society in Baltimore, Maryland, a place I had played before with Art Blakey. Roy asked Woody Shaw to help him get a band together, so Woody called me right away. Roy had recorded an album at that same place a few months earlier with a band that included George Coleman on tenor sax, but he wanted a different sound this time around. For this gig, Brooks brought in Harold Mabern on piano and Cecil McBee on bass together with Woody on trumpet. Those last two were kept from his last band, which had performed right there at the Left Bank Jazz Society not long before.

For the show, we did a version of my song "Taurus Woman" and also a few songs by Woody and Roy. The music was very intense, serving as a true reflection of what we were doing in those days. We weren't holding anything back, and the crowds loved it. My Black brothers and sisters were getting together to enjoy the moment, using our performances as a way to vent their problems while we played our asses off for them. The music we performed that night was structured but free. Even back when I was with Art Blakey, the live shows were more open, placing less importance on the chord structures, as in the manner of Ornette Coleman and John Coltrane's innovations.

I was young and coming up but felt confident, in part thanks to Woody because he would encourage me to do more and to take more risks in my blowing. Woody was younger, but he was a virtuoso from a young age. Musicians knew and respected him a lot, so it really meant something to me that he liked my style as much as he did. He and I developed a

Carlos Garnett on tenor saxophone (photo by Raymond Ross, used with permission, Raymond Ross CTSIMAGES).

Part 1. Panama Roots

language between us because of the many hours we had already accumulated playing alongside each other.

Roy had an original sound too—very intense but controlled. As mentioned before, Roy had a great career even before I started with Freddie Hubbard. His playing was very on the edge but at the same time measured. What is sad is that according to some people I knew, he had some mental issues, but in the end what really counts is that he was able to overcome some of those difficulties and perform the way he did.

First Return to Panama

I hadn't been in Panama since I left in 1962, so it was time to visit my family. I returned to see my parents for the first time in many years and took Ayo with me to celebrate New Year's Eve. We walked all over the popular "Avenida Central" street in our funky clothes and hats. I would tie some bell chimes around both my ankles and make music using my flute while jumping to a rhythm, using the bells as percussion. People thought I was crazy, but I couldn't care less!

During my trip, I sat in and played with the Exciters, a popular band in Panama. I really don't remember where, though. Horacio Adams played drums with them back in those days, and Carlos Alfredo Brown played bass. Carlos Brown and I both have the same first and second name, and we were both born in December (I'm on the 1st and he's on the 12th). I would take my horn around and check out the local shows; that's how I got to play with the Exciters as well as with various groups around town. We all had a great time.

What I was really interested in was getting some of the famous "Panama Red" marihuana that I had heard so much about for years. Finally, through three of my friends from back in the day (Pooch, Bully and someone else), I was able to get some. For New Year's Eve, I bought a bunch of that "Panama Red" and got blasted. We smoked weed around 1:00 p.m. Ayo and I then went home and ate before going to bed, for we planned to go out and party that night. We later woke up, showered, dressed and were on our way to the city right before midnight. On the bus, I asked Ayo whether we had just smoked a joint, and she said no; then it dawned on me that I was still high after all that time. Since 1:00 p.m.! That was some good stuff—no wonder that in New York everybody wanted "Panama Red."

That New Year's Eve was something else. Panama was bumping back then! Ayo and I went to this popular club called the Rancho Grande in an area of the city known as "Rio Abajo." I took my flute, jammed with some musicians and had a great time. In "Rio Abajo," you could find bars, cabarets and all sorts of places with some great local bands playing jazz, soul, funk, salsa and everything in between.

Also during that visit, I got together with my good friend Carlos Jordan, a singer I knew from my early days in Paraíso. He and another friend, Lenny Daniels, later played with a Panamanian soul group in the United States called Love Warmth and Affection with my friends Carlos Brown and Ralph Weeks.

The Universal Black Force (UBF)

Back in the United States, I was seeking gigs at all of the Black colleges around New York City, New Jersey, Connecticut, Boston, Philadelphia, Baltimore and Washington, D.C. The word spread from one Black college and Black Student Association to another about my revolutionary Black music. All the colleges back then were hiring white musicians, but through the Black student unions, I was able to take the Universal Black Force concept to these places full of young Black minds. Playing Black music to spread love to my Black American friends made me feel like I was promoting a change in these young guys. It was important for me to let them know about our beauty and worth!

The first set of musicians I had with me when I formed the Universal Black Force were Olu Dara on trumpet, Kiane Zawadi on trombone and euphonium, Khaliq Al-Rouf and Russell White on flute and alto/soprano sax, Harry Constance on piano and Ron Warwell on drums. I later got Norman Connors on drums because I wanted someone who could give me a little fire like Elvin Jones. Hakim Jami and Stafford James were on bass at the same time. My

Part 1. Panama Roots

band sometimes had two bass players and two drummers before Norman ever attempted it with his groups. I also had Neil Clarke and Charles Pulliam on congas and percussion, Reggie Lucas on guitar, and Ayodele Jenkins (with her sister Cora and friend Mona) on vocals. My two Panamanian friends Carlos Jordan and Carlos Chambers were also in the group playing the ukuleles. This was a large ensemble, and I thank all of them for their loving vibes, for with a large group the money was little. Later, I met Dee Dee Bridgewater, and she began singing in my new group.

We used to play a song I wrote but never recorded named "Congo." I can still hear the band singing the chorus in my head:

> *Congooooooo.*
> *Congoooooooooo.*

The song was written with the Republic of Congo in the motherland of Africa on my mind. I also wrote another song called "The Future Is Ours" around the same time I wrote "Mother of the Future." You can see the pattern in my writing in which being Black and proud is the main theme. I drew inspiration from African rhythms, as well as music made by Africans in America like calypso, Afro-Cuban, rock, jazz, and so on. Then I decided to add lyrics to my songs so they would have an even bigger impact whenever someone listened to them.

The message was strong and clear on another song I wrote for the UBF called "Africa Is Here." It went something like this:

> *Africa is here. Africa is near....*
> *It's in the air.*
> *Can you feel it everywhere?*
> *It's in the atmosphere.*

Just to please the jazz guys a bit, I would play "I Want to Talk about You" by John Coltrane with the changes to "Misty." Another jazz standard we used to play was "Softly as in the Morning Sunrise." I changed it to "Morning Softly Rising" and altered the melody completely over the same chords. Wrote my own!

This one time at the Village Gate, the UBF was doing a presentation in one of the concert halls. The place had two big halls, and in

The Universal Black Force (UBF)

Carlos Garnett with the Universal Black Force (unable to identify musicians) (photo by Ron Warwell, used with permission).

the other one, Ray Barretto was performing with his group, which included a young Panamanian called Rubén Blades on the vocals. At that time, Rubén was not famous yet. One way or another, he heard about my group having three Panamanian musicians and came all the way back into the dressing room. He was very excited, telling me how much he loved that we were all there. The "Panameños" (Panamanians) together performing in New York. Who would have thought? It was quite an event in Panamanian music history if you think about it. This new Black spiritual concept music played next to the swinging Latin sound of Ray Barretto with Rubén Blades in his early stages before he got the big ego.

New York had a sizable Panamanian community, especially in Brooklyn and Queens. There was another Panamanian saxophone player in New York who had a very good style and technique and was a good friend of mine; his name was Carlos Ward, and he sometimes played with my group too. He played alto and flute really well and complemented my affairs on the tenor. We never did record, which

Part 1. Panama Roots

Flyer for Carlos Garnett and the Universal Black Force at the East, 1970 (art by Ron Warwell, used with permission).

is a pity. However, he recorded with Rashied Ali, Dollar Brand and others. He also played for Crown Heights Affair and had several hits with the soul group B.T. Express. On top of all that, he played with organist Jack McDuff. Since we are both named Carlos and played

The Universal Black Force (UBF)

the sax, people get us confused sometimes. I never played with Jack McDuff, but some credit me as if I did; however, it actually was Carlos Ward. He had a great career playing with Don Cherry, Dollar Brand and drummer Ed Blackwell.

One day, I got a call from a writer asking whether he could interview me for the new edition of *Downbeat* magazine. He wanted to do a piece on me as a new up-and-coming saxophone player, to which I agreed. I was now set to appear in the top jazz magazine as one of the best fresh talents in the world! To make things better, I learned this issue would feature my idol Sonny Rollins (one of my favorite tenor players ever) on the cover. When I think of it, I guess I was an interesting character to interview. You could find me around Brooklyn with a secondhand flute walking with sandals and a strap of bells around my ankles, making those chime sounds that I liked while I played my flute to the rhythm. Not only that, but I was a Panamanian making it in the big city, you know? As for my strange behavior, I did not care what people thought! If *Downbeat* magazine put me inside its pages, why would I care about other people's opinions? I was doing the right things.

For the June 1971 *Downbeat* article, a guy called Mark Durham interviewed me. He was interested in my upbringing and stories about my days playing with the Gay Crooners, Black Majesty and Vincent Ford, in addition to growing up in the Panama Canal Zone. We talked about why I came to New York as well as the different musical experiences I had encountered. That article made me feel very proud, because not only was I in the same edition as Sonny Rollins, but I also really got to talk about a lot of things from my past and also the present with the UBF going strong. The only problem with that article was that Mark put somewhere in there that I played with Jack McDuff, which just wasn't true, as I mentioned earlier. I guess he confused me with Carlos Ward.

Pharoah Sanders, another well-known sax player, was also a frequent performer at the East, the cultural and education institution where I often performed. He would come onstage during my shows and jam, and I did the same when he was featuring live with his groups. He dug my sound and invited me to record with him on

Part 1. Panama Roots

his *Live at the East* album, although he wanted me to play flute and I'd have rather played tenor sax. For that particular record, I felt like I didn't get a decent sound because music—and especially this spiritual Black music—should be fun to play, but Pharoah had me limited. But what the heck. I liked Pharoah a lot. He had a different style, and I had my own style.

Pharoah did call me again to play on his next record titled *Black Unity*, also for Impulse Records, and for this one I did play more tenor, but I don't recall much about that session except that it had some top musicians, guys like Stanley Clarke and Cecil McBee on bass with Norman Connors and Billy Hart on drums. There was also my friend Joe Bonner, who would later record with me. The music was a long, collective improvisation with layers of solos, using a lot of percussion and African instruments—a combination that I always enjoyed.

There was this other time when I recall sitting in with Pharoah's group at the Knitting Factory. I remember Pharoah on sax, Ron Burton on piano, and I think Steve Turre on trombone. With Pharoah, there were a couple of times when I would go to a show to hear him and he would invite me on stage.

One of the founders of the East was Jitu Weusi, also known by his original name Les Campbell. Jitu and some other guys formed "The East Cultural Center," which used to be the Arlington Inn before it got renovated. It was a big place! I used to come around all the time because I constantly played with Leo Price across the street in the Baby Grand.

Jitu also led the "African-American Teachers Association" in New York. He was the union representative. One time, they had a big strike and shut down the New York school system for almost three months. Most people involved with Jitu changed their names to African names, but I never did that. Carlos Alfredo Garnett is my name, and it will stay that way.

Jitu was always at my shows and loved the UBF because of the Afrocentric mentality, so he booked my band constantly. We were very popular at the time, especially at his place. Every week he had some different people—sometimes Leon Thomas, sometimes Freddie Hubbard, sometimes Gary Bartz—but the mainstay was "The

The Universal Black Force (UBF)

Cover of *Downbeat* magazine featuring an interview with Carlos Garnett, 1971 (property of *Downbeat* Magazine Maher Publications, used with permission).

Part 1. Panama Roots

Flyer for Rufus Harley, Joe Henderson, the Last Poets, Gary Bartz NTU Troop, and Carlos Garnett and the UBF at the East, 1971 (art by Ron Warwell, used with permission).

The Universal Black Force (UBF)

Album cover for *Alkebu-lan: Land of the Blacks* by Mtume Umoja Ensemble (copyright Strata-East Records).

Universal Black Force" every month. When we performed, people were always singing and dancing.

There was another popular group that catered to the Black communities led by James Mtume. He sometimes worked in my group and I in his. Mtume arranged for a live album called *Alkebu-lan: Land of Blacks* to be recorded at the East, in which I played tenor and flute ("Alkebulan" is an ancient name for Africa). For that occasion, Mtume got together some of the best musicians who performed regularly at the East, including Ndugu, Gary Bartz, Buster Williams and Stanley Cowell, who had just started his own label called "Strata-East." People loved the music, but I think my band was more popular at that time because of the name "Universal Black Force."

Part 1. Panama Roots

The UBF played all the colleges we could: Rutgers, Cheyney State University, Camden University and Lincoln University. At Camden, I used to stay with my good friend Tony Fonedilles and his wife; they always treated me right in their house!

One time at Amherst College in Massachusetts, the white student union didn't want the UBF to go in and perform, so we performed outside. People were singing and dancing everywhere, even up in the trees. Seems like yesterday when we were experiencing this sort of racism right in the faces of everyone in the government (still do!). Many of those people protesting against Black awareness music being played at colleges are still alive today. Let's hope they repented.

The group also played quite often at the Left Bank Jazz Society in Baltimore, Maryland. This was a very important place for the development of creative music, and I would return to play there at the Famous Ballroom quite a few more times during the coming years. Many musicians came along with my group to play there, including Guillermo Edgehill, a Panamanian bass player who was more widely known for his work in salsa and Latin jazz groups. I recall clearly that at one of those gigs at the Left Bank Jazz Society, my spiritual brother Charles Pulliam left the group because he had some trouble with his wife and kids. He should have been in all of my albums to come, but instead I had to go and get Neil Clarke in the group, who at the time was living with his mother. Neil was kind of young still but such a great player regardless. I will never forget having to talk to his mother to ask whether she could please give him permission to play in my group!

Miles Davis!

Mtume was constantly playing in my group, and I was in his, so we developed a close musical relationship. At some point, he got a gig with Miles Davis, and when Miles was looking for a saxophonist, Mtume recommended me. Next thing I knew, the man himself wanted me to go to the next rehearsal at his place. I think me being from Panama had something to do with that. Miles loved Panamanian boxers.

Miles Davis!

I heard once that Miles had punched one of his musicians because he didn't like to talk to people or something, so when Mtume called me to tell me about the gig, I thought about whether it was a good idea because I wasn't going to take shit from anyone, even if it was Miles Davis! But I went. Of course I went; it was Miles Davis! Who says no to that? There I was, the Mango Tree Musician up from Panama, in the band with the legendary Miles Davis.

Miles didn't really compliment me or talk to me much about my playing. He wasn't that kind of person with me. He dug the stuff I was doing but never really suggested or told me what to play except for some of his ideas. The majority of the rehearsal was jamming on ideas without Miles playing. He wasn't even there! He would be upstairs with some fine women hanging out and come down suddenly to engage with us for a while before going on to the same thing.

My first rehearsal with Miles was at his big brownstone house on West 77th Street. When I became a member of the Miles Davis band, I immediately got close to him because I used to snort a lot of cocaine and Miles did the same. At the rehearsals in his house, he would call me to his room to check out the stuff he got because he knew I always had the really good stuff, and I could tell the difference better than anyone else. He lived close to Harlem, and he would send for this one guy to bring him the coke.

One time, he called the guy from Harlem and told him to bring some cocaine. Miles then called me up and told me to check it out, so I snorted a bit. I told him right away that it was bad coke and that I had better stuff with me. He yelled at the dealer to change the shit and sent the cocaine back! When the guy brought the stuff the second time around, Miles told me to go and check it again. This one, though, wow, yeah, shit man, this time it was good. The guy went to change it and came back with "flakes." I don't know if you all understand, but flakes (or fish scales) was what we sometimes called top-grade cocaine.

Miles was a character. There are three guys who frightened me in my life, and he was one of them. Miles once told me to take out a dollar and passed me the pack of cocaine. I did some and put the dollar back in my pocket while I returned the packet to him. Well, next thing I knew, he took the whole packet down! That frightened

Part 1. Panama Roots

me. I still remember it, just like I remember Charles Mingus eating a five-course meal and drinking a gallon of wine after the sets and Art Blakey shooting heroin down in the basement in one of the jazz clubs on 113th Street with the rest of the band downstairs in the bathrooms. That really scared me. I loved my job, but I didn't feel good about using heroin. I used to skin pop, as injecting under the skin was better than putting it in your veins, but I stopped using it because I didn't like the way it made me feel—made me vomit and stuff like that. As I said, in all my life, there's three guys who frightened me: Miles Davis, Art Blakey and Charles Mingus.

Miles hung out with me because I knew about good cocaine and, on top of that, because of the Panamanian boxers. He loved boxing. That's one of the few things I knew about him before I joined his group. He used to call me and say, "Hey, Panama, Panama, the best fighters come from Panama." He loved and respected Panamanian boxers, so from the very beginning I was in with him. I got to see his gym, and we talked about amateur boxers because he used to be one. He was very knowledgeable about the sport. He loved Roberto Duran, one of the best to ever fight.

Despite all the rehearsing and messing around at Miles' house, it was at the studio that I really learned what to do with his music. While I was with Miles, we always recorded very early in the morning. His producer, Teo Macero, would call all of us and tell us to be at the studio for a specific time to record, sometimes as early as 5:30 a.m.! Miles used to say that the morning was the best time for recording because, according to him, you had more energy. We knew we were going to record at some point, but not the date or time. My first date at the studio for the *On the Corner* album was very interesting in that the huge Columbia Records studio was filled with top musicians. I encountered a lot of what I was doing with the UBF, like two drummers, two percussionists and electric guitar to top it off. There were Jack DeJohnette and Billy Hart with Don Alias and James Mtume. I remember John McLaughlin and some other guy there on electric guitars. Miles did his thing differently in the studio, and he would book many musicians, but not all of them would make the cut for his tours.

Miles Davis!

The same day of that recording date, Miles told me he wanted me on his next tour. It was an incredible feeling to have that opportunity arise for me after all that I had experienced in my life—to be where I was, on the way to start a tour with Miles Davis and his new group. The next day, after the session at Columbia Records, I got a soprano saxophone because Miles wanted that sound. I went straight to Sam Ash and asked them to make an attachment to wire the soprano to the wah wah pedal. Miles needed the wah wah sound.

In those days, Miles used mostly electronic instruments. His trumpet was electrified with a wah wah pedal, as was my new soprano sax. For the live group, he had Cedric Lawson on electric piano, Mike Henderson on Fender bass, Reggie Lucas on electric guitar, Badal Roy on amplified tablas and other Indian percussion, Khalil Balakrishna on electric sitar, James Mtume on percussion and Al Foster on drums. I played tenor sometimes, as well as a lot of soprano sax. It was a heavy and very different crop of players. There are some unreleased recordings of this group that I heard much later in which you can hear me blow my tenor well. It was a very innovative format and changed Miles' sound from the earlier period that had Gary Bartz and Keith Jarrett. This music was out there but funky.

I don't recall Miles telling us what to do very much. You had to kind of have a feel for it. He gave very few suggestions. Most of the time it was freelance, and his great producer Teo Macero recorded it all. Back in those days, John Lennon and the Beatles were listening to sitar and Indian music. I speculate that Miles wanted to do something like that but make it funky and Black. He was going through that era in which he didn't want to swing, so he went in the direction of fusing the Indian and Black American influences with great jazz players.

Teo Macero recorded for hours every single day, and afterward Miles would go into the control room and choose what he wanted to put out and what to keep in the vault. That vault over at Columbia must have so much good shit from those days. We just recorded non-stop. We had sort of an idea from the rehearsal sometimes, but that's it. I never had a clue about what was going to come out on the record until I heard the LP.

Part 1. Panama Roots

Around the same time as recording *On the Corner* with Miles Davis, Norman Connors came out of my band to record his own debut album. Norman got a recording deal with Buddah Records, a subsidiary of CBS Records, with a producer named Skip Drinkwater, who happened to be from his own hometown in Germantown, Philadelphia. Norman asked me to help him arrange his composition "Dance of Magic" for his debut album of the same name. He had gotten some heavyweights for the recording session—notably Herbie Hancock, Gary Bartz, Art Webb, Airto Moreira, Eddie Henderson, Stanley Clarke, and Billy Hart. I had to lead the band with my arrangements, and I always felt honored to work with the best of the best.

In those sessions, I met Joe Fields, who was the executive director and was still working for the CBS recording company. He noticed that I was directing Norman's group and doing most of the arranging. He informed me that he was getting ready to open his own recording company and that he would like me to join it and record for him. What Joe told me made a lot of sense, so I decided to wait for that opportunity to come around because Joe was going to give me complete musical and artistic control over the albums I made with his label. That, to me, was the most important part, besides the fact that I would own my compositions, not the label.

The Norman Connors session was done quickly, and soon enough I was traveling with Miles. On that tour, we performed at the 1972 Ann Arbor Jazz and Blues Festival in Michigan, where we played in front of something like 50,000 fans. That is still the largest crowd I've ever performed for. The huge crowd was no concern to me; in fact, that night I felt I could express myself really well on the horn. I remember arriving on the plane and going straight to the show from the airport. On the way to the festival, I saw a sign on the turnpike that said "Brooklyn" with a big arrow next to it, which got me thinking a bit because I had been living in Brooklyn, New York, for several years. Well, it so happens that there is also a Brooklyn, Michigan. There's probably a Brooklyn in Alaska too! Looking at that highway sign on the way to the biggest show in my life made me feel kind of like I was at home. Just reading those letters that spelled "Brooklyn" brought a sense of calm.

Miles Davis!

This Miles Davis group also played several nights in a row at Paul's Mall in Boston, Massachusetts, right after a run of shows at some place called the Spectrum in Philadelphia. The next stop was a packed show at the Philharmonic Hall (now called Lincoln Center) in New York City, which was recorded and released as a full double LP titled *In Concert*. At the time, we didn't really know the performance was being recorded for an official album. The music we were playing at that time was very rhythmic and repetitive, but very rich. It was not about the solos; it was mostly about the feel of the rhythm. There were slow vamps, but also heavy and fast layered grooves—very African and psychedelic at the same time. Cedric Lawson had a lot of effects on his pianos, and it mostly sounded nothing like a regular

Miles Davis *On the Corner* album cover (copyright Columbia Records).

Part 1. Panama Roots

Miles Davis *In Concert* album cover (copyright Columbia Records).

piano. Once the *In Concert* LP came out, I got to understand Miles' approach a little better. The music was strange at times.

Both album covers for *On the Corner* and *In Concert* had artwork appealing to the younger audiences, with cartoons of pimps, prostitutes with big afros and stuff like that. Miles Davis was going somewhere new, and the critics didn't know where that was, so they hated it, but young people loved it. He had those critics scratching their heads, as they didn't even know what sort of instruments we used in the albums (Miles had no credits inserted in them).

A few days after the show at the Philharmonic, we played Stanford University in Palo Alto, California. While staying at the Hollywood Hotel, I opened the door to my room and saw Cedric Lawson butt naked, just hanging out. He was always pretty crazy, and for some reason the only person in the band who could stay in the room with him was me. I used to do crazy things, but Cedric was crazier. Cedric used a bunch of keyboards with effects that layered on top of each other. It was mostly textures, not really solos. When that was paired with the Indian instruments, it created an interesting blend. Everyone except the percussionist had a wah wah pedal too.

After those shows in Palo Alto, we were packing up to go to the LAX airport. I carried a big Sony tape recorder box, which had light meters with very nice volume monitor buttons for left and right channels. It was a top-notch recorder! It even had volume adjustments for each side, allowing me to balance it all. Everywhere we went with Miles, I had it. That day at Palo Alto, I was packing up the tenor, the soprano and the big recorder into the taxi, and for a minute, I placed the soprano sax on the hood of the car behind me. I was more worried about the recorder! Before I knew it, I had left the soprano behind. When I got to the airport, I realized what I'd done, and shit, we went back and it was gone. I had to get another horn.

We also visited the city of San Diego, where we had some time off, so we all took the bus to the border in Tijuana and bought some cheap leather jackets of all different kinds for a good price. Michael Henderson and Reggie Lucas and I got some nice ones.

Once we got back from the tour, Miles broke his leg by crashing his Lamborghini on the West Side Highway. During the time I recorded and toured with him, he was usually limping because of hip problems. The car accident made him stop working with his previous regularity. The group had gotten into a nice rhythm, but it all stopped and this particular band dissolved. Back then, I thought the group was going to continue and had no idea that show at the Civic Theatre in San Diego would be my last with Miles. You see, we kept recording a few months later, when Miles started feeling a little better, but he wasn't thinking about touring. He then got Dave Liebman into the group.

The UBF was going strong, playing almost every week, so my mind was already heading in that direction. I wasn't thinking about Miles Davis anymore. My recordings with Miles ended up on four of

Part 1. Panama Roots

his albums: *On the Corner, Get Up with It, Big Fun,* and *In Concert.* In almost all those gigs and recording sessions, I played soprano sax, usually wired for effects. That was what Miles wanted, not so much tenor sax. During the year 1972, I went to the studio about four times with Miles Davis.

Working with the Miles Davis group for those months taught me a lot, especially about the music business. Whenever we did a show or traveled with Miles, they put money in our hands before we got on stage. Management wanted the guys to be happy, and I was definitely happy! We had a lot of fun doing his new music, but, to my/our dismay, we did not swing too much in the traditional sense.

Carlos Garnett with soprano saxophone (photo by Ron Warwell, used with permission).

Miles was breaking new ground, and I would come to understand his approach much later.

It was great while it lasted.

More with Norman Connors

I was also back in the studio recording with the Norman Connors group, first for his album *Dark of Light* and then for another one titled *Love from the Sun*. This became a bit of a habit for me over the next few years, as I would record a few more times with Norman in between recording my own albums. These sessions gave me the opportunity to arrange for another set of top-notch musicians like Herbie Hancock on piano, Eddie Henderson on trumpet, Gary Bartz on alto and Ron Carter on bass.

Skip Drinkwater, Norman's producer, offered me the same deal that he gave Norman, in which he would have control of all my music for five years. He would also own all of my original songs and the

Painting of Carlos Garnett and Art Webb (art by Ron Warwell, used with permission).

Part 1. Panama Roots

From left: Carlos Garnett, Charles Sullivan and Charles Pulliam at Studio Rivbea in 1973 (photo by Raymond Ross, used with permission, Raymond Ross CTSIMAGES).

publishing. I turned that down and waited to go with Joe Fields' new company, Muse Records. Joe gave me a great deal in which I owned my songs and had my own publishing company, along with the freedom to record the songs I chose with whatever instrumentation I wanted. I was doing different kinds of music, experimenting with African and Latin stuff, with total artistic freedom.

After the release of his album *Love from the Sun*, Norman decided to use most of my group to travel with him when he started to get gigs. Many were musicians with whom he had played before, and they included Hubert Eaves on piano, James "Fish" Benjamin on bass, Neil Clarke on percussion and me on reeds. He used Jean Carne on vocals too. On *Love from the Sun*, Norman would use a song of mine called "Carlos II." This song was named after my son. I also arranged other songs of his for that release.

Around this time, I did a session for saxophonist Robin Kenyatta. Robin was well known in and around the New York scene, and I had seen him play a couple of times. His producer, Michael Cuscuna, contacted me to record a couple of tracks for him, and I was pleasantly surprised when I arrived at the studio and heard the music. They were sort of funky reggae tunes with a calypso flavor, which took me back to my roots. I wasn't involved in any gigs that required playing that style, but I was happy nonetheless, as it made me feel my Caribbean roots. The songs came out on an LP of Robin's titled *Terra Nova* and featured some great musicians like Ron Carter, Ralph McDonald and the funky lady Betty Davis, who was Miles' second wife.

Black Love

In the beginning of 1974, I recorded my first album for Muse Records, which was titled *Black Love*. For this album, I used several songs that the Universal Black Force had been playing for the past few years in and around the scene, plus a few new tunes. There were compositions like "Taurus Woman," which I wrote for my woman many years before. That song was actually one of Art Blakey's favorites to play during our 1970 Japanese tour. We played "Taurus Woman" all over Japan in its original form, but I worked out a fresh idea for this new record. Alex Blake was the bass player, and I told him to use a fuzz and wah wah pedal. My friends Charles Sullivan and Mauricio Smith handled the harmonies on trumpet and flute, respectively.

Part 1. Panama Roots

My concept was based on the idea that too many Black artists were too busy doing their thing, and white people were robbing them of their art, so I wrote "Black Love." To top it off, Black brothers and sisters were still treated as inferior in many places. I was reading Black history, while listening to Black and proud songs. My song "Black Love" came out of those thoughts, and I wrote it with vocals to express my feelings. "Ebonesque" was for the mother of my son. For my song "Banks of the Nile," I was thinking about our origins—the origins of my Black brothers and sisters in Egypt, along the Nile River, with all the crocodiles, pyramids and mythical stuff. "Mother of the Future" is one of my most recognized compositions, and it came from thinking about all the Black sisters raising the next generation of our beautiful Black societies, always fighting for their young ones.

On that album, I had the time to sit down and break down the meter and write out all the notes. The musicians I chose were in and around the New York scene, and when I called them up, they were all very excited to work on my tunes. Most of them knew me: Norman Connors and Billy Hart on drums, Buster Williams and Alex Blake on bass, Mauricio Smith on flute, Charles Sullivan on trumpet, James Mtume and Guilherme Franco on percussion, Onaje Allan Gumbs on piano and Reggie Lucas on guitar. I also had my good friend from Panama, Carlos Chambers, as a guest yodeling with his voice. He had come from the Vietnam War not long before. I remember he had a big piano with all the keys in the world but couldn't play shit. For my debut album, I played mostly alto, but my approach was different from most others because the idea was to play it as a tenor. The tone wasn't fine, fine, but more of a broader sound.

Ayodele sang on the record after I taught her how to improve on what she already knew about singing. She had a strong voice because she used to sing in a church. I used Ayodele and her sister Cora, along with one of their friends named Mona, as vocalists in my new venture. Dee Dee Bridgewater also sang on my first album. When I first met her, I showed her around the different music circles I was involved in, and she turned out to be a top singer, one of the best. She did the lead on one of the songs, "Banks of the Nile." Ayodele sang

Flyer for the East announcing Sam Rivers, Max Roach, Betty Carter, Edwin Birdsong, and Carlos Garnett, 1971 (art by Ron Warwell, used with permission).

the lead on the title track "Black Love," which became the rallying song at many Black affairs events, colleges and universities on the East Coast, but especially at the East in Brooklyn, the cultural, educational and entertainment establishment that for years had brought

Part 1. Panama Roots

Flyer for the East announcing Betty Carter, the Visitors, and Carlos Garnett (art by Ron Warwell, used with permission).

in top jazz artists to perform. It was after a night playing at the East that I had lost my gig with Freddie Hubbard, but now the UBF was a regular there, and we always had the place jumping!

Before we got to the studio to record *Black Love*, the band had

Black Love

Flyer for the East announcing Carlos Garnett, Chief Bey, McCoy Tyner, and Collective Black Artist Band at the East, 1971 (art by Ron Warwell, used with permission).

Part 1. Panama Roots

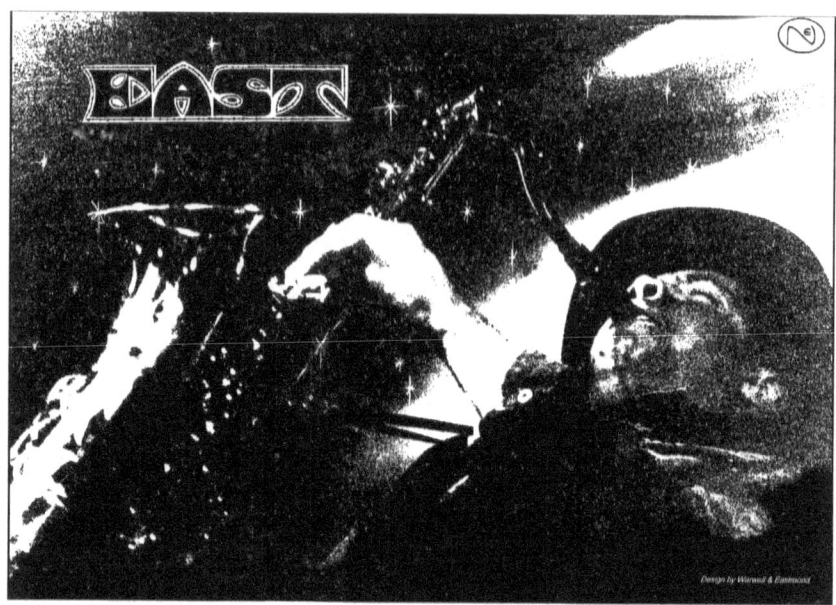

Concept art for the East featuring Carlos Garnett (art by Ron Warwell, used with permission).

to rehearse all the songs. I conducted several rehearsals before we went in because I wanted to make sure everyone had the music right. My compositions were very different from the stuff they were accustomed to playing. The musicians were in fine form, and they played their asses off for me. That is something I will forever be grateful for because everyone involved took the music very seriously.

Black Love was a big hit in the Black communities and colleges. The UBF played all around New York, New Jersey, Philadelphia and Boston. I was also working and traveling with Norman Connors as the band director in addition to leading my own group. I was very busy indeed, playing and practicing all the time on all my instruments. By then, I had bought a Selmer soprano saxophone. I found a way to play all three of my horns on the *Black Love* album.

My good friend Ron Warwell did the cover and graphic work on that album, and Clarence Eastman took the photos. That *Black Love* cover photo I think was taken in my apartment by Clarence. Ron is a very talented and gifted brother. I met him around 1965 when I was

Black Love

playing with an organ player named Henry in a club by Bushwick Avenue and Halsey Street. Henry was a fuckup, but he could play well. He had this guy John, a drummer from Indianapolis or Detroit, I can't remember. When I finished one of those gigs, I wanted to smoke a joint and went outside. While smoking my thing, I ran into Ron with this other guy, Jim Doudy, who had just bought a house right by the jazz club. Jim invited me to go jam in his new basement. Ron was renting the first floor at the same place. It turned out that Jim played piano and Ron played drums. After finishing my gig at the club, I went over to Jim's and jammed until the morning, playing all kinds of music with Ron. He and I built a friendship that has been very strong even up until now.

Carlos Garnett *Black Love* album cover (copyright Muse Records).

Part 1. Panama Roots

Ron is my best friend, always looking out for me and never a pain. He was usually there with me and kept a lot of my history in the form of drawings, flyers, newspaper cuttings and more. The other day, I was trying to remember the names of some musicians who played with me at the East with the UBF, and Ron sent me the flyer—with all the names and everything! His artwork was a blessing for my music.

Many times I get down in the dumps, but Ron tells me, "Carlos, think of all the work you have done. People in Russia, people in Japan, people everywhere love your music! Think about what you have done!" I told him I loved him because he always gets me up when I'm down. He told me he loved me too.

Journey to Enlightenment

A few months after recording *Black Love*, I was back in the studio for my second album titled *Journey to Enlightenment*. My mind was working very fast, and it seemed new songs were coming out of it almost daily. My friend Ron Warwell once again did the cover design and photos for the album. Ron's covers are legendary. He made a painting of me with my tenor sax with a prehistoric bird up in the sky and all this other crazy stuff. I wanted the "ankh" symbol on the cover because my father was into a cult back in Panama called "Rosicrucianism." I used to wear one of those symbols all the time. The title *Journey to Enlightenment* was because of my spiritual connection, African connection, metaphysical connection—you know, spirituality.

The title of the last song in the album puts it well: "Let Us Go (Into Higher Heights)." Need I say anything else? There are different concepts of feeling in the songs I write. The whole concept of my music is spiritual, and sometimes I can get inspiration from someone like "Chana." "Chana" is a bad, bad tune. It's got this heavy Latin stuff going on with a magnificent bass line. The song was written for my daughter who carries that beautiful name. When we finished recording "Chana," I asked Joe Fields to play it back for me. After I heard it, I told everyone we were going to do it again because I didn't like a

Journey to Enlightenment

Artistic interpretation of Carlos Garnett playing his soprano saxophone (art by Ron Warwell, used with permission).

bad note that I had played on the solo. Reggie Lucas stopped me right away and told me I was crazy. He loved the "bad note." So did everyone else but me. Sometimes you've just got to listen more.

Another great song from this album is "Caribbean Sun"; the name came from the fact that I am from a Caribbean country: Panama! That's why it has a calypso flavor. All those experiences playing with Black Majesty and the other great Panamanian calypso singers are present in "Caribbean Sun." I wanted to record jazz with ukulele, so here I made it possible. I also wrote the vocals and decided to sing them myself. Years later, Betty Carter recorded "Caribbean Sun" but with a very different arrangement. That was an honor for me. For this record, there was only Ayodele and me on vocals. We were both working on songs all the time at home. She had developed a good singing style, complementing my arrangements. You can hear her sing very well on a song titled "Love Flower."

"Journey to Enlightenment," the title track, is a highly spiritual song, with Ayodele and me doing some nice harmonies. For this album, I used great musicians like Reggie Lucas on guitar, Anthony

Part 1. Panama Roots

Jackson on bass, Hubert Eaves on piano, Neil Clarke and Charles Pulliam on percussion and Howard King on drums. Joe Fields decided to use a different studio than where we had recorded *Black Love*. It was the Minot Sound Studios, where I would also record another album the following year.

One of my problems during this period was that I was doing everything by myself. I didn't have a manager, agent or anything. Joe Fields helped with the sessions and all the record-related stuff, but I was dealing with everything else on my own. That's why I never got a penny for my songs, I guess. The only thing that mattered to me was making great music. I wasn't thinking about selling lots of

Carlos Garnett *Journey to Enlightenment* album cover (copyright Muse Records).

records—just making music that had meaning by channeling all of my experiences. *Journey to Enlightenment* is an album that I get praised for to this day. I really liked what Joe wrote in the liner notes: "Carlos' music is mysterious, streetwise and of other places.... There is a message, a theme to Carlos' songs. It is a search for Nirvana."

Let This Melody Ring On

Ayodele had a piano in our apartment that helped me a lot when it came to putting whatever I had in my head into musical language. It was in this apartment that I wrote, arranged and composed all the music for *Black Love* and *Journey to Enlightenment*. It was only natural that this was the same place where I also began writing music for my next album, *Let This Melody Ring On*. Musically, all of my creative powers were going in the right direction with a new album in sight, but the rest of my life not so much. My career as a musician was good, but I was messing around too much with drugs and women. Ayodele and I separated around this time because of my insanity! I then moved into another apartment located on East 19th Street. One of my saxophone students and a good friend, Akum Ra Amen-Ra, moved into a side room and split the rent with me.

The rehearsals for my new album began with calling in some of my favorite musicians, like Charles Pulliam, Reggie Lucas, Hubert Eaves, Anthony Jackson, and more. They dug the music right away, and soon we were at the studio recording my songs. Joe Fields had everything ready at Minot Sound Studios once again. I had a new vocalist called Prema doing the rounds. She did the lead vocals on the songs "Samba Serenade" and "Let This Melody Ring On." I wrote all the lyrics for those songs. Sometimes I look back and give thanks and praise to the Almighty Creator that those ideas came into my head. The music, the words just flowed out. I used to write in a book every word that rhymed—"bear, fear, dear, wear, tear"—and put them all down meticulously. "Son, mom, don, fun." I used that book a lot. I still have it somewhere.

Prema, my new vocalist, was recommended by someone I can't recall, but she was fairly unknown. To my surprise, she tore the shit

Part 1. Panama Roots

out of "Samba Serenade"! She could go really high! Higher than I thought. When she joined the band, I was studying yoga, and so was she. I realized Prema was another one with a spiritual mentality. I tried to get with her one time in my apartment, but she wouldn't do that; she was very spiritual. She told me she only wanted to hug. I wasn't into that. She came to Panama once, many years later, to the "Parque Omar," where I was practicing, and showed up together with some other girl. I think she had something with that one girl. I didn't make a move, but back in Brooklyn I did try. In those days, she was married to a trombone player, so she didn't want to have anything to do with me.

I remember that I played baritone on *Let This Melody Ring On*—overdubbed it. Muse Records did make a mistake, though: they didn't credit me as the flute player. I played the flute on "Panama Roots," a song that is among my favorite compositions. That song has the only flute solo I ever did on record. I was always extending my knowledge on the flute, but I guess I didn't feel I really got the sound I wanted on it until the time of "Panama Roots." The flute is an instrument that was very close to me, but for some reason I didn't record with it as much as I would have liked.

I wrote "Ghetto Jungle" as a mixture of things. First, I put myself in the context of the song because I came up from the jungle, but it also was about the Black kids who couldn't play anywhere in Brooklyn. When I first moved to New York, kids played soccer and everything in the street—in the concrete jungle. When I was a kid growing up, I made my toys with a saw. I remember in Paraíso I made my own gun with wood. Those memories were very much present as I wrote "Ghetto Jungle." This was another of those songs that I decided to sing for myself.

I had the opportunity to bring Carlos Chambers and Carlos Jordan, my friends from Panama, into the recording studio. We were all raised in Paraíso, and we were all in Brooklyn at the same time! We all played ukuleles at the same time too! One day, all of us went to Riis Beach in Brooklyn with Ron Warwell specifically to take a photo with the ukes. I wanted to record jazz with the ukulele, and I did it!

On *Let This Melody Ring On*, I played some nice solos while

Let This Melody Ring On

From left: Carlos Jordan, Carlos Garnett and Carlos Chambers with ukuleles at Riis Beach, New York (photo by Ron Warwell, used with permission).

enjoying my sound on the tenor sax. Musicians all over the world were starting to recognize me as a fiery saxophone player with my own ideas. My albums then didn't have any covers of other songs, standards or remakes. None of that! It was all original music that sprang out of my brain. My experiences in life were caught up in these compositions.

I used most of the same guys from my previous recording session. As you can see, I liked to do that as much as I could. For *Journey to Enlightenment*, I didn't use any other horns, but for *Let This Melody Ring On* I brought them back, with Olu Dara on trumpet and Kiane Zawadi on trombone in some tunes. I also told Joe Fields that I wanted to use some strings, so he got me a string quartet right away. The strings brought another color to my music, but I had to sit down to write everything in detail, breaking the time slowly and giving the players all the music to record my songs.

I am grateful to Joe Fields for giving me not only the opportunity

Part 1. Panama Roots

to record but also the freedom to write, arrange and keep ownership of all of my music on the albums. The artistic liberty I had at Muse Records allowed me to create these compositions without worrying about the commercial part or what critics had to say. Thanks, Joe!!!

The cover photo for *Let This Melody Ring On*, which showed me holding my flute, was taken in Central Park. You can't see it, but I was standing up on a big rock. Ron Warwell took that picture. He came to my home one sunny day and told me to get ready to go to the park to take some pictures. It turned out to be a great photo. Bless you, Ron!

Let This Melody Ring On was recorded around the same time as my final album for Norman Connors' band, titled *Saturday Night*

Carlos Garnett *Let This Melody Ring On* album cover (copyright Muse Records).

Special. This was the last of a series of albums I did with him like *Dance of Magic, Dark of Light, Slewfoot* and *Love from the Sun*. With Norman, I got to play with some of the best musicians in the business. I rearranged "Mother of the Future" for Norman's *Slewfoot* album, and it was a big hit in Europe. I still haven't seen a penny from that.

The Tony Silvester Era

I don't remember how, but that same year, in 1975, I got hooked up with a character named Tony "Champagne" Silvester, who was a singer formerly with the famous Main Ingredient group. Tony was Panamanian, and his group had a big hit in the early 1970s with the song "Everybody Plays the Fool." Cuba Gooding (the father of the famous actor of the same name) was the lead singer in his group.

Tony was a producer for the CBS/April Blackwood publishing company, which managed several hit catalogs. The company hired Tony as a writer, as well as producer, so he got a group of talented musicians to write, arrange and be part of his production team. The crew consisted of Dwight Brewster, Stan Lucas, Harvey Lesesne and me. Dwight and I quickly became really good friends.

Dwight Brewster was from New York, but he had a deep connection with my country because he had lived in Panama for several years. He had a funk and soul band called the Jungle Rat, which played all over Panama in the early 1970s. Dwight had a big career in the Latin and salsa circles before I met him. He was the guy who put together and directed Willie Colón's first band. He arranged all of Willie's early recordings, including his first album for Fania Records.

Tony Silvester knew he could count on us both to do a great job, so we were contracted to write 10 songs each for $15,000 a man. Since I loved composing songs, this deal was great and a lot of fun. We had to compose, arrange the songs and record them as demos first. Dwight and I also became the lead composers for Tony's band. Basically, we were in the recording studio every day and night. Tony would rent the studios and give us free rein to make what we had in mind happen. Sometimes he would show up, but most of the time he did not.

Part 1. Panama Roots

We were making a union-scale payment, and for that we had to join the musicians' union. Pay was $100 for the first three hours, but after that it was time and a half. Sometimes we were in the studios all day and night, making a lot of money. This was good news for all of us, especially me, for I was also able to record my compositions and listen to them on the same day. I was doing most of the solos and was having a great time doing so. Soon they began calling me "One Take Carlos," for when I did my solos, it would be accepted after the first take. And it wasn't just on my tenor; I was also doing some great stuff on the alto and soprano saxes. Imagine, doing what I loved to do and making good money at the same time!

Tony had connections. We were writing and making demos for the likes of Prince, Marvin Gaye, Kool & the Gang, the Imperials, the Kay-Gees, and so on. For the Imperials, I recall recording a nice soprano saxophone solo on their hit "Who's Gonna Love Me." Dwight and Harvey did the arranging on that one. Dwight was always in and around those recordings too, as in those sessions I did for Kalyan, a group from Trinidad that Tony Silvester was producing.

Eventually, Tony got a multimillion-dollar deal to write songs for a French artist who sold millions of albums. We were to write all of the songs for that project. Everything was set, and I had two or three songs on the deal. Tony was supposed to fly in for a meeting with the artist in France on a Monday, but he chose to go three days later to fly on the new Concorde supersonic jet. He arrived late and blew the deal. After that, he lost his CBS/April Blackwood contract, and that was the end of the team.

Cosmos Nucleus: *The Big Band Experiment*

As soon as I finished *Let This Melody Ring On*, my head kept pointing me in a new direction. The work with Tony was steady, but I decided that I wanted to do something I had never done before. It was in my heart and mind to do a big band recording. I was living on East 19th Street in Brooklyn listening to Duke Ellington and Count Basie constantly. I always thought I could write classical music too,

Cosmos Nucleus: *The Big Band Experiment*

so that was also in my head, but at that moment in time the big band sound was all I could think of.

Ever since moving out of Ayodele's apartment, I had no piano, but I was still writing every free moment I had. My pinky finger even got a big corn blister on it from all the writing. When I write my music, I'm always in the sky, and when I play my sax, I play a lot of high notes. Throughout this time, I was doing a lot of yoga and meditation too. I believed I could do anything. When putting together the big band scores, I had a song called "Cosmos Nucleus," so I decided to use that name for the big band and, ultimately, for the record itself. The cover was done once again by Ron Warwell, who created an iconic painting that everyone (especially record collectors) loved.

All of the compositions and arrangements on the *Cosmos Nucleus* album were done on the flute and sax because I had no piano. I would take the ruler, cut the staff in half, and then write these tiny notes because I wanted to save paper! Every musical thought was interpreted through my reed instruments and written in these small music sheets. I never went to school, so I give much thanks and praise to the Almighty Creator because I feel I have been blessed.

Besides writing and arranging new material for my big band experiment, I needed to recruit a lot of people to form the Cosmos Nucleus 24-piece band. I knew many young, upcoming musicians and asked them whether they would participate in my experiment, and they all agreed. Kenny Kirkland was a notable one, as was Cecil McBee, Jr. They both joined the band, and we started rehearsing at my apartment. Before I knew it, a flood of young musicians wanted to record with me. Some would recommend others, and that was how I formed my 24-piece big band. I could not ask professional musicians to rehearse every week for nothing, especially with no gigs, as I could not afford it. Cecil McBee carried his father's name, and (can you believe it?) both played bass. I had played with his father before, so he knew about me.

I got busy; every waking moment I had was spent composing and arranging. Something that helped me a lot was looking through a book on arranging by Russell Garcia called *The Professional Arranger Composer*. This information was all new to me, and I

Part 1. Panama Roots

found myself submerged in the content, as I loved fourths and fifths. I implemented them in my voicings all the time. This was all done by trial and error and common sense!

I had to do a lot of rehearsals to record my work so I could listen to it later and check out how the arrangements sounded. It was hard work, but I had the commitment of the young musicians, and it was one of my passions, so I continued. My tape recorder was my best friend for quite some time before recording this album.

The apartment was now too small to rehearse with this big group, and I couldn't afford a big hall to practice, so I ended up getting everyone together at Prospect Park right across the street from my apartment. People would gather and watch me direct the group and the entire practice sessions. One such day, I saw one of my former girlfriends, Lucille, walking in the park, so I went to her and told her that I wanted to see my daughter Sheila. After Sheila was born in 1965, I didn't have a chance to meet her because Lucille left me and hooked up with another guy. She didn't want my daughter to know I was her real father. It had been 10 years.

Lucille told me she would bring Sheila to the park, but only if I would agree not to tell her that I was her father. I didn't approve of this deception, but I really had no choice and agreed to her terms for the meeting. For the next rehearsal, she brought Sheila and we played a little bit, but it was strange to me because I couldn't say what I really wanted to say. Regardless, I was very happy to meet my beautiful daughter.

After that encounter, I was able to call Sheila once in a while at her home. I remember calling Lucille one time to ask about Sheila, and while waiting on the phone her Muslim husband kept telling me that he wanted to play saxophone, so I promised to send some patterns for him to practice. I took the time to find some printed music that could help him and wrote out a few simple patterns for him to rehearse, and I sent the printed sheets in the mail to him. He was nice to me at that time, but then, all of a sudden, he stopped talking to me. This development affected my relationship with Sheila.

At the beginning of the summer, I felt the band was ready because we had rehearsed as much as I thought was necessary. Now, if I was

Cosmos Nucleus: *The Big Band Experiment*

going to record this music, I wanted to hear it! So, I put together a live gig. Steve Turre, the trombone player, played with us on that occasion. He was part of the big band initially and should have been on the album, except he had a tour or something to attend for the session date.

During the entire experience, I enjoyed listening to the band playing my music. To me, that was the most interesting part of my role as director. I was very happy that this huge ensemble of great young musicians was playing my music as I envisioned it, and I also very much enjoyed making sure it all was exactly the way I heard it in my head.

I had many bright and upcoming youths on this album. Just to mention a few: Kenny Kirkland; Zane Massey; Cecil McBee, Jr.; Charles Dougherty; Angel Fernandez; Sheryl Alexander; Cyril Greene; Andrew Washington; Akum Ra Amen-Ra, Warren Benbow; Wayne Cobham; Curtis Fowlkes; James Stowe; and of course my good friend Neil Clarke on percussion.

While writing "Saxy," I was thinking about calling it "Sexy," but then I decided to call it the way it is because the saxophone is my lover. When I put my mouth on the mouthpiece, she responds. If I put a finger on the keys, she does what I want, and she screams. That's the closest I've come to writing anything sexy.

The "Wise Old Man" was me. If you know history, the wise men are always standing next to kings and queens. When you think about it, they also all have a good woman beside them. But the song is also about Africa. They don't have books or computers in those small towns, so the griot tells the villagers the stories of their ancestors and their history with the big pipe in his mouth. The griot was the wise old man in these villages.

> *When you are sick,*
> *they know the cure.*
> *They are welcome in any door.*
> *Wise old man.*

I thought about the "Mystery of Ages" in my studies of the Bible. When I think about life and death, I interpret it as a mystery.

> *Nobody knows,*
> *Mystery of Ages.*
> *Who am I?*

Part 1. Panama Roots

Where did I come from?
What am I here for?
Where am I going?
All the wise men of the world don't know the answer,
Is there life after death?

"Mystery of Ages" is one of my most beloved songs around the world, especially in Japan. Musically, you can hear what I was digging when I made that long line for "Mystery of Ages"; the way the line works is that I end up in a different key, letting the drums do a solo and starting again in the same key from the beginning. Years later, I got this book also called *Mystery of Ages* by a guy named Herbert Armstrong, who was an American preacher with many articles to his name. His book is what I call a bunch of crap. I read some of it and kept it just because of the title.

Another song on the album was "Kafira," which is a wordplay on "Afrika." (Most of us back in those days liked using a "K" instead of a "C.") I used to do a lot of that, playing with words for the titles of my songs. When composing, I would sometimes have a whole song finished and no title, and I enjoyed the process of coming up with original names. At other times, it was the other way around: I thought about the title, and then the musical idea developed.

"Bed Stuy Blues" was written to honor Brooklyn and all it had given to me since my arrival in 1962. The Bedford–Stuyvesant neighborhood has been a center of African American culture for many years, and living there changed my life. The song is a swinging arrangement! Al Brown opens with a burning alto sax solo. Wayne Cobham has a great solo in this piece too. Wayne happens to be Billy Cobham's brother. Billy was another top musician with Panamanian roots, like Eric Dolphy or even me. However, Billy left Panama at a very young age, so he never really grew up in that culture.

After *Cosmos Nucleus*, I was burned out from dealing with problems coordinating the rehearsals, staying up all night getting the charts ready, managing different personalities, and so on. It was very hard work, but I got it done and I was most certainly pleased with the outcome of the album. *Downbeat* magazine even reviewed the album in the April 1977 issue, in which the writers were very impressed

Carlos Garnett *Cosmos Nucleus* album cover (art by Ron Warwell, used with permission).

with the outcome of the big band recordings and how the young guys performed for me. Guess who was on the cover of the magazine once again? Sonny Rollins!

The Girl at the Warehouse

Back when I was still living with my roommate Akum Ra, he had fallen in love with a young Panamanian lady who also lived in our apartment building. Before I knew it, they got married and Akum Ra moved out. I stayed in the five-bedroom apartment by myself for

Part 1. Panama Roots

a while afterward, but after recording *Cosmos Nucleus* I decided to leave because I was paying the rent alone. Not long after, and for reasons unknown to me, Akum Ra and his wife broke up, so he ended up living by himself. Who knows why his relationship collapsed? It all happened so fast! Since I had given up that large apartment, I went to stay with Akum Ra at his new place for a while.

One night, while lying down on a big stack of pillows on Akum Ra's floor, I started thinking of what I wanted to do next with my life. I decided that I would go out dancing that night because I felt something special was going to happen to me. My pockets were hot because Joe Fields had given me some money earlier. I got dressed and went to a popular disco club called the Warehouse. The club was jumping. As usual, I looked around to see which woman I wanted to dance with and maybe have a conversation with. I went to the bar to get a drink, and I noticed two fine young ladies sitting there, having a drink and talking.

As I perused the club while watching these two ladies, I noticed that most of the guys were asking only one to dance. The one they asked to dance was dressed up too much for my liking. After standing next to the ladies for a while, I offered to buy them a drink because I had some money. I went ahead and sat down next to the one I liked; after some talking, I invited her to dance, which she accepted. She could dance very well, and, needless to say, we danced and conversed all night. It was evident that we both liked each other, and I was able to get her phone number. She told me her name was Janis. We danced every song together until she and her friend had to leave. I had a great time! Janis and I started dating, and the more I knew her, the more I liked her. She lived with her parents until she moved in with me a few years later.

Mario Bauzá

Latin jazz was something I enjoyed playing my entire life, and it was around this time that I had a short stint in Marios Bauzá's Afro-Cuban jazz orchestra. Bauzá was the lead trumpeter and director of the band led by the great Cuban artist Machito, the famous musician from the mambo and Cubop era. I remember listening to his songs in Panama and liking the percussion and great horn arrangements.

I ended up in Bauzá's group because one day I was at a record store and this guy Rolando Briceño, whom I knew from the Latin scene, yelled at me from the other end of the store, "Hey, Carlos Garnett! Why don't you come join Mario Bauzá's group?" I knew about Bauzá's Afro-Cubans, so I told him yes right away but, at the same time, made it clear that I was not a good reader. He told me not to worry, because I played much more complicated stuff, and gave me his number. If Rolando told me I could do it, then no problem.

I went to a couple of rehearsals and joined the group for some shows. I would take the charts, go home and learn what to play. Never sight-read—never ever. It was a fun time. I got to play with a few Panamanians like Vitín Paz on trumpet and Guillermo Edgehill on bass. Mario Bauzá also had Graciela on vocals. She was Machito's sister and also Bauzá's sister-in-law. With Bauzá's group, I played a couple of shows at the Latin venues with crowds going crazy and dancing all over the place. The arrangements were always tight, and I kept myself in the pocket until it was my turn to take solos, when I could really go out showcasing my style.

Playing that music reminded me of my days in the 1950s and early 1960s in Panama. The local scene back then had music everywhere with some heavy Latin groups like Chachi Macias' "Nueva Alegria" big band and Victor Boa's orchestras. There were some good local musicians in those big bands who I wished could have gotten more recognition in their careers.

The Kidney Stone

While staying at Akum Ra's, one day I went walking around Parkside Avenue, looking for a new apartment for myself. I saw a nice building to my liking with a real estate sign outside. I had saved enough money to get a luxury apartment in Brooklyn, and I felt this was the place. As I was walking closer, I saw a guy I kind of recognized. Once I got a good look, I realized how I knew him: his father

Part 1. Panama Roots

used to sell cocaine to me. He recognized me as well, and it turned out that he had become a real estate agent. His office was right there on Parkside Avenue. We talked, and I told him I was looking for a nice apartment. To my surprise, he said he could help me and took me to 160 Parkside Avenue. I wanted a good apartment with a nice view because in my last place, every time I looked outside, I saw a concrete building, which was disappointing. My guide showed me apartment 3A, and as soon as I walked in, I was convinced right away to take it. This was where I would stay for the next 19 years. At my new place, I had Prospect Park across the street, which was the biggest park in Brooklyn. I loved parks—still do.

While living a mad lifestyle of music, women and drugs, I suddenly began to have a lot of pain in my stomach. I was suffering, but at first it was intermittent. It would bother me for a few days and then stop. Sometimes I would not feel it for weeks, and out of nowhere it would bother me again. That went on until this one time when the pain was so bad that I stayed in the apartment for a whole week lying down! I had a mattress on top of some milk crates, and I just lay there. Before, I had tried all these holistic methods like shiatsu, acupuncture, drink this, drink that, but it didn't work for shit.

I could not take the pain anymore and decided to call the musicians' union so they could help me get an appointment to see a doctor. They did, and I finally went to the Downstate Medical Center in Brooklyn. The diagnosis was a clear kidney stone, so I blamed the big band. Can you imagine dealing with 24 characters while writing, producing and playing all that?

While I was in the hospital, I had a girl staying in my apartment (Janis was not living with me yet). Let's call her VD. She had a big black dog, and I hated dogs in my home. She could sing well, and my idea was to have a musical relationship, but then things got complicated. She was going upstairs to the neighbors' place to snort cocaine while I was in the hospital.

The guy at the penthouse in my building was a friend, and he always got the best cocaine. VD visited me in the hospital and brought me a little packet. This was in early 1977. Fortunately for me, the musicians' union paid for my operation. I was very blessed, for I had two of the best kidney surgeons in New York City taking care of me. One was Jewish, and the other was a doctor from India. After the operation, I felt no pain whatsoever and refused all of the painkillers they wanted to give me. When I woke up in my bed, one of the first things I did was blow my flute to see whether I was still able to. Janis and I were going steady by then, and she would later become my wife. Janis visited me as much as she could and gave me her support.

After I was released, I was no longer going with VD but still submerged myself in more drugs and madness. I was depressed over the fact that many of the musicians who were former members of my group were making good money with good contracts and I was not. My music made it through the doors of many big recording companies, but none signed me. I just could not understand it. So, I used more women and drugs to ease the pain and disappointment.

Suddenly, a few weeks after the operation, I checked my mail, and in there was a check for $6,000! The union made a mistake and paid me directly instead of the hospital. Me! A cocaine head! The hospital must be still waiting on that $6,000. I got it, and I used it—paid rent and spent the rest on more cocaine. It was probably insurance money anyway.

The New Love

That same year, 1977, I went back to a small group setup and recorded my fifth album for Muse Records titled *The New Love*. It had Joe Bonner on piano, Alphonse Mouzon on drums, John Lee on bass, Terumasa Hino on trumpet and Otis "Junior" McCleary on guitar (Otis was the only musician I kept from the Cosmos Nucleus band). I also had two percussionists; one was Guilherme Franco, who had played on my *Black Love* album. He was a popular Brazilian musician at the time and played with some other groups regularly too. For the sessions, Guilherme brought along another percussionist named Timana, whom I barely knew.

Otis McCleary, who was Ayodele's nephew, was a vital part of my life in Brooklyn. He was learning all these songs from me because he couldn't read very well. Junior, as I called him, was always at my

Part 1. Panama Roots

home. He helped come up with funky lines all the time. I would try different stuff with him because, as I said, he was always at my home. He would play stuff I taught him so I could practice arrangements on top. I was writing music with whatever I had. Most of my jazz tunes were written in my mind out of spontaneous ideas. I blew, I liked it, and I started writing. For *The New Love*, I composed all of the songs, as it was a custom for my records now.

When I started working on *The New Love*, I was fresh from my operation for the kidney stone, but I could blow just as hard as before. Alphonse Mouzon, whom I booked as the drummer, was playing some hard stuff too. We all did. Terumasa Hino was one of the guys I recruited for this album because one day in New York, I bumped into him at the Blue Note or one of those clubs. We knew each other from years back when I toured Japan with Blakey; Terumasa and his brother Motohiko Hino had come to a lot of the shows and jam sessions. From what I recall, Terumasa was around town and came to one of my shows. One way or another, he ended up on the record. I don't know why I didn't give him more time for solos in the album—the great Japanese trumpet man Terumasa Hino.

Once all the music was rehearsed for *The New Love*, Joe Fields booked the Dimensional Sound Studios in New York. The album had compositions like "Dance of the Virgins," which is really three songs in one. The melody and structure changes. I don't know why I called it that, but I do know I should have made Terumasa solo on that one more.

As I said before, sometimes I write a song and then look for a title, like in "Little Dear." The title can mean anyone or all of my seven daughters. It was originally written on the ukulele, as were many of my other songs. When composing, I would sing the melody and play the uke behind; then, when I was ready, I would write the chart and finally give it a name. That's how it happened with "Little Dear."

I like to play with words too. Take "Bolerock," for example—if you take away the "ck," you have "bolero"; take the "Bole" away, and you get "rock." Otis did a great solo on that song. He's one of the guys I always used to give a hard time to because of eating pork. I

The New Love

didn't want anything to do with pork—still nothing to do with pork. Sometime around 1974, I was reading a book by Paramahansa Yogananda because I was interested in practicing yoga. I bought the book and read some profound statements the author made. He was talking about what a man puts in his stomach. People buy the best car and put the best gasoline in the tank, but they put the worst food in their stomachs. Then, around 1978, I started to vomit from eating all this different bad stuff, so I stopped eating pork, bacon, and eggs, and that, together with the yoga, contributed to this long life I have had. Or so I would like to believe.

I really liked the name "Uncle Ben and Aunt Jemima" for a song, so I used it for *The New Love*. Two different sides: one was rice, and the other was pancakes. I thought they were funny if I put them together. White and brown—whiteface, brown syrup. In a way, you can say it's a song about unity, about being together no matter what your skin color is.

I also recorded "Memories of Coltrane," which was, in a way, because John Coltrane's love remains. A lot of people say that he influenced me. Well, he did. Back when I was starting, most people were influenced by Charlie "Bird" Parker, but not me so much. I never really played any of his songs to practice. Bird was incredible, but I listened to Trane day and night. There was a tune that Trane played beautifully called "Out of This World." I loved that song and found myself playing it all the time. Trane blew the shit out of that number. It was a different language. If you ask me, I could understand his feeling because I was Panamanian with a different worldview. The African and Panamanian influence was powerful. Listen to Coltrane, my brothers and sisters. Those arpeggios changed everything for me. I used to sit with Jerry Warfield and listen to that music in Brooklyn all the time. Jerry wasn't a musician, but we shared the same love for music.

When the recording sessions for *The New Love* were done, it was time to start working on the layout of the album. One day, Ron Warwell came to my apartment to hang out, as he usually would. I was smoking a joint, and he took a few pictures. One of those pictures actually ended up on the album's cover. In the photo, a background

Part 1. Panama Roots

painting is visible behind me. I painted that on the wall in my home! I was working with triangles and circles. I made it because I also wanted to be a visual artist. You could say I came up with the cover for that LP. Sorry, Ron.

Much was happening during this period, in which I found myself still recording with Tony Silvester earning good money, doing my thing with Muse and at the same time playing around at a few bars and small club gigs. Together with Tony and Dwight Brewster, I remember recording some solos for a record by the disco reggae band Kalyan—a fine group from Trinidad.

(Apparently I also recorded an album during this time with a jazz trumpet player by the name of Milt Ward. I really don't recall

Carlos Garnett *The New Love* album cover (copyright Muse Records).

this session at all and only learned of it many years later thanks to Mr. Jaime "Jota" Ortiz.)

Roland Alphonso at the Apache Restaurant

I love fish. It's my absolute favorite thing to eat. There was this Jamaican place at Prospect Place and Nostrand called Apache Restaurant, which I frequented to get my fish. Jamaicans know about fish, so they sold escabeche, fried fish, fish patties and even fish tea with some spices. I went there all the time and stood in these long lines just to get hard dough to make patties at home. This restaurant also had the best fish stew. Beyond the restaurant side of the business, this place functioned as a vinyl record store. They even had some of mine for sale, and the whole staff knew me.

This one time I went over to get some fish as usual and met a guy selling records inside. He introduced himself as Roland Alphonso. I told him I'd heard his name before but didn't really know who he was. He would talk to me about how he had a famous group back in Jamaica and even played some of his early recordings for me—funky, upbeat stuff with a raw sound. As it turned out, Roland was a Jamaican saxophone player who was an original member of a band named the Skatalites, a very famous group in Jamaica and also in England.

We formed a good relationship since we could connect on many levels—as Black musicians in the city of Brooklyn, as immigrants with Jamaican roots, as saxophone players and, of course, as regulars at the Apache Restaurant. Roland's son played drums for another Jamaican musician by the name of Denroy Morgan, whom I would later work with for many years to come.

Downward Spiral

Janis and I had been dating for a while now, and she decided it was best for her and her children to move in with me. She worked in a bank, and we were doing okay. Then my mother sadly passed away on October 16, 1978, from colon cancer. It was a very difficult period

Part 1. Panama Roots

for me, especially with that to deal with. *The New Love* finally came out that same year, but I was not doing too well in many respects. Things got worse when an agent friend of mine, Paul T., introduced me to crack.

One morning, on what turned out to be one of the craziest days of my life, I woke up and I needed to get cocaine. I had spent the night over at Paul T.'s place after partying, and when I walked out to his living room, I detected a different smell. I asked him what it was, and he said he was smoking this stuff that, as he said, "I did not want to try." I told him to give me some of that shit right away. I thought that my system could handle it. Nothing could have been further from the truth. I was hooked immediately. I became super paranoid and could not slow down my heartbeat and was sweating like crazy. Nothing I did helped; to make matters worse, in a few hours I was set to appear on the Joe Franklin TV show. It was a big day for me, and the show had a big audience. What was I thinking!?

Here's how it had happened: Paul T. had a good friend who worked as the agent for the famous soul group the Commodores. Both of these hotshot agents were also friends with my drug dealer. One day, as all three of us happened to be getting some good stuff at the same time, my dealer told both the agents about working to get me on the Joe Franklin TV show. Well, they listened and pulled some strings, and soon enough I received a call from the offices of Joe Franklin to book a date for me to appear live on set.

Unfortunately, when the day finally came for me to appear on this famous TV show, I was really messed up because of the crack. I cursed myself for being so stupid, but that did not help in the least. I ran down to my apartment, washed my face, took deep breaths and began blowing my horn, but nothing helped. When we got to the studio at Channel 9 WWOR–TV, I was taken to the green room, where the guests waited for their turn to come on the show. While in the green room, I kept telling myself that I was only high and that everything would be all right. A lot of crazy thoughts were going through my mind. The paranoia started to creep in, and I thought to myself, "Shit, Garnett, you can't control this." I was sure everyone on the show and the viewers would know that I was stupidly high. Once I

Downward Spiral

got called to the set, however, the nerves went away a bit. It was kind of like when I would perform at a really important gig; there would be some nerves, but when I blew that first note, it all went away. The show aired nationwide, and I guess I made it through all right. Joe Franklin mostly asked me stuff about my career. That was it.

You'd think that I would have learned my lesson, but no, I continued with the madness. I was pawning everything to get that crack; I was hooked for good. I used to go to some dangerous spots to get the garbage, but I did not care. My craziness even led me to pawn my beloved Selmer tenor, the one I got from Crystal D. back in 1965. That horn had been with me through my most notorious adventures, with Freddie Hubbard, Art Blakey, Charles Mingus, Miles Davis and beyond. I would never blow it again.

PART 2

Life After Life

The Miracle

Some things were getting out of hand in my life, but I kept on playing as much as I could. My friend Carlos Chambers was in a reggae group playing organ and piano, and he recommended me when they were looking for an arranger and sax player. The group belonged to a Jamaican singer named Denroy Morgan. They were called the Black Eagles and even won some kind of famous reggae festival contest. I knew about Denroy from before because he used to sell a lot of weed. He was supposed to be Rastafarian. He believed in all that 12 tribes stuff. Shortly thereafter, I got in the band and became the director because of my notoriety.

Denroy was well connected and had a lot of money. He owned a couple of houses, one in Brooklyn and one in Massachusetts. He stayed mostly in Brooklyn, though. Denroy's songs weren't the most inspirational compositions, but he paid good money for my services, giving me the chance to dig myself deeper into my own hole. By this time, my girlfriend Janis was living with me. Stupidly, I had turned her on to crack, so now we were both hooked. Sometimes I sent my lady to buy the garbage at very dangerous drug dens; luckily, nothing happened to her! Every time the garbage was finished, I prayed ardently, asking the Almighty Creator to help me and my woman stop the madness.

Finally, there came one important day that I remember vividly. On this particular day, I pawned a Haitian drum that I had kept with me for years. I sold it so I could get high with a crack dealer who lived in my building. When I cooked the cocaine, it dissolved in the water, and we ended up with nothing to get high on. Later that evening, on

Part 2. Life After Life

the way to a gig with Denroy Morgan and the Black Eagles, I decided to check on one of my younger brothers, whom I had gotten hooked on the garbage as well. As I was walking down the street, I recognized my brother's car immediately but with some guy I didn't even know driving it. I stopped him and told him to give me a ride to my brother's place. Once there, my plan was to see whether I could get a hit or a loan from him, but my brother had just paid his rent and was low, so he had nothing for me. I had gone through all this trouble, but no matter what I did, I could not get high!

In the middle of this mess, I missed the gig with Denroy. So, I decided to stay and play dominoes with my brother and friends to kill some time before I went home. My brother and I were partners, and we knew how to really play. Call it what you like, but during the game my guardian angel began talking to me in my mind: "You'd better stop killing yourself with that crack and come to worship your Heavenly Father, or you will surely die." These words were resonating in my head while everyone else did their thing. I was in my own world. It made me get up from the game and head home. My brother was mad because we were blanking the other guys.

On the way home, thoughts started coming from every place in my brain—the good things and the bad things. I started feeling very bad about some of the stuff I had done in my life and thought about how I could make it all better. As usual, I was involved with other women besides Janis (at this point, three), and so, before I got home, I stopped to see the one who lived directly behind my apartment building and turned her loose. I then called the other two, met them and turned them loose as well, explaining that I was not going to see them anymore, and then I carried on to my home.

When I finally arrived, Janis said to me as I entered the door, "I see that you did not go to the gig." I did not lie and told her that she was right. She said that she already knew, for she had seen earlier when I had gotten in my brother's car. She went on to tell me that she had received a message in her mind while I was gone and wrote it down. What a coincidence! I told her that I knew what she had written. Sure enough, it was the same message that I had heard in my head while playing dominoes! Wow!

The Miracle

That night we dumped every piece of drug paraphernalia that we had in the apartment. It was a Friday night, as I remember, and instead of getting high we threw all the bamboo papers and pipes into the incinerator. The next morning, we woke up free, like two little children. On Sunday, we went to Prospect Park for the first time in a long time and ran around shouting "Halleluyah!" and giving thanks to our Heavenly Father. We were free from the poisonous crack pipe by the grace of the Almighty Creator. The craving for crack was miraculously gone!

As we lived across the street from the park, we began going out very early in the mornings, running and throwing frisbees like kids without that relentless desire to get high. For us, that was a miracle. We did not need any rehabilitation center; Yahweh heard our cries and prayers and cured us overnight! We had been living in that building for over two years, but we had never been to the park until around 1:00–3:00 p.m. or later because we used to stay up all night with the sickness and would not get out of bed until late in the afternoon. I will and I must testify as to how the Almighty Creator whose name was given to the Hebrew people and prophets as Yahweh, whose name is everlasting and will endure forever, had mercifully saved us.

That same Sunday, we noticed two men entering the park with their Bibles; they sat down and began studying. I told Janis that I was going to listen to their conversation and give thanks to God with them. At that point in time, we did not know of our Heavenly Father's true, everlasting name. As the two guys, one Jamaican and one Trinidadian, were talking in the name of Jesus Christ, a Muslim heard their conversation, stopped and interrupted them, saying that the name Jesus is incorrect and that his name was Esau.

As they were having this heated discussion, another man walked by with his three children and stopped for a minute before walking a little farther into the park. He sat the children down and returned. He then told the two Christians and the Muslim that they were all wrong and that the Heavenly Father's name was Yahweh and the short form of His Holy name was Yah! He continued, stating that the holy name was also in the names of most of his prophets and in the

Part 2. Life After Life

word "Halleluyah," which was a testament to His true name. He went on to say that the name of his son is Yahshua. He also explained that the Messiah said that He came in His Father's name, and yet Christianity used the names "Lord," "God," "Jesus," and "Christ," none of which matched. He explained that he came in his father's name, Lewis, as I came in my father's name, Garnett. Everything that he said made sense and seemed to be true, but I was always a man who just did not take anyone's word for the truth.

Janis and I stayed for seven hours listening to him. On Sundays, the park was always full of people from every walk of life and many different denominations. Many stopped and listened to what this man was saying. Some even challenged him, and he rebuked them all with the truth. When I got home, I checked out the dictionary, and what he stated was the truth: the name Jesus was a Greek word, and with my limited knowledge then, from when I was studying with the Jehovah's Witnesses, I knew that the Messiah was born a Hebrew. I also learned that there is no "J" in the Hebrew language/alphabet. I had gotten the man's number and could not wait for the next day to ask him more questions. I went to his home very early the next day, and he answered all of my questions, backed by the Bible. When I was leaving to go home, he gave me one of his Holy Names Bibles, which had the Heavenly Father and His Son's true names in it.

Janis and I began going to the park every day to study with our new Bible and the Webster's New Collegiate Dictionary. Every time we had a problem about something we did not understand, our guide would show up, as if he knew we needed some answers to our questions. Our lives had been changed forever. Every day that we went to the park, we were attacked by the adversary—again I repeat, every day—and we were always protected by Yahweh.

Back in 1973, while studying with the Jehovah's Witnesses, I had bought a book titled *Aid to Bible Understanding*. This book had a lot of excellent information in it, and I had kept it over the years. There was also a lot of misleading information in it, but while studying, you will soon discern the truth from the lies. And we did.

One time my lady Janis and I were in the park studying, and a drunk Haitian man who roamed the park daily came up to us.

The Miracle

Everyone was afraid of him. He had a park ranger stick used for picking up beer cans and trash. The stick had a long nail in it, which he would use to menace everyone. The bully got to the bench where we were sitting and began molesting us, but luckily standing nearby was a man we knew who lived in the park. On many occasions we helped him by giving him food. He was a big man. Everyone called him "Panama" because he was Panamanian like me. "Panama" intervened by shouting at the crazy drunk Haitian man, telling him we were his friends, so leave us alone or else! The madman turned his attention to "Panama" and began threatening him, but the big man soon made the mad Haitian follow him out of the park while still warning him not to molest us. Both Janis and I started saying "Halleluyah!" and praised Yahweh for sending an angel to protect us.

Janis and I were now free of the desire for all drugs and had changed our lifestyle. However, we were still far behind in our rent, owing around $1,800, and neither of us were working. We were praying and studying the Bible daily and did not worry too much about the rent. We knew that somehow we were going to be all right. One Friday, we were sitting in the park studying when our daughter came to us with her hands behind her back. She told me that the mailman had given her something for me. I asked for it. She gave me an envelope, and I knew it was a check. She said that there were two more. Lo and behold, I had gotten three checks from the musicians' union for some reason or the other, totaling $2,000! Janis and I shouted out, "Halleluyah!"

To make matters even better, Janis went back to the unemployment office to inquire about some checks that she had been waiting on for over two months. Each time she had asked about them before, the office people had told her that her checks were not there. This time, she started complaining to the person at the window where they distribute the checks; a supervisor just happened to overhear her complaint and told Janis that she would go and investigate to see what the problem was with her checks. When the supervisor returned, she handed Janis six checks and apologized for the problems that the unemployment office had caused her. I was still in the park when she returned, and as I saw her approaching, I saw a big smile on her face. She then informed me of what had happened. We shouted "Halleluyah!" over and over again, for now we had close to $4,000, enough to take care of our rent, other bills and more.

The New York State Division for Youth

The weekend after the miracle, I was in Prospect Park and saw a friend of mine walking his dog. His name was Fitzgerald Taylor. We started talking about what each of us was doing, and I told him that I was looking for a job. He happened to be working at the New York State Division for Youth, so he sent me to see his supervisor to try my luck.

The day that I went in for the job interview as Fitzgerald had suggested, there were three other gentlemen waiting for their own interviews. They all had college degrees in social services, just what the job description wanted. When it was my turn to talk to the supervisor, he recognized me right away and started to tell me how he had all of my albums! He had even seen me performing with Charles Mingus at the Village Gate! Needless to say, I beat out the three other applicants for the job at the New York State Division for Youth and was hired first. You can say what you want, but do not tell me or Janis that Yahweh does not exist!

Now I had a good job and a steady income to complement my gigs. It may seem like I wasn't as "qualified" as the other applicants, but no college degree could get those guys the knowledge about real life and hardships that I had. I started out working part time; after two years, I became a permanent employee. Doing this sort of work felt good, as I was giving back to the community and working with a lot of Black youths.

I started to concentrate more on my work as a counselor. I had experience with drug use, so it was easy for me to show the youths what I went through in those dark moments, something I did not want them to experience. No book or movie was going to get the message through to them, but I could—I was there! I was there with Miles Davis, Lee Morgan, Woody Shaw, Art Blakey and all of those guys who sometimes struggled just as I did to keep their lives in order. So I could tell them it was no good! I am not ashamed to talk about it. As a matter of fact, I'm proud to say the Heavenly Father cleaned me up.

Janis and I joined a study group called the Assembly of Yahweh. We studied and prayed together, and everything was great. It was the happiest time in my entire adult life.

Black Eagles

I was still in Denroy's band at this point, and he decided that he wanted to record some new material. One night, Denroy came to my home and was smoking weed nonstop as usual. I was blowing some ideas to him, and right then and there I came up with the line for "I'll Do Anything for You"—his first real big hit. There is a synth line in the song that I also came up with in my head at my apartment.

A couple of days later, we were at the studio putting everything together. Bert Reid was the producer. He heard everything I was doing and liked the rock and funk flavor. For "Part 2" on the B side of the record, we did an instrumental version. When Denroy sang, he had to do something like 15 takes. Denroy couldn't sing worth shit, but he paid for the studio. He had the money. That's how that hit was made. They wanted me to play it funky. The three girls who sang backup for Denroy's hit were Bert Reid's girlfriend plus another two friends. At this point, I was doing little music aside from playing for Denroy's band, for which I served as the director. My only horn at this point was my alto sax, which I must say I wasn't playing as much as I would have liked.

Around 1983, I recorded a song of mine titled "It's Summertime." Bert Reid, the same producer for Denroy's first hit, produced my song as well. Denroy himself was also involved in the production of this track. We used his girlfriend and the same two lady friends from "I'll Do Anything for You" as the singers. I later found out that Janis was credited in the record as a writer. I guess I put down her name for her to get some kind of money and credit. When I wrote the song, we were in my apartment. Janis wasn't involved in the writing process, but she's still credited. She was a good lady and helped me with many things. She worked at a bank and was smart, but she didn't know the first thing about music.

Part 2. Life After Life

Carlos Garnett "It's Summertime" 12-inch single (copyright Top Flight Records).

After more than seven years together, Janis and I decided to get married. We got the preacher from the park, Yohannan Lewis, to officiate. I decided that it was time for another change as well, so, after a little while, I decided I was done with playing in Denroy's group. That group was a great experience for me. With Denroy and his Black Eagles, I had the opportunity to play in Bermuda, Jamaica and Trinidad. We toured with a famous reggae group named the Third World. Later, we went on across the country opening for rock'n'roll artist Frankie Beverly. We crossed the entire United States in a bus.

One time, during Denroy's second tour of Jamaica, I recall driving from Kingston to Saint Mary Parish; on the way, we stopped to get some food at a stand because Denroy was very hungry. They told me they were going to get cow cod soup. Then they had to explain what it was because I had no idea. It was bull testicle soup. I told them I would get juice or something else instead. My old friend Carlos Chambers was on the tour as well. He was still in Denroy's group. Another time in Jamaica, he and I went on a little adventure, looking for a place to dance. We got into this place, and it was full of guys inside. The smell of sweaty men was strong, as we usually found in the places we visited in Jamaica. Carlos and I called the smell "the badge of honor." He and I were one and two in Brooklyn (and in Panama too)—really tight. I was "nighthawk," and he was "the rambler." That's what we called each other. While he was driving, whenever a red light was coming, we would both put our feet out of the car. He would put it in neutral, and we'd stop the car by slowing it down with our own feet—just something we did. Things between us changed later in Panama when I moved back. It seemed as if he were jealous of me. He wanted to be like me so bad that he ended up sleeping with a few women I left behind.

Photo of Carlos Garnett in the early 1980s (photo by Ron Warwell, used with permission).

A Note on Self-Defense

The job at the New York State Division for Youth required special self-defense training. I had studied kung fu initially when I got the job because I had to be able to defend myself. After my shift, I would work out in the park, going over different defense techniques with my friend Abdul Mohammed. The main thing between us was to talk about kung fu and to practice it.

Another part of the job was being a teacher, and in one of my classes there was this kid called Ocasio who bothered everybody. One day during class, I was working with Yolanda Martin, who happened to be from Colón in Panama. She and I were both in the classroom, and this boy was making all these problems, so she suggested we take him out of the class. I took him to a separate room we used for studying and we both sat down, but he was still troublesome and would not settle down. My plan was to talk to him calmly, getting him to understand the importance of behaving and following the rules set for him. He didn't care about what I said and wanted to go back to the class. I stood in front of the door and told him that he needed to pass me first. That was when he made the mistake of putting his hand on me in an aggressive manner, so I struck back with a right hook to his chest.

Ocasio was shocked, and so was I. The supervisor came in, and I explained everything right away. The hierarchy had to intervene in this situation because children between the ages of 12 and 17 were protected by the state. Counselors got special training to deal with them, and if we did something that went against those rules, we would have to go see a judge with the kid. The director, Mr. McGregor, liked me and knew I always handled myself correctly, so he suggested to the judge that he fine me $100, and that was it. I was lucky because I could have easily gotten fired. After that incident, I was more focused than ever on the job. The supervisor position was offered to me, but I did not want to take it. It would have interfered with my music, and I always thought that was my only road to becoming a millionaire one day, even if I wasn't as active as I once was.

No Sax Carlos

In 1987, I managed to buy a brand-new car for the first time. I remember the car well: it was a Nissan Maxima. I was making

No Sax Carlos

around $600 a week working for the New York State Division for Youth, which gave me financial stability with a steady income, and with that came credit opportunities I didn't have as a musician.

A little while after I bought the car, I was coming home from jamming with some friends, and I put my sax in the trunk of my car so I could go get some groceries. After parking the car on the street right in front of my apartment building, I carried all the groceries up the stairs. I left the saxophone in the trunk, figuring it would be safe there; after all, I could see the car from my apartment window. I was wrong. Later that night, I heard some loud sirens. So I ran to the window to look out; my trunk was open, and I saw some guy running down the street with the saxophone case in hand! I yelled and ran downstairs. I was pissed and went out trying to find him with no luck. The police didn't do shit either! I couldn't believe it.

To make matters worse, the stolen saxophone was not mine; it was my student Akum Ra's Selmer tenor horn. I had borrowed it for some gigs because the songs were better for me on a tenor and its B-flat tuning. I was slowly coming back to the jazz scene and wanted that tenor sound. Beyond that, after so many years of blowing, I always considered myself a tenor player mostly, but I didn't have one. It had been so long since I owned a tenor. My main sax after recording *The New Love* and during this period was the Selmer alto that I got from Bunky Green's brother years back while in Art Blakey's group. That alto was featured extensively on my *Black Love* album, and most recently I had done all the work with Denroy Morgan with it. However, I had no choice; I told Akum Ra that I couldn't pay for his stolen tenor, so, in return, I gave him my alto sax. The alto and I had been through so much together, but it was time to part. Akum Ra told me not long ago that he sold it for good money.

At this point, I had no saxophone. My soprano had been pawned long before my Selmer tenor, and my alto was now in the hands of my student. Fortunately, this awful period didn't last very long. I got lucky one day when I met an old friend of mine by the name of Abdul Salam. By coincidence, I ran to him on the street and we started talking. Back in the 1970s, Abdul had an apartment close to the East, where everyone got together. We got along well because he played saxophone too. Now Abdul started telling me how he had no job, so I suggested he apply for work at the New York State Division for Youth where I was working. He liked the idea and told me he was going to look into it right away. I then told him about how I had no saxophone, and he pulled out two pawn tickets—one for his tenor and another for a soprano sax. He then told me to take them, get both horns out and use them for as long as I needed. Getting both was too much for me, and the tenor was what really interested me, so I took that ticket only. I went to the pawnshop and got his horn out. A beautiful Selmer sax! That horn would go all over the world with me in the years to come. Sadly, Abdul passed away a few years later, indirectly making me the owner of the horn, and I must say at least it ended up in good hands. God bless Abdul.

Slow Cook Back

My grandson Dawid was born in 1988, and about one or two years later, he came to live with Janis and me. My daughter Lisa thought that he would have a better life with us. There were many battles that confronted us, and we overcame them all together. I finally started playing music a little more and found a group of young kids who started to jam with me. I called the group "The Quicksilvers" and started to write songs again. This made me quite happy, especially coming after a period when I decided to focus on my regular job at the New York State Division for Youth and not much was happening in my life musically.

There was a point when I had a small relapse with drugs. It was gradual, and then I stopped. It didn't even last six months. It all started with smoking cigarettes lined with cocaine, then another day marihuana, and sometimes marihuana and cocaine (it doesn't give you as much of a charge), but it also progressed to snorting some coke. I had to go to Narcotics Anonymous and had a sponsor who I could talk to about my urges. I could call them any time I needed, and that person was supposed to be there anytime too. Jerry the counselor and I became friends. We used to go to the same meetings. These sessions helped me to stop, and I began playing tenor again in the park.

Slow Cook Back

Sometime around 1990, there was this drummer I knew named Valentino from Colón in Panama, and he saw me practicing in Prospect Park as usual. A couple of times he passed by and told me how much people were missing me and how everyone wanted to see me play again. I really missed my music and playing for people, so I decided to form my first quartet for the return. I called Ron Warwell on drums, Bill Ware on vibes, and Badoo on bass, and we started to play every week. I also had Al Hicks sometimes on drums. My pianists when I first started gigging again were Jeff Lawrence, Terry Conley and Anthony Wonsey. A year or so earlier, I had performed at St. Mary's Church with an ensemble put together by Ron Warwell that included Bill Ware, Shamek Farrah, Jeff Lawrence and a bass player called Brad Jones who would go on to perform steadily with me.

Soon after these musical forays, I decided to go to a famous Panamanian club in Brooklyn called Club Michelle. It was a very popular place, and everybody went there. I knew the owner, Junior, who was friends with Sorolo, a character from back in Panama. Junior and Sorolo would attend the "Black Christ of Portobelo Festival" in Panama almost annually. We were all good friends, so I went to Junior and talked about playing on a Tuesday or Wednesday. He approved, and my new group began playing regularly.

One day, I passed by this place called Sistas' Place with my grandson Dawid. I used to take him to preparatory school in Brooklyn when he was about four. I drove him to school all the time, going on Bedford and making a right on Jefferson Avenue. This one time passing by Sistas' Place, I saw they had a tribute to Coltrane in some sort of amateur jam session. They did not feature professional live music in that place at all, so the next day, after dropping off Dawid, I stopped by. The owner was there, so we talked and I gave him the idea to have a real group for the tribute. I told him I could do that for him! The owner agreed, and my group became the house band every week from that point onward. Later, the demand for live music at Sistas' Place grew so much that I also started booking all these different artists like Gary Bartz, Reggie Workman, Bob Cunningham, Bill Saxton and others. They are still having jazz there, and I started it!

Part 2. Life After Life

My chops on the tenor saxophone were improving by the day. The urge to get back to the studio was starting to surface. Everything was lining up, with my compositions flowering as well. I was feeling great now, playing constantly.

Resurgence

In the mid–1970s, I used to hang out with my friend and tenor player Roland Alexander. For some reason, he didn't get as much exposure as me. My guess is that I had more recognition thanks to my prolific writing and Joe Fields' vision. He had an important career nonetheless, playing with some top musicians like Max Roach. One day, I went by Roland's house, and there was his seven-year-old son Taru on the drums. Roland had taught him music really well since he was a baby.

Now, well into the 1990s, Taru had grown into a top musician, and I was starting to hear about him in and around the scene. The sound I was looking for now required a kind of Elvin Jones style on drums; that's why I liked Norman Connors in my early days. Ron Warwell and Al Hicks played too sweet. One day at a jam session, I ran into Taru and ended up talking to him about playing together. He agreed to join my group, which at that point had Hakim Jami on bass and Terry Conley on piano. Taru was an older teenager then. He played for a while with me all around Brooklyn. My old friend and bandmate Neil Clarke also became a part of this new group. This one time for a gig, Badoo the bass player didn't show up, being a pain in the butt, so Ron Warwell reminded me about his cousin Brad Jones. I called him up right away. He came for the next rehearsal, and soon enough he became my regular bass player.

I started to think about getting this new group together for a recording. I had Brad Jones and Neil Clarke, whom I liked, and had somewhat of the sound I was looking for on the drums with Taru. For the piano, I ended up getting a guy by the name of Carlton Holmes, whom I first saw playing with Roland Alexander's group. Before Carlton, I felt there was a missing piece in my band. Luckily, one night I went out because I felt like hanging out and hearing some music,

Resurgence

so I went to the Kingston Lounge. My friend Roland Alexander's group was playing. That night was the first time I heard Carlton. I saw his introspectiveness and how he played inside. Taru Alexander was playing drums in his father's group as well. A few weeks later, I called Carlton, and he joined my band. Roland would always tell me for years afterward that I stole his piano player (sorry, Roland).

My routine was to practice in Prospect Park right across the street from my apartment. I was there all the time! One of those days, this guy came up to me because he heard me blowing. He started asking questions, and we began talking about what I was playing on the sax. He introduced himself as Steve Neil. Soon Steve started to bring his bass to play with me in the park. My regular bass player was Brad Jones, but I was practicing in the park with Steve all the time now. There was a new song coming along really well between Steve and me. The "Resurgence" was closer and closer.

There was steady work for me around the scene now, so I took my music more and more seriously. Taru Alexander ended up coming late to a couple of big gigs at the Blue Note in Manhattan, and I decided that I needed to look for someone else. Coming late was not acceptable to me. The group needed a specific sound, but my search led me to many candidates who did not have what it took. One night, I went to a jam session that happened every Friday at Dean Street Cafe. I had been there a couple times before with my horn to jam, but this particular night I left my horn at home because I went there with one thing in mind: finding a drummer.

When I got to the jam session, a small group was performing, and I happened to know a few of them, so I got a shout-out as usual from a couple of the guys when they saw me walk in. The band was good, they were playing some nice stuff, but nothing out of the ordinary. After the intermission, the group comes up, and there's this Asian guy now on the drums. Immediately after the first few bars, I knew this Asian guy was too good! All the other drummers' jaws dropped. When the players took another break, I went over to him. He had no idea who I was at this point. He told me his name, Shingo Okudaira, and started to salute me. I told him that he played well and that I liked his style and proceeded to introduce myself. I told him my name at

Part 2. Life After Life

the same time he was doing the traditional Japanese kowtow—you know, like in Japanese movies, when they meet somebody, they bend down. Next thing I knew, Shingo was almost on his knees, telling me excitedly how his father had talked to him about me so many times. All this with his hands clasped together. I had to tell him to get up and thanked him for his kind words. His father had seen me several times with Art Blakey when I played in Japan in the 1970s and had been a fan of mine ever since. Would you believe it? Growing up, Shingo had heard about me, and there we were now together, talking about him joining my group. Shingo accepted the challenge in no time.

We did a few gigs until I felt we were ready, and Shingo was always there before me and everybody else. That's a testament to Japanese culture and his very serious personality. Since we were on the right track, I had been speaking to Joe Fields about maybe going back to the studio to record new material. When I finally felt we were ready, I told Joe I wanted to record a new album at Van Gelder Studio. I requested that of him personally. I remember in Panama, and in Brooklyn also, reading the liner notes to all the great jazz albums. I was buying all this vinyl and noticed that most big cats recorded with Van Gelder. This was going to be my first time working with Van Gelder with my own group, because I had worked with him before, but under Andrew Hill's band, not mine.

I wrote the song "Resurgence" because of my comeback. Yahshua, the Messiah, came back from the dead. The day of the session, everything went well. However, after the recording, Steve Neil, one of the bass players for my group, came up to my apartment, and we listened to the solo for the song "Resurgence," which I didn't like. I called Joe Fields right away and told him I needed to do that one song again. I felt I could do much better, but it's a tough tune, even for me! I made it that way because I was just coming back, and I wrote this song for the return, so I had to play stronger than ever. Some licks were hard! I was still living across from Prospect Park, and I kept practicing it for weeks with Steve, and then I went back and re-recorded it again at Van Gelder Studio. I was happy this time around. Hey, you know what? John Coltrane recorded at least four takes of "Giant Steps."

For the *Resurgence* session, I had two drummers and two bass players. Steve knew my songs from coming to the park twice a week. Out of loyalty, I took him to Van Gelder's together with Brad Jones. Shingo was a steady member of the group now, so I wasn't going to use Taru, but I talked to Carlton about it, and he suggested having him on the record as well. Taru played a different style than Shingo. Taru and Steve recorded several songs each.

I wrote "Panamoon" as another play on words (Panama + moon = Panamoon). That was my thing. I didn't like "Panamoon Part 1" very much, but some of my friends did, so I put it in there after all. We also did "Song in My Head," which is a song that had come to me years back when I was working for the New York State Division for Youth. I happened to be on the midnight to 8:00 a.m. shift, as I was many times. This particular night I lay down for a bit, and I kept hearing this song in my head. I wanted to write it down, but I had no music paper. I got a ruler and drew the staff on a regular paper sheet I had lying around. I used "solfeo" to figure out the melody in my head and then finished it.

My friend Ron Warwell was always recommending songs to me to record for this new album, but I was hesitant to do so. All my albums featured my compositions, and I had many of them already rehearsed, so why record a cover? However, after much insistence, I decided to do my version of "Maiden Voyage," which came out very nice.

Resurgence was recorded sometime in 1995, but it wasn't released until a year later on Joe Fields' new label High Note Records. The album received many good reviews, with people enjoying my new sound.

Fuego en Mi Alma

The same year as the release of *Resurgence*, I recall performing at the African House in Queens, New York. At that show I blew my ass off playing "Take the Coltrane." Shingo put the performance on YouTube many years later for anyone to see. I asked Shingo who had recorded it. He said it was me because I had a woman there recording

Part 2. Life After Life

at one of the tables up at the front! My memory sometimes fails me. What can I say? I didn't even know it was recorded! The day Shingo showed it to me, I was impressed.

All the songs I was writing at that point in my life were straight-up jazz. That's all I was looking to write and play, so all the songs for my next album were again swinging jazz. I recorded my second album after the comeback and called it *Fuego en Mi Alma (Fire in My Soul)*. For inspiration on the name, I was thinking and reflecting on things from Panama. I'm from Panama, and the "fire in my soul" is from Panama. I used both the Spanish and the English names, because it was going to appear in the English-speaking markets, but, at the same time, I wanted to reflect my origins. The name also referred to the inner urge I had to make music even at this later point of my career. The musical fire kept burning inside me.

I chose two songs for the record that were not of my writing: an original by Carlton Holmes titled "Eternal Justice" and another song called "Little Sunflower" by Freddie Hubbard. "Little Sunflower" was one of those tunes I played a lot while in Freddie's group. The rest of the compositions were all mine, including "Mystic Moon," "Love Thy Neighbor," "Catch Me If You Can" and "Shalome." "Shalome" at one point had another name, but I changed it at the last minute. It was supposed to be dedicated to a woman, but that wasn't to be. Another song I wrote for that album was "URD14ME," which is just another one of those wordplays that I enjoy a lot.

Joe Fields booked the Acoustic Sound studio in Brooklyn. It was no Van Gelder, but the place had top-notch equipment. I had a good time; the music was tight and we all felt great during the entire session. I felt my sound was in a great place; ideas were coming together with ease, and the band that was backing me was tighter than ever. Those days seem like a long time ago now, but I remember clearly that I felt very motivated with what was happening musically, even if the life of a jazz musician can be very difficult from time to time.

There was an incident around the time that *Fuego en Mi Alma (Fire in My Soul)* was released that's worth noting. My group was performing at Jazz 966 on Fulton Street. It was a big building, and on the top floor the place had live jazz with different groups every week.

We were booked for a show at which the MC for the night was going to be this jazz critic I knew from the scene. This guy was even going to write the liner notes for my next album. This so-called critic came over before the show to say a few words to me. We talked about the guys I had in the band, and he made a remark about how my drummer was not Black. That shit really got to me, and I even cursed him on the microphone that night by expressing how we as Blacks have been fighting discrimination and prejudice for a long time, but if we discriminate, it makes no sense! Later, I told Shingo that I wasn't going to use that critic for the liner notes, which was initially part of the plan. Throughout my entire career, my groups always had Black musicians. I was known all over the world for writing music for my Black brothers and sisters. Why would I have to take shit from this guy after all I had done and accomplished? It pissed me off. I had to set him straight. And besides, Shingo was in a way African to me because he grew up in Kenya, where his father had worked and owned a restaurant for many years.

That show at Jazz 966 ended up being a great performance and credit to my friend and spiritual brother Charles Pulliam, who played four congas masterfully. Charles was the first percussionist I ever used in my own group and a founding member of the Universal Black Force. I would have loved for him to continue with my group for many years, but he was having some issues with his wife and kids and had to leave the group. He had a very unique sound and personality as an artist. I am very glad he was at least able to record on my *Journey to Enlightenment* album, on which he formed a formidable team with Neil Clarke on percussion. Neil became my main percussionist after Charles had to leave the UBF.

Much Change

Shingo told me one day that he wanted to do a tour of his native Japan, so I told him I was in. He planned everything with his contacts over there. And off I went to Japan for the first time after my days with Art Blakey. I had so many great memories of the country and its people. We played almost a dozen shows with Shingo's group,

Part 2. Life After Life

which featured Fumio Karashima on piano, Ikuo Sakurai on bass, Shingo and me. That tour took us to places like the Black Saint in Narashino, Rag in Kyoto, the Paltia in Niigata and many more clubs. I remember going to the city of Mito, where we played at the Mito Art Hall with Japanese vocalist Mari Nakamoto. Another of the shows was at the Pitt Inn, one of my favorite clubs in Japan. Every show was packed, and the Japanese loved how I played. No matter how much time I spent in Japan, I always planned to return.

The following year, I kept myself really busy. This was a period of much musical exploration, but at the same time, some stuff in my life was beginning to change. After two decades together, Janis and I separated. Our relationship had been long and very fruitful. It was now time for me to get a new place to stay, so I found a nice three-bedroom apartment just right for me and my music equipment.

Several weeks later, while performing at the Dean Street restaurant and jazz club, I noticed a very good friend of mine whom I had not seen in over 20 years. He entered the club with two ladies. One in particular caught my eye. On the set break, I went to sit with my friend, and he introduced me to one of the ladies by the name of Marva Mitchell. We hit it off immediately. She was beautiful and very sexy. We connected and started dating, and eventually we lived together. She was amazing but very jealous. Marva, whom I called "Pudding," was totally supportive of my music. I liked her very much. We both loved to dance, and almost every weekend we would go out dancing and socializing. Unfortunately, wherever we went, she accused me of looking at other women when I was not, and that destroyed our relationship. The men would admire her, even some women looked at her with envy, so why would I be looking at any other woman when I had the most beautiful, sexy lady in my arms? I guess she was predisposed to think that way because of my past behavior with other women. Eventually, her accusations became a self-fulfilling prophecy, because I would go with other women, but I must say it was after the relationship was already not so good. One good thing, though, was that Marva was also a fantastic cook and fixed many delicious dishes for me.

Most of my writing and creating was done with the saxophone. There were a lot of patterns in my head, and so I started writing them out on the computer. I also bought an eight-track recorder, a mixing board, a Roland XP-50 synthesizer, microphones and all the accessories to start my own small recording studio. It was my intention to write some original music, arrange it all and invite some Panamanian artists who were living in New York to record.

Some Panamanian artists whom I invited to join me were Natalia Clarke, Alfredito Payne, Ralph Weeks and a few more. I was able to record them and made some sales to other Panamanians. I have that CD somewhere; my brother Nando sent me copies recently. I produced that recording in my little home studio. Ralph Weeks sang on a piece I wrote with Natalia Clarke called "Meet Me at the Parkway." That song was hot! In that same place, I wrote a song called "Panama La Patria Mia." I played and recorded all the instruments myself on that Roland XP-50 synthesizer workstation. I did trumpet, conga, and piano and even recorded my voice singing in Spanish. This one was a kind of "salsa" sound.

I remember another song I did in Spanish called "La Primera Vez Que Te Vi" with some great vocals by Ralph Weeks. I made around 100 copies of this self-produced CD and sold them all, mostly to the community of "Panameños" living in New York. It was great having other Panamanians on a record doing my originals. Natalia Clarke lived close by, and we did a lot of music together. She had some hit songs in Panama, and she's a talented composer as well.

The music scene in Panama was always very vibrant, even after I left. Many musicians like Natalia Clarke, Alfredito Payne and Ralph Weeks left Panama just like me to find better opportunities in the United States. Mauricio Smith and Felix Wilkins did the same. Many of us Panamanians would have the chance to get together, as there was a big community of us all around New York. That community supported my group, coming to shows and buying some of the new releases coming out.

Back to Van Gelder's

Even though I was almost 60 years old, my enthusiasm for making music remained very strong. All the practicing, gigs and recording sessions made sure my tone was sharp while also allowing me to channel my ideas quickly into my playing. One of the highlights of this period of my life was another fun recording session at Van Gelder's legendary studio.

Joe Fields called me up one day and suggested I record for a session with the great organ player Charles Earland. I liked the idea from the start. I immediately wrote a song called "Organyk Groove" for the session. I loved that song! It's the only song I've written for an organ group that has been recorded. I had composed some tunes decades earlier for a session I was supposed to do with the famous organist John Patton for Blue Note Records, but that never materialized. Ron Warwell and I even had rehearsals with John Patton, but for some reason Blue Note didn't continue with the album.

This was the first time I ever recorded with an organ-oriented jazz group. Joe Fields made all the connections in order for this session to happen. Joe at this point had sold Muse Records and was running his new label, called High Note. This session with Charles Earland featured Bernard Purdie on drums, Melvin Sparks on guitar, Charles on organ and a few other guys. The album was called *Slammin' & Jammin'*, and it was released on another of Joe's new labels called Savant Records.

The music that Charles Earland brought to the session was swinging, which you know thrills me, and playing with Bernard "Pretty" Purdie was the icing on the cake. He is one of the baddest drummers on the planet! He has recorded with everyone in the business, so it was great to play with him on this album, especially given the fine way in which he approached the drums on my composition "Organyk Groove."

Just Like Kenny G

After recording at Van Gelder's with Charles Earland, I went back to Brooklyn. Shortly thereafter, my group was booked for a gig in Florida. You see, some years before in Brooklyn, I had met these ex-military guys from Panama. They organized a reunion for people from the old Panama Canal Zone who were spread all over the world.

Just Like Kenny G

Every year this event was hosted in Orlando, Florida, and they had different musicians play at this special party. For this particular year, the event organizers invited my group to play.

A friend of mine heard about my trip and gave me a contact for a jazz radio station DJ in Tampa. Since I was already going to be in Florida, the idea was to get this DJ to book me a gig. I called him, and, sure enough, he put together a gig for me at a local jazz club on our final day in Florida. Many different things happened during this "tour." For starters, Steve Neil canceled at the last minute because he had a gig with Pharoah Sanders' group that paid him more money. I had to call a guy by the name of Leon Dorsey to fill in, but I already had a plane ticket under Steve Neil's name, so I told Leon he was now called Steve. (In those days, you could pull off things like that on domestic flights.)

We got to the airport right before departure time, and the place was very crowded. While at the counter, the lady assistant was giving me some trouble with the extra charge for the big upright bass case, until suddenly some staff member at the back asked, "Are you jazz musicians? I love jazz, and I always listen to Kenny G's smooth jazz! He's my favorite!" At this point, all I wanted was to get through without anyone noticing Leon's real identity, so I immediately said, "Yes, that's what we do! So please let the bass case check in at no extra charge!" When Shingo heard me saying that I was playing the same music as Kenny G, he nearly blew up.

When we got to the hotel, to our surprise, they had booked only one room, and the hotel had no more rooms available, so my musicians had to sleep on the sofa and around the room, while I stayed in the bed. Everyone was hungry and we decided to go eat, but when we got to the dining room, we realized it was an "All You Can Eat" special for $40. That was a lot of money when you added all of us together, so Leon had the idea to go to the farthest table and have one of us order the "All You Can Eat" option and share, while the rest only ordered drinks. We did that for the entire stay at the hotel. That's the kind of stuff we had to go through because something as basic as food wasn't included for the artists.

The next day, we were waiting around for the performance until a staff member finally guided us to the venue. To my surprise, it was

Part 2. Life After Life

a conference room inside the hotel—no piano, no drums and no bass amp. There were only a few conference microphones and a microphone stand. Everyone was at a loss. I took the tenor sax out of its case, and Leon took out his bass. Shingo had brought a cymbal, snare, and stick case, but there were no cymbal stands or snare stands. He ended up putting a cymbal on top of the microphone stand in the room and the snare on a chair, but it sounded like shit. The bass didn't have an amplifier, so Leon tried to pick up the sound with a conference microphone, but the speakers were all over the ceiling, so we could barely hear anything. Carlton Holmes could do nothing but sit there without a piano. Even in these terrible circumstances, we tried to play a song as a piano-less saxophone trio—that is, until I stopped everyone and told them that we weren't going to continue because this was ridiculous. Since nothing was happening for us music wise, we just hung around the pool watching a local group play as if we were having some sort of vacation. At the party, I had a good time meeting old friends from my days in Panama. A few days later, we were set to go to Tampa for the final date of our "tour." We all left in a car, but Leon had to go separately because his big bass case would not fit.

When we arrived at a local jazz club in Tampa, pianist Anthony Wonsey had already arrived from New York. You see, I had agreed that he would come for our gig in Tampa because Carlton had to head back to New York and could only play for the Panama reunion event in Orlando. Now this jazz club in Tampa was a long-established club with a good atmosphere, and of course there were pianos, drums, and bass amps, and the room sound was great. On that evening, a local radio station transmitted a live broadcast of the show, and the room was packed. The DJ at the jazz radio station put it all together wonderfully! (I wish I could remember his name ...) What a sight! Everything was set for our performance, and we definitely tore the place down. Without knowing it, Anthony the substitute snatched the best part of the tour away from under Carlton's nose.

When we got back to New York, I called my musicians and thanked them for their patience, also telling them I was sorry for the inconveniences caused by the lack of preparation, amenities and basic equipment to exercise our vocation as musicians.

Under Nubian Skies

My recording activity was on a streak that year (1999), as I was back in the studio for my third album after *Resurgence*. I called it *Under Nubian Skies* because, as you should know by now, I was always an Afrocentric guy. This record could have been called "Egypt," or "Ghana," but then I thought about the name Nubia, which is a very beautiful Black name. A strong African title was important to me, I guess. Just as with *Black Love*, I now had *Under Nubian Skies*.

For *Under Nubian Skies*, I used my regular group, except this time Joe Fields suggested a young trumpet player named Russell Gunn who was hot on the scene. Joe told me to bring him into the group, so I did. I enjoyed Russell's playing very much on my record. The album was recorded at the Tedesco Recording Studios in New Jersey, where I would also later record my final album made in the United States.

I wrote many songs for this album since I was feeling really good and had been practicing my technique daily. "Dancing Daffodils" was a song that my grandson loved. It always reminds me of him. He liked the drums and also the piano as a little boy. When I played with Freddie Hubbard, we always performed "Little Sunflower." It was a song I liked to play. When I recorded *Fuego en Mi Alma*, Ron Warwell had suggested I record that song and I did, but I added a funky flavor to it. Now, for *Under Nubian Skies*, I told myself I would write something in 3/4 time and call it like a flower because I viewed flowers in a spiritual way. Later, when I finished the song, I thought about daffodils. Thoughts about my grandson dancing and daffodils came together for the title. It's a swinging song!

All of the compositions were written by me, except "My One and Only Love," which was composed by Guy Wood and Robert Mellin. It was the version recorded by John Coltrane that really got to me. That's a song I listened to many, many times and also performed a lot with different groups. I have enjoyed playing that song since my early days, and it's one of my favorites, so I chose to do it for this particular album. I also decided to do a tribute to Coltrane once again on this record with a blues song I titled "Blues for Mr. C."

Part 2. Life After Life

Sometimes songs would come out of thin air, like "Happy Children Song." When I wrote it, I was practicing the tenor and suddenly played a couple of lines that made me go "wow!" So, I worked on those to make a song. Back then, I was still living with Janis, my second wife, and my grandson Dawid. He was listening to me play it, and I asked him what it sounded like to him; he said it sounded like happy children, so that's what I named it. That song reminded me of Charles Mingus, because of the way the chords and the melody go together. Just reminds me of Mingus for some reason. I wasn't inspired by him or anything, but I realized later that it made me think of him, especially how Brad and Carlton used the melody, not to mention the great bass playing.

Just like the song "Happy Children," which came out of nowhere, I wrote "What." In the middle of writing it, I hit this dissonant chord, and right away thought that chord was like a '"what?" in my head. I hummed the line and could hear that the notes were off a little, a flat fifth or sixth. You can hear that "what?" moment clearly on the recording. Russell Gunn played a great solo on this one.

Back in the 1970s, I had this friend, and we used to make up words together. We started with just a few letters, and each of us would add more letters until we had these very long words. I made some with 13 letters in them, and that's how the title "Epitapher Zackerism" came about. It has no meaning, though maybe it's an earthling, but who knows? I had written this tune a long time before, but for some reason I didn't remember it until this period. Maybe it was the jumping seventh that brought it to mind. Anyway, it's a musical word.

The Trip to Jamaica

Sometime in 1997, I received a call from my brother Stevens asking whether it was okay to give my phone number to a Panamanian guy called Wendell "Papito" James, who was interested in taking my group to a jazz festival in Jamaica. Of course, I was very interested, and so we connected. He informed me that Jamaica's top trumpet player, Sonny Bradshaw, was putting together his annual jazz festival

The Trip to Jamaica

and that he could get me in on it. He gave me Sonny's phone number. I called Sonny, and we made a contractual agreement for me to perform at the festival. I was happy and excited because I wanted to visit the homeland of my forefathers. I was to do a show at the festival along with a couple of jam sessions the week that I would be in Jamaica.

The very first night that I checked into the hotel, there was a jam session in one of the lobbies. I went down to have a drink and maybe join the jam after freshening up. In the lounge, I was introduced to many of the musicians; for the most part, they were very friendly, and some knew a lot of my accomplishments. There was one tenor player who seemed cold to me, for it appeared that he was the main attraction before I got there, but now I was the center of attention. I joined the jam session and was burning up the place, receiving a lot of applause. I was having a great time! I met and talked with some of the other musicians except that white tenor player who was from somewhere in Europe like Sweden, Denmark or some other place. He was acting really cold toward me.

The next morning, I was informed that there was a marketplace nearby where I could buy all sorts of gifts, souvenirs, and so on. After I had my breakfast, I decided to visit the market for a gift or two. In those days, I had some long dreadlocks, and in the marketplace, there were a lot of Rastafarians who greeted me with love and respect and, of course, tried to sell me anything.

While walking around shopping, I ran into a beautiful Jamaican woman at one of the stands. The rain began falling as I was talking to her. When it started to pour down too hard, she invited me to stay in her tent until the rain stopped. More than half an hour went by, so we kept talking. Since she was so nice to me, I asked her whether she would like to attend the festival with me. Her name was Jasmine, and she kindly accepted my invitation. She was very beautiful with cinnamon-colored skin. A fine, beautiful Black woman indeed! I invited her to have dinner at this swank hotel, and as time went by, I knew she had to be mine. She let me know that she liked me very much from our conversation in her tent and was with me every free moment she had.

Part 2. Life After Life

On the day of the festival, I performed with some notable musicians; among them was Ernest Ranglin, Jamaica's number-one jazz guitarist. Jasmine and I watched him and the other performers who were part of the show. She agreed to be my companion while I was there and to show me around. I was having a wonderful time! Ernest Ranglin was leading a jam session later that night after the festival, and he invited me to play with him. Jasmine and I dressed up and went to the jam session at a nearby town, and she brought her child along.

We arrived at the club, and the jam session was in full swing. The white tenor player from before who didn't like me was blowing. I ordered some food for Jasmine and her child and then went to the bandstand to let Ernest know that I was there. After the group finished the song they were playing, he called me up to the bandstand and asked what I wanted to play. I told him to do "Impressions," a song by John Coltrane that had only two chords. I figured that everybody knew the song, so we could have fun doing it. The white guy began fussing that he did not want to do that song, but Ernie told him that he had invited me there and he was going to do the song I chose. The guy took his horn and walked off the stage.

Ernest counted off the song, and we began swinging. The audience was very receptive and gave us a strong round of applause. I then suggested we play the ballad "Lover Man," and we grooved on that. Once again, the audience was very receptive. As we were about to play a third song, the white tenor player walked up to the bandstand drunk with a beer bottle in his hand, acting like he was going to throw it at me, but what he didn't know was that I had met some Jamaican guys earlier that day at the festival, and they were in the audience. Two of them walked up to the white tenor player immediately and escorted him from the bandstand, taking him to the back of the club. When we took a break, I asked the guys where the tenor player was. They said that he went back to the hotel, for they had warned him that if he messed around with Ernest or me, nobody would ever find his body, so he split. Isn't that something? His ego got in the way of making friends and having fun jamming with other musicians.

Jamaican Diabetes

One of the friends I had made earlier that day was a man named Strickland, a member of a rich family who owned the Strickland Lumber Company. While the other groups were playing in the festival, I sat down on the grass near the stage and happened to sit next to him. We got acquainted with each other and watched the festival while talking about music. He informed me that he would like me to return sometime in the near future to perform at a jazz festival he planned on having. There was no hesitation on my part, and so I gave him my contact information.

Jasmine and I had a whirlwind romance, seeing each other every day and hanging out during my stay in Jamaica. We went to the Dunn's River waterfall and also to Montego Bay. I had a great time, but soon the week was up and I had to return to New York. I had gotten Jasmine's home and cell phone numbers and promised that I would stay in touch with her, which I did when I returned home. I was also now in contact with my new friend, Mr. Strickland.

Jamaican Diabetes

When I got back to the United States, things got back to normal. I was still living with my woman Marva ("Pudding") in Brooklyn. Once a week, I would buy a calling card and call Jasmine in Jamaica. We stayed in touch because I planned to see her again. Mr. Strickland also called and kept me up to date on his jazz festival. Several months later, after agreeing on my fees, plane ticket, hotel, transportation and other things, he sent me my round-trip ticket. This time I would be staying in a hotel on the beach in Montego Bay, right next to the ocean, which sounded great to me.

Like I said before, Marva was an excellent cook. One of the drinks she made that I loved was "Sorrell" or "Saril," a sugary West Indian drink that I always liked from my early days in Panama. I drank it daily, not knowing I was on the verge of becoming a diabetic. Finally, the day arrived for me to return to Jamaica to do the festival and to see lovely Jasmine, my long-distance Jamaican lover! When I was settled in my hotel, I went to the bar and ordered a rum punch. Later, I had another while waiting for Mr. Strickland at a

Part 2. Life After Life

nearby restaurant. We had to discuss how the festival would be set up and the different venues. He informed me that I would be doing two concerts: one at the Grand Hotel in Kingston and the other in Montego Bay. I ordered a fish dinner but hardly touched it, because I felt something was wrong. We intended to celebrate my arrival with some drinks, but I told Mr. Strickland that I did not feel well and would rather go back to my hotel and rest. Stupidly, I ordered a rum punch sent to my room. I was really feeling bad.

I called Jasmine to meet me at my hotel. Unfortunately, I soon began hallucinating. I saw all kinds of monsters in my mind; my mouth was dry, and I was sick as hell. Finally, Jasmine arrived, but I was so unwell (now with chills on top of all my other symptoms) that I could hardly kiss her. I was very concerned by this time, wondering how I was going to do the concert the next day given the condition I was in. I had been thinking for months of making love to Jasmine when I saw her, but that could not happen, so we cuddled, trying to keep me warm.

The next night, I tried to do the concert because Mr. Strickland had spent a lot of money bringing me to Jamaica. I tried my best to do my thing, but I was too weak and did not give a good performance like I usually do. I got through the first night sick as hell! Afterward, I was really too sick to do anything but curl up, stay warm and sleep. Everyone could see that I was very ill, and I kept telling Mr. Strickland that I wanted to go home to New York, so he changed my flight. They had an ambulance take me to the airport, and they got me on board in a wheelchair. When I landed in New York, Marva met me. When we got home, she called the hospital for an ambulance; they came and took me straight to the emergency room. When the doctors examined me, I was informed that I had diabetes and my blood sugar was over 400; had I waited one more day, I could have fallen into a coma. My life as I knew it changed immediately. I had to take insulin twice daily. I changed my diet and started watching my weight. By the grace of Yahweh, I am alive. Halleluyah!

I was very grateful to Marva for sticking with me during those tough times, but our relationship was in trouble a long time before I started seeing other women. Then we decided ourselves it was time to go our separate ways.

"He Said" in Swahili

Shingo and I did a record called *Alisema* at the beginning of March 1998. According to Shingo, "Alisema" meant "He Said" in Swahili. Shingo had a strong bond with Africa because his father used to work in Uganda, and Shingo lived there too. I think they had some restaurant or something. They were a very tight family unit. Everywhere we played in New York you just knew Shingo's father and mother would be there.

For that album, we did a duet for a composition of mine titled "Fifthology" based on some patterns I had been working on at high tempos. The song then went into some changes in fifths, hence the name. I blew the shit out of that one at 60 years of age! Shingo played some killer stuff too, driving forward and hitting hard like Elvin Jones style. On the rest of the record, the alto sax player was a guy named Justin Robinson, and I remember I liked his sound very much. He was good. A Japanese guy called Yosuke Inoue played the bass and a young brother named Mark Cary was on the piano. We did this record at a place called Systems Two Studios in New York. I remember Shingo brought in some nice compositions of his own like the title track "Alisema" which featured a very good singer called Mari Toussaint. I was very impressed and at the same time proud of the sounds Shingo created on this album. It's not talked about enough even though the concept is very unique. It's an African album by a Japanese drummer.

Right after recording *Alisema* Shingo invited me to Japan once again to perform. We did a residency at my favorite spot in Tokyo, the Pitt Inn, with pianist Fumio Karashima. The week-long affair was called the "Golden Week Special 5 Days at the Pitt Inn" and it featured Fumio Karashima on piano, Shigeo Aramaki on bass, Shingo Okudaira on drums and me on tenor sax.

The crowds poured into the Pitt Inn night after night and they loved the music we played for them. The Japanese certainly made me feel at home. There will always be a special connection between myself and the wonderful people of Japan.

Part 2. Life After Life

The Motherland via Ghana

Upon returning, I kept playing all around Brooklyn and keeping myself busy with gigs and writing music. One musician I started working with was Torrie McCartney, also born December 1 like me. Torrie was a very good jazz singer. I used to do gigs with her all the time. Her husband Mike Howard organized the African Art International Festival with Jitu Weusi, my friend who ran the "East" back in the day. Mike was a promoter, and he produced a lot of shows for his wife. I performed many times in their events and he was always present. Mike promoted shows for a collective known as the Brooklyn Jazz Emporium which ran jazz festivals and concerts and wrote articles on mostly Brooklyn–based jazz artists. He even nominated me to the Brooklyn Jazz All Stars.

Later in 1999, Torrie and Mike invited me to go to Ghana in Africa with her group to play at the Pan-African Cultural and Jazz Festival. I couldn't believe it. The motherland Africa! A place I had always wanted to go. When the opportunity came to go to Ghana, she wanted good musicians with her and I jumped on the idea right away and said yes. Playing in her group gave me the beautiful opportunity to visit the motherland a few times. The destination was always Accra, in Ghana. We played at a place called W.E.B. Du Bois Cultural Center, named after the famous black writer. Torrie's group back then had Onaje Gumbs on piano, a good guitar player called Gerry Eastman, and a nice white boy named Jim Dooly, an Irish bass player. The drummer was a funny guy, Greg Bandy. He and I used to hang out a lot. He always fooled around with me with the name Ghana. "What you Ghana do? When are you Ghana meet me? We Ghana have a good time" ... funny stuff.

That first time in Ghana, I went on an interesting tour of the different slave castles down the coast. Ghana has the largest slave castle in the world. All the slaves were sent from there to the United States, the Caribbean, Mexico, Panama and beyond. After visiting a few of the castles, I could not go into them anymore. At the first stop, Elmina's Slave Castle, I had a guided tour, and the guide kept talking about all the slaves and deaths. I swear I could smell the blood, sweat and tears of my Black ancestors. I felt very strange in these places because I knew about all the suffering witnessed by those walls. This slave castle was the oldest one built in Ghana in a country that has the most slave castles in all of Africa. Tens of thousands of slaves passed through this gate of no return. In the last stop of the tour, I met a young guy named Joshua and told him that his real name was Yahshua, the name of the Messiah in Hebrew. I took out my Bible and started to teach a little Hebrewism and people gathered around to listen. Even though I felt very strange at these places, a very beautiful thing would happen at the Elmina Slave Castle a few years later.

Moon Shadow

It had been many, many good years since I began working at the New York State Division for Youth (NYSDY), but it was now the end of the millennium and I felt it was my time to retire. I always give many thanks for the opportunity I got to work there for so long and all the young boys I was able to help by straightening out their paths in life. It made me feel very good about myself. There's something magical in helping others, and we all need to do more of that. Help one another. If my music has been doing that for people all over the world, then I cannot ask for anything more.

Later that year, in September 1999, Shingo organized another tour of Japan to support the release of *Alisema*, this time with Yutaka Shina on piano, Yosuke Inoue on bass and me. This would be my third tour in three years down in the Land of the Rising Sun. I remember spending pretty much the entire month over there! It was great and we got to play at the Keyboard in the city of Toyota, Monk Club at Matsuyama, the Country 99 at Isahaya and many, many more cities. Japan made me feel special once again!

The late '90s were some of the best days of my life as I was returning regularly to Japan and playing with local Japanese musicians who loved my music and performing for crowds that were more engaged with the music than any other I have ever experienced. Thankfully, I would make one final trip to Japan more than a decade later.

At the end of the year, after the touring was done, and after I

Part 2. Life After Life

finally retired from the New York State Division for Youth, I felt just right to record another album with my group, only this time I would use an extended band for the arrangements on most of the songs. Right before Christmas, on December 23, I went in to do my final album for High Note/Savant Records. At that time, all over the news you could hear about the last lunar eclipse of the 20th century which was going to manifest itself anytime. This happened to be in and around the very same time I was writing music for my new album, so I named one of the compositions "Moon Shadow," and that's how the name for the album came about.

The title song had a Latin feel to it as did most of the other songs on that record. I recall using Robert Trowers, a Panamanian trombone player and teacher based in New York. Brad Jones was working with the Jazz Passengers, so Carlton Holmes recommended George Mitchell, a bass player from Canada. It was all in all a septet with Derrick Gardner on trumpet as well. There was a lot of Latin flavor in this album, evident in "Salsa Blue," one of the few compositions of mine in this record. I did all the arranging, but for the first time in my career, I was recording more covers than original compositions. We did a composition from Shingo titled "McCoy Next Block."

I did a Latin arrangement of "Giant Steps" that got great reviews from some critics. Even Ron Carter had some nice things to say about it! I also did my version of "Delilah" popularized by Clifford Brown and "Manha de Carnaval" from Black Orpheus. "Moon Shadow" would actually take quite some time to come out as an official release. To be exact, the album finally came out in 2001. Many things in the label were transitioning and I wasn't pushing hard either. The pace of my life had certainly slowed down.

Katy, Texas

In 2000, I relocated to the city of Katy in Texas. I had intended to move back to Panama, but I met a woman whom I had not seen in a long time called Caroline Small, which changed the course of my actions. We both had grown up in the same community of Paraíso in the Canal Zone. We ran into each other at a class reunion dance in

Panama at the "Bohio Florencia," a place where people went to dance and which I frequented while in Panama. I liked the fact that she knew and used the Holy Everlasting name of Yahweh and his son's name, Yahshua, the Messiah.

Caroline and I spent the rest of that vacation together in Panama. She then invited me to visit her in Texas, so I did. I spent two weeks at her house, and when I returned to Brooklyn, I changed my mind about going to Panama and went to Texas to live with her instead. She was a member of the Institute of Divine Metaphysical Research, and I soon began to attend it with her.

Over in Texas, I had a "pick a side" band in which I just chose some of the best musicians in town and played mostly standards. Eventually, I got a gig at a club called the Red Barn. I knew a guy there who played drums, and soon enough I was working there every other week. At this juncture, I also met percussionist Will Cruz, and we formed a group called the Latin Jazztet. He and I were both band leaders, but I was doing the arrangements and writing songs. We had a good piano player from Peru and a trumpet player we called Tiger Lewis who practiced martial arts.

Doing anything I could and playing every gig possible would eventually lead me to play a couple of shows alongside pianist Joe Sample, a Houston local and original member of the Jazz Crusaders. Joe had a great career, playing with some of the top artists in the business and making his name around the same time I did. We had a lot in common. I would also go to Houston and play in places like the Red Cat Jazz Café, Cezannes, Ruggles and the Iris Jazz Resort. In addition, the festivals in and around Houston were booking me, and I got to play a few such as the Kemah Boardwalk Jazz Festival, the Houston International Jazz Festival and the Texas International Festival. There were also gigs at important universities like the University of Houston–Downtown and Rice University.

Mighty Sparrow and Montego Joe

Torrie McCartney invited me once more to go to Ghana. I never had to think twice about going to the motherland for the Pan-African

Part 2. Life After Life

Cultural and Jazz Festival. I remember staying at the Ravico Hotel, where I ran into the famous calypso singer from Trinidad called Mighty Sparrow. We happened to be opening for him.

As a vegetarian and pescatarian, I liked to eat very early in the morning, so I was having breakfast at the hotel when suddenly Mighty Sparrow came and sat at my table. He didn't know who I was, but I knew him. You see, there was this song he made that was very famous in Panama, and I knew it, so I sang the lyrics out loud: "Chubby girl you like too much money, you driving me crazy." He was shocked and immediately asked me whether I was from Panama! Chubby was a pretty girl from Panama who had played Sparrow around. (I knew about this story from my days in Paraíso.) Sparrow was very big in Panama and had calypso battles with many Panamanian calypsonians like Lord Cobra and Lord Kitty.

While in Ghana, an opportunity came to record a duet on film with percussionist Montego Joe. Joe was an experienced musician, and he had been playing with Torrie in our group for these gigs in Africa. We talked it over with a professional photographer and filmographer named Benjamin who had the duty of recording all the shows for the festival. Joe and I decided to do an improvisation at Elmina Castle, a place I had been to before and where I had smelled the blood of my people.

When we got to the castle, the sun was out, with birds singing everywhere. It was a beautiful day. Montego Joe started playing an intro on his African drum, and then I joined on my horn with what I liked to call the "Tribute to the Ancestors." Joe began improvising, and I started blowing. This video was released on YouTube by the photographer Gentle Benjamin on his channel, and you can see me looking over at the ocean while playing, because all I thought about in that moment was playing these melodies to the souls of my ancestors who left for America. This improvisation was made up on the spot, and I played what came from deep in my heart. Afterward, I thought I could have done better, but I liked it regardless. This event in Ghana inspired me to write a song later in my life titled "African Lament."

Later that year, I was back in Texas, where I did a show for the Houston Jazz Festival. I performed with a blind drummer called

Whitiker. I also played a set with some local guys and felt I blew my horn really well. One time, during an intermission, I was still blowing my horn backstage, and this one young guy came to the dressing room. He entered and approached me, saying he had heard some of my records and knew about me. As it turned out, he was there performing at the festival, and his name was Jonas Kullhammer. He played tenor and baritone. Out of nowhere, he told me that he would like to take me to Sweden to play! I gave him my phone, email and everything, but I didn't hear from him until later.

Back to Panama, Like Mother Wanted

I was returning to Panama at least three times a year and continued doing so after moving to Texas. I met a young man named Guillermo Herrera, and he loved jazz. He and I began producing local jazz shows in Panama. He booked me whenever I returned, sometimes two or three times a year. I thought that my West Indian Panamanian friends and fans would support my shows, but it was not so. They would promise to attend but never did. When I saw them later, they would have all sorts of excuses. Eventually we stopped putting together the shows, much to my disappointment.

On one occasion during my visits to Panama, I played at a spot called Club Bombardy. The place was packed. Danny Clovis got me that gig. Danny was Victor Boa's drummer, and I used to play with him in my early Panama days. We used to speak all the time on the phone from Panama to the United States, and vice versa. One of those days on the phone, I told him I was coming, and he went to talk to Jose Banfield, the owner of Club Bombardy. He booked me to play with Danny's group. I always thought he paid me well, but this time he gave me $300 to play, and I used that money to go party a little.

My mother had always wanted me to return to Panama, and I finally made the move in 2003. I was tired of the stress, difficulties and pressures of living in the United States. It had been more than 40 years since I left Panama, years in which I accomplished much more than I ever thought was possible for me inside the music world. My mother must have been proud. She had been gone for much too

Part 2. Life After Life

long, and I certainly missed her. I arrived in Panama on February 10, something I can remember clearly because the next day, February 11, was the birthday of Raquel, the mother of my last child, Shekinah. Raquel and I started going out during my last visits to Panama, as my relationship with Caroline came to an end.

Back in Houston, Texas, I had no choice but to leave a lot of my belongings in a rented private storage facility—my *Encyclopedia Britannica* and *Encyclopaedia Judaica*, all sorts of books, and even a few gallons of nice shea butter. After paying storage fees for a while, I had no choice but to leave everything behind. What really hurt was losing the hundreds of cassette tapes I had with recordings I had made all over the world with my little Sony tape recorder. (Maybe somebody kept those?) There was no other choice for me at that point, so what could I do? They were just material possessions.

Since I was now established in Panama, my very good musician friend Victor Boa and I decided to do a record together. Victor had two strokes before I moved back home, so it was important to do it as soon as possible. He was one of Panama's legendary musicians and someone I was very happy to have worked with as a youngster. Victor was a gifted composer, arranger, orchestra leader and jazz pianist. I knew that he had a lot of original compositions that were never recorded.

We called the album *Legends of Tambo Jazz*. Victor had written some music in which he combined one of the types of country music from Panama, called "Tamborito," with jazz—or, as he called it, "tambo jazz." I produced the recording together with Guillermo Herrera, but the idea initially came from my good friend Ricardo Richards. One day he got us to go to Victor's house and talk to him about recording. A guy who would go on to become a good friend was also there; his name was Charley Anderson. He videotaped the meeting and took some nice pictures of Victor.

After speaking to Victor, we got the group together for the recording, which included musicians like Reggie Johnson, Dino Nugent, Juan Berna, Mario Beccabunco, Wichy Lopez and Stanley Bryan Cox. The rehearsals were at a place in the area of "El Dorado." When we were finally ready, I booked the Riba Smith Studios. Guillermo and I paid for the session.

We recorded that CD in 2003, and it was very popular in Panama. That recording was extremely important, as Victor was sick and we did not know how long he would be with us. Sadly, he passed away on December 4, 2004.

Panama Jazz Festival

When I first moved back home, I met with jazz great Danilo Perez, who informed me that he had just started the Panama Jazz Festival and invited me to perform in it. In that first festival, the headliner was a good friend of mine, Kenny Barron. We worked and recorded with the late, great trumpeter, Freddie Hubbard. On the same bill was another friend of mine who also played with Pharoah Sanders: the trombonist Steve Turre. He had played in my Cosmos Nucleus big band too! I stopped by his clinic at the University of Panama, and when he saw me, he stopped the seminar to inform the students that they were fortunate to have me here in Panama, for I was an exceptional musician. Everyone stood up and clapped for me. That was very nice of him.

There are some things I would like to get off my chest about my experience with Danilo and the Panama Jazz Festival. I met Danilo back when he was a "young buay" because Mauricio Smith took him this one time to the annual Marcus Garvey birthday celebration held at the Lodge Hall in Brooklyn. That event was put together by Rex Archibal, who was from Colón in Panama. Mauricio was from Colón too. Mauricio played that event every year, and he always invited me to go and play with him and some Puerto Rican musicians—all heavy Latin jazz guys.

From what I recall, young Danilo was very happy to meet me that day in Brooklyn. We did not have much of a professional relationship after that, but I thought he understood my achievements. I knew he was moving up in the jazz world and was happy for a fellow Panamanian to achieve such recognition. Fast-forward twenty-something years later, and we ran into each other one day in Panama at a restaurant called Manolos in Via Bennetto. He started telling me about the jazz festival he was putting together and said that he wanted me to be

Part 2. Life After Life

featured. I thought it was great! We kept talking about it and eventually reached an agreement.

When I finally got to see the flyer for that first Panama Jazz Festival, it had Danilo, Mike Stern and Steve Turre way on top. Then came Kenny Barron, Regina Carter and the Panama Big Band—all with big ass letters. After all of that came the local musicians, and guess what? My name was way down there below Panamanian Reggie Boyce or something. I went up to Danilo and asked him about that. I told him I would never have put his name down below the locals for the first Panama Jazz Festival. Come on, I toured with the greats—with Blakey, Davis, Hubbard and Mingus. Danilo never swung like me. He liked to play all mysterioso and stuff with Wayne Shorter. I knew he wasn't happy with me telling him off like that, but I did what I thought was right.

The night of the festival opening, a TV crew interviewed Danilo, and I heard him say something about "not having egos at this moment," which I believe was aimed at me. Some people might think it's not a big deal. But I did. That night, when it was time for my performance, people wouldn't stop clapping for me. The crowd loved my show so much that it allowed me to cool down and think about the situation a bit further. It wasn't okay in my eyes to put me way down there on the flyer with small lettering and in the middle of a bunch of Panamanian musicians who hadn't been through what I had experienced. It's nothing personal against my Panamanian brothers and sisters but really about the producers doing things right because I had paid my dues as a professional musician. Anyway, it got me to consider that maybe Danilo didn't have too much time to think about every detail; I mean, he was putting together a jazz festival and all. I can take back a little bit of what I said about him, considering that he deserves a lot of credit, and of course he could swing. What I felt then was in the heat of the moment.

Danilo Perez did invite me back several times in the future to his festival, so I guess he appreciated what I brought to the event. However, I feel it was not only because of my shows that he would invite me but also because my methods and my local musical activity were making homegrown musicians improve remarkably. In those days,

I devoted a lot of time and effort to teaching, giving musicians an opportunity to learn from someone who had been to places many could imagine only in their wildest dreams. When I was a boy starting in music, just like many of these "likibuays," there was no way I could picture myself in Japan touring with Art Blakey, one of the greatest jazz drummers ever, much less alongside Miles Davis, the most famous, iconic and revered musician in modern history.

The Panama Jazz Festival was a success, and although I was happy playing with a group made up of locals, there was always the idea in my head to bring my band from Brooklyn. That opportunity would arise later.

Soon after that show at the first Panama Jazz Festival, I played a show with the great piano player Fumio Karashima. He and I knew each other very well, as we had played many times together in my tours of Japan during the late 1990s. Fumio played with Elvin Jones in the 1970s and was one of the most highly regarded pianists from Japan.

Fumio was on some kind of South American tour and planned a stop in Panama. Shingo Okudaira had called me months earlier and told me all about it, so we arranged for me to perform in two shows with Fumio's group at the Teatro Balboa located in the old Canal Zone town of Balboa. It was packed both nights, and the band sounded great. Years later, Shingo would let me know through my dear friend Mr. Jaime "Jota" Ortiz that Fumio had passed away in Japan. He was certainly a great pianist, and I felt very honored to have played with him many times around his homeland of Japan as well in my motherland Panama.

Who's Got the Key?

Barbara Wilson, Victor Boa and I were given the key to Panama City for our dedication and accomplishments in the field of music. That honor was bestowed on us by the "alcalde" (mayor) of Panama, Juan Carlos Navarro. Apparently, everything was lined up for only Barbara to get the key, but Mayor Navarro insisted that if she were to get one, then Victor and I also needed to receive it. (Thank you, Mr.

Part 2. Life After Life

Navarro, that's more than any other mayor has done for me!) I believe this event was held on June 23, 2004.

Barbara Wilson was the leading vocalist in Panama, in my opinion, and not only was she the best jazz singer for many years, but she also sang a wide variety of music. She kept active on the scene but did not record much, as far as I know. There were several good musicians in Panama who suffered the same fate—a lot of talent but not too much recognition, and since there's no recorded music, newer generations cannot appreciate these artists in posterity.

Granting Victor Boa the key to Panama City was a long-overdue honor. Victor had been an influential band leader since the 1940s and had created new styles of Panamanian jazz. Victor—the "High Priest of Jazz," as he was called—was always on the forefront, leading his own groups, writing his own songs and arranging. He was a true innovator. He could really play music through reading or improvising, but he also composed and arranged beautifully.

Not long after we were granted this honor, Barbara died of cancer and Victor likewise passed on. I learned a lot from Victor. He took the time to teach me a few things when I was younger and he was already an established figure on the scene. That led me to realize that I needed to do much more of what I was already doing with the younger musicians.

I was living in "Altos de Pradera" in San Antonio, Panama. The great trumpet player Vitín Paz came over for three months; then he never came back because he didn't want to practice the patterns I was teaching him. He told me he wanted to learn how to really improvise. I had to explain the way I used fourths, fifths and diminishes. He was a great player, one of the best in the business, but he wasn't big into improvisation like I was. Vitín Paz was another great Panamanian musician who was just on another level from everyone else. He played trumpet for Dizzy Gillespie's big band, the king of that instrument. What more can I say?

Vitín was also awarded the keys to the city of Panama, which was the least the government could do for him. He passed away just recently, and I didn't see any specials on national TV about him. Guess what's going to happen when I'm gone?

Tearing Up the Festivals!

Many local students like Wichy Lopez and Luis Carlos Perez were coming around to my place to get lessons from me. Luis Carlos went to the New England Conservatory and even wrote his thesis on me. Many young local musicians really wanted to develop their jazz skills, and a few of them began to study with me. They heard I was home, so they looked me up. Some of them studied locally, but others were from big schools all around. I had some students from Berklee in Boston, others from the New England Conservatory. I even had one from a Puerto Rican school. In my mind, it is always important to pass on knowledge and experience to the younger generation.

Tearing Up the Festivals!

One of my best concerts in Panama was in 2006 with my local group. That show was great, and I happened to record it. It was the third Panama Jazz Festival, and the headliner was Randy Weston. Performing with him were two former members of my first group, the Universal Black Force: bassist Alex Blake and percussionist Neil Clarke. Alex Blake is Panamanian, but I met him in the States, not Panama. It was great seeing all of them. My band consisted of Juan Carlos De Leon on piano, Eduardo Crocamo on bass, Anibal De Leon on drums and guest Rodrigo Denis on guitar. After our performance, Alex, Neil and Randy came to my dressing room. Randy gave me one of the best compliments of my musical career when he said, "Your tone on the sax is the best I've ever heard." Wow, now that boosted my ego, of course! Then he invited me to perform with him that same week on Saturday at the open concert held in the historic Casco Viejo cathedral.

On that Saturday, the plaza of the cathedral was packed! Everyone was having a good time with their drinks and dancing to the music. I was very happy my group was scheduled to play! There was an audience of more than 6,000 expressing their appreciation during the whole show. Even Mayor Juan Carlos Navarro was jumping up and down in the front row. We had a great time and a fantastic show. After I played with my quartet, Randy Weston came on stage, and I got to play with him, Neil, Alex and the rest of his group. It was an

Part 2. Life After Life

amazing experience for me. Randy even asked me to go to California with him for a concert, but it never happened for one reason or another. I would have loved to do that concert with him!

Ironically, on one hand, we had jazz giant Randy Weston giving Carlos Garnett the best compliment he could give to any musician, and, on the other, there was Danilo Perez, who at this festival was paying a tribute to Mauricio Smith and wanted to play some Panamanian jazz, or "tambo jazz," but instead of calling me up to the stage, he invited Puerto Rican David Sanchez to play saxophone during the jam. Victor Boa had invented "tambo jazz," and I recorded with him. We even played together in the 1950s! I had also played with Mauricio Smith many times. Remember, Mauricio was also a sideman playing flute on my album *Black Love*. I had a musical bond with those two, but David Sanchez got the call to the stage instead (it's okay, but I must admit that got to me).

The next year, 2007, Danilo brought some of Panama's most famous jazz musicians together to perform for his festival. The "Panama Jazz All Stars" included Jorge Sylvester, Danilo Perez, Santi Debriano, Renato Thoms, Billy Cobham and me, among others. What a lineup! Unfortunately for me, my diabetes was acting up and I could not see well at all. I had problems reading Jorge's great compositions and arrangements. We were invited to the U.S. ambassador's home for a dinner and reception, and I passed out there. I was losing my sight, and, stupidly, I continued drinking rum and Baileys mixed, which made matters worse.

A funny incident happened the day before my performance with the Panama Jazz All Stars that year. A select group of musicians was invited to the presidential palace for a cocktail dinner and buffet with the then president of Panama, Martin Torrijos. Since my days in Paraíso, I had always carried a knife with me, and that day I had a big ass blade with me with a nice ivory handle made in Costa Rica. I wanted to leave the knife behind before going to the presidential palace, but as I was about to open my car to store it, another car pulled up; it was Danilo Perez, Randy Weston and David Sanchez, telling me to hurry up and get in the car! I had no time to do anything, and so the knife came along for the ride.

The Selecter

When we got to the president's palace, we headed downstairs to security, and they asked for our IDs. I gave them my Panamanian "cedula" ID, and we sat in the waiting room for half an hour, until they escorted us upstairs to the buffet. During this entire time, I had the knife with me! Shaking hands with everyone, taking pictures, eating dinner with the president and all that shit. I even hugged the president. I thought that was funny.

Even though I wished there were more gigs for me happening in Panama, I was grateful for what I had. That same year, in 2007, a beautiful opportunity arose through my connection with the cultural events director for the province of Chiriquí. His name was Antonio Singh, and I met him at one of my shows. He had the idea of starting an international jazz festival in the small town of Boquete, a beautiful community located in the hillsides of the Baru volcano. Singh told me that he could use my help, so I agreed. We began planning and advertising, and things went well. For that first Boquete Jazz Festival in 2006, I was the host because there was no presenter. Apart from covering as the MC, I also played with my group.

The festival featured many different blues artists, some from New Orleans, and was a big success for such a small production. Just playing in that magical place was something special in and of itself.

During the festival, I also met a Panamanian friend called Andy Berger. While visiting a packed restaurant in Boquete, Andy was kind enough to invite my woman and me to sit with him at his table. Turns out, he was the owner of a big music instrument company called "La Nota," which would help me later with my musical needs.

The Selecter

I met my friend Charley Anderson through Ricardo Richards, since they were both dreadlocks. We became good friends right away. As I said before, Charley had accompanied me to Victor Boa's place in 2003 to talk about recording *Legends of Tambo Jazz*. He must have some very good footage of Victor, because he went with a video camera in hand. Charley's wife worked for the World Health Organization and was stationed in Panama. Charley used to play bass

Part 2. Life After Life

and guitar with a top reggae group in England. It was actually a ska music band called "The Selecter"; they used to be very famous back in England, with several hits in the early 1980s.

Charley once let me know that Roland Alphonso, the Jamaican saxophone player, had told him that he considered me one of the saxophone greats. That made me feel really flattered. The world is a small place for sure, because when I met Roland back in Brooklyn, I would have never thought we would be connected in the future thanks to a dreadlock from England as our mutual acquaintance!

I remember that Charley helped me get my first car in Panama. He took me to buy it over at the "El Dorado" area—helped me choose it and everything. I got a red Toyota, which meant I could now go out to bars and play around much more easily because I was living in "Condado Del Rey," and that was a little far from the places I frequented.

Charley lived in an area called "Clayton" in the Canal Zone. That place used to be an old U.S. Army installation, and I had passed by it all the time back when I lived in Paraíso. After the American military left Panama, it was turned into a residential area with lots of schools and universities. Charley had a little music room in his house where we used to go and record different ideas. His style was mostly reggae oriented, but I liked to solo on top of his forms. People enjoyed it. I made a lot of music with him.

Charley even took me to Europe one time. He invited me since he had to go do some big shows over there. In a sense, I became his musical director together with a friend named Hugh Lawrence. Charley had quite a following in England because of the success of "The Selecter." I soloed the shit out of those reggae and ska tunes his group played. People had never heard anything like it. I also enjoyed it because those guys had to look good all the time. As a matter of fact, the best suit I have now is one I bought in Europe on that trip. It was a custom-made suit from a haberdasher. They took all my measurements, and I looked slick. It reminded me of the days in Japan with Art Blakey when I always looked fine with the highest-quality tailor-made suits.

We spent around two weeks in England with Charley and performed at three to four big shows. Since I was already making the long trip, I found a way to put together a jazz gig on the side at this one club I can't remember the name of. I performed with some white guys from Birmingham University. Hugh Lawrence, who was in Charley's group, helped me get that gig because he knew the club's owner. I had to rehearse with these guys. They were all right.

After coming back from that trip to England, Charley and his wife moved to Colombia. He tried to get me to play at some Colombian jazz festival, but I couldn't make it. Fortunately, before he left, I recorded a few things for an album of his titled *Ghetto Child*.

Oh No, Rubén

My bass player and then friend Eduardo Crocamo worked for the most prominent airline in Panama, Copa Airlines. He had a very good job there, and every time there was a corporate event, the Carlos Garnett Quartet played. One time, Copa was having an event for the owner, and, as usual, they hired us to play. Everyone loved it! Afterward, while I was packing up the horn, Crocamo told me to look over my shoulder, so I gave this individual a really good look; turns out, it was Rubén Blades. Of course I knew him! He had come over to my dressing room that night in 1971 when I was at the Village Gate with the Universal Black Force and he was working as Ray Barretto's singer. I told Crocamo I was going over to him to say hello. Rubén was now very famous all over the world. His salsa music compositions had brought him stardom. At this point in his life, he was working as the Panamanian minister of tourism, so I figured he could help me out with getting some gigs for my quartet in different parts of the country. As I approached, I called his name, and he turned around. I asked him whether he remembered me, and he did. After some meaningless conversation, I went to business and asked him whether he could help me get some gigs around Panama in addition to giving him a card with my number. I asked him whether he could please give me his number as well, but he didn't, telling me that he would "call me." That never occurred.

About a year later, my quartet was performing at a private event in a very nice house located in the luxury neighborhood of "Costa Del Este." My drummer, Anibal De Leon, had a sister, and she and her husband owned the house and hosted the affair. I had a student, Giulio

Jimenez, come and play guitar because there was no piano player and there was no bass. People were having a good time, and I went over to the bar. There were some people ordering at the bar, and I saw Rubén Blades, so I went straight to him to talk and greeted him cordially. We talked for a bit; I asked him if he had lost my number from the previous time we met and eagerly gave him my card again. Once again, I asked him for his number and received the same reply: "I will call you."

I'm still waiting on Rubén Blades to call. While at the Village Gate in New York more than 30 years earlier, he was all excited because of our Panamanian connection, but now he was all big stuff. He could have helped me with anything; anything at all is better than nothing! Musicians and artists need the support of as many people and institutions as possible, especially in the later stages of their careers. Rubén was in a position of power, with the ability to help someone like me as well as many others. Getting some sort of support at that time would have been important. Whatever—Rubén didn't call.

Ana, My Purum

One day, on the way to play some dominoes, I stopped to get gas. Then, in the middle of the road, my car stopped. Turns out, I had put the wrong fuel in the tank because I was in a rush and didn't pay enough attention. I used diesel instead of gasoline, and now my car had come to a full stop in front of 15th Street, "Rio Abajo." Soon enough, I found a guy to help me get the gas out of the tank, and while he did that, I waited around. All of a sudden, I saw a nice girl walking in tight dungaree shorts and a *Dukes of Hazzard* shirt. She was a nice, beautiful lady, so I asked her name, and she said, "Ana." I asked her what she was doing, and she told me that she was going to the store. When she came back, I looked to see where she was going, and she went another way to avoid me! I went around the bush, caught up with her and asked for her number. She started to tell me the wrong number, but then she gave me the right number (as I learned from her later). We agreed to go out to the Johnny B on 14th Street. Soon enough, we started a romance that lasts until today.

When we first started going out together, I went to pick her up, and some guy who used to date her threw a rock at my car and broke my window. I used to be frightened to go to 15th Street, "Rio Abajo," because it was always a dangerous street, even for me. When this guy broke my window, I went straight to the police, but nothing happened. Later, Ana's uncle Lucho heard about the incident, and I asked him whether he could please go talk to the guy who had assaulted my car since he knew the guy. Sometime later, Lucho ended up threatening him and got me a brand-new window from the guy. Not only that, but he also got me the money for the new license plate tag stickers that, by law, I had to have on the windshield. Thanks, Lucho!

Life was good for me at this moment with Ana (my Purum, as I like to call her) and my music going strong. Purum is my woman to this day. We have been through thick and thin together. Back in those years, I was doing gigs constantly around Panama at different places. One such place was the Take Five bar, where I played regularly with the Fidel Morales group. People used to fill that place up to see the band, which had very good musicians from the Panama scene like Wichy Lopez, Dino Nugent, Juan Carlos De Leon and Carlos Ubarte. There was also a bass player called Eusebio Dinza who, from what I remember, passed away in a car crash coming from Chiriquí. His wife fell asleep while driving or something—a real pity.

Take Five used to be called "Platea," and I used to do a lot of gigs in this same place. Most of the time it was with my own group, and we had many guests show up. It was the place to be in Panama for jazz. I remember Santi Debriano showing up and playing with me; Danilo Perez also sat in many times. It was good because the younger upcoming guys could come see regular shows and actually jam with the older musicians like me. A lot of my students would come there every night to hear my band and to join in for the jam sessions. There was a nice scene starting to build up in Panama.

Sonny Rollins, My Brother

One day I got a call from musician and saxophone player Jonas Kullhammer, whom I had met before at the Houston Jazz Festival. He told me that Sonny Rollins was being awarded the Polar Music

Part 2. Life After Life

Prize in Sweden and that he wanted me to do a few gigs for him and assist as a guest to the gala ceremony with the Kings of Sweden. I said sure! A couple of days later, he sent me the contract, and we agreed for me to go.

Now the interesting part of the story begins. To start, they sent a ticket for me to fly first class. I was surprised. I knew right then and there that it was all going to go great. I couldn't wait to leave. I hadn't felt that excited about traveling in a long while.

The day of the flight, I left for the airport very early because my plane departed at 12:00 for Newark, and from there I had to catch another plane to Sweden. While at the airport in Panama, an announcement came from the loudspeakers that there were some changes in my flight, so I headed to the counter, where I was told the pilot for my plane had a long trip, and according to the rules and regulations he needed more hours of rest between flights. My plane from Panama to Newark was now running late because the pilot had to sleep. Ana came to pick me up and took me back home to wait. Around 6:00 that same day, I returned to the airport. Everything went fine and the plane took off, but when I finally got to Newark, the earlier delay had made us miss the connecting flight, and the airline had to put me up in a hotel.

Very early the next morning, I returned to the airport and sat down waiting for the flight to leave. While waiting, I saw a guy getting pushed in a wheelchair with a tenor sax case in his lap. There was a girl next to him and another guy pushing the wheelchair. I remember thinking to myself that the guy looked like a sax player from New Orleans or something. I didn't pay too much attention, and they sat down behind me. After a while, I stood up to go to the bathroom and passed by them while taking a good look, and shit! To my wonderful surprise, it was Sonny Rollins! One of the greatest saxophone players ever, if not *the* greatest. I used to listen to him back in Panama and in Brooklyn. I couldn't believe it. Right away I approached him, asking, "Excuse me, sir, are you Sonny Rollins?" He said, "Yeah!" I was amazed! Starstruck!

My happiness was such that I then asked whether I could shake his hand, to which he happily agreed. I told him that I had listened to his music for many years. We had even appeared together in *Downbeat* magazine in June 1971, but he didn't remember that. We talked a little bit, and I let him know that I was going to Sweden, which was obviously his destination too. After our small talk, I went to the bathroom and then said goodbye to everyone.

When I got on the plane, I sat in my comfy first-class seat. Suddenly, Sonny Rollins boarded with his people, and he sat in the first row, right-hand side. I was in the second row, left side, sitting by myself. The guy who pushed the wheelchair came over, said hello and sat next to me. As the flight was underway, Sonny Rollins came over and told his friend that he wanted to exchange seats so he could talk to me! All he knew was that I was going to Sweden, but I guess he decided to change seats since he saw me walking around with my tenor sax. It must have helped when I had told him earlier that I was going to play for him. The fact that he told the guy that he wanted to sit with me was very nice. We both played tenor sax, and I had admired him for years!

We started talking about many different things. At one point, I mentioned to him that I didn't practice as much as before, and he told me to start rehearsing more. I also mentioned Louis Jordan and James Moody as some of my influences on saxophone. He told me Louis Jordan was his inspiration too! He was older than me, but we were both inspired by Louis Jordan.

The flight was long, so we kept talking, and I was running my mouth nonstop. He answered everything, so I asked him, "Am I speaking too much, Mr. Rollins?" He told me, "Naw, man, I don't want to sleep, so keep on talking!" And we did precisely that from Newark Airport across the Atlantic Ocean. That was an inspiration, not only talking to my idol man to man for so long but also having him encourage me to practice and worry about my saxophone.

Many hours later, we landed in Sweden, and Sonny told me to follow him out of the airplane. We went through customs, and none of us were bothered with any documents. I was about to say goodbye when Sonny abruptly told me that he was giving me a ride to the hotel! Once outside, a fine limousine picked us up. I told the driver the name of the hotel, and they took me there. I was in heaven! After

Part 2. Life After Life

arriving at my destination, I said a warm goodbye with much appreciation to my new friend Sonny Rollins and got out.

At the hotel, I met Jonas and thanked him for the first-class accommodations. We talked, and I told him that I didn't eat chicken or meat, and he arranged everything for me. He also took me to the restaurant for a jam session with Marcus Strickland, which included Jonas and another good tenor player from Sweden. There were four tenors on the bandstand for this show. While eating, we had pleasant conversations with lots of wine, and they served me a nice fish dinner. The place was loud, with everyone in the restaurant talking and enjoying themselves. Then Jonas told me it was time to go to the bandstand; as soon as we got up, all the noise coming from the people in the room stopped completely. Everything went into total silence in just a second! That was amazing to me. The place got really quiet, but people were very receptive as soon we started playing, and everybody had a good time.

On the night of the gala affair dedicated to Sonny Rollins, I was invited, though just as a guest. Jonas played with his group as Sonny Rollins sat down next to the Kings of Sweden—a real sight to see! In the interim, I sat at a table with some other musicians while another artist called Steve Reich was being honored for some weird music. As I was socializing, this young guy came up to me and started talking, but I couldn't remember who he was. He said, "I am Clif Anderson. I played trombone for your big band." Turns out, he was in my Cosmos Nucleus big band and was also the nephew of Sonny Rollins! Crazy connections. We went by the bar, and Sonny was there talking to all the young tenors and other musicians. I have a photo somewhere of Sonny Rollins, Marcus Strickland, Jonas Kullhammer and me.

Sweden is a great country, and I got to see a little of it in the coming days after the gala. I remember walking around the streets and running into some Black folks. I never thought I would meet other Black folks in Sweden! I stayed around for a week or so and ended up doing two shows at the same hotel and restaurant. I also played in a few jam sessions backed by Jonas' group. A few years later, Jonas would go to Panama, where I booked him to play in the beautiful mountain town of Boquete.

"La Magnolia"

There was this place called "La Magnolia" where I used to hang out and play dominoes with my friend Alvin Moeyson from Colón. He, like many other Panamanians, left the country to live in New York around the same time I did. Alvin sold good cocaine in Brooklyn. One time, I was at his apartment with Janis, and she saw some gold bangles she really liked. They were $300, a little too expensive for me, so he told me to take them and pay him little by little, which I did. Janis was happy with that gift.

I had lost track of Alvin until I moved back to Panama and went by "La Magnolia." This is where I saw him again; after that, we hung out almost every day. People asked me why I was always with "Moey" (that's Alvin), but they didn't know what he had done for me in Brooklyn. I always had a special place in my heart for people who helped me or were a positive part of my life, especially back in the early days.

Moey and I played dominoes at "La Magnolia" all the time. Sometimes George Allen (the famous calypsonian popularly known as Lord Panama) would come and sit with us. We all drank "Caballito" gin. I felt right at home because I could talk to many people whom I knew from back in my early days in Panama. Most remembered me and addressed me with much respect, as if they knew or had heard of my achievements. Throughout my career, I always stayed very humble, and my friends appreciated that aspect of my personality.

I hung out there pretty much every day. Listening to salsa while playing my favorite game. Dominoes in Panama is a big deal, so people get together to play in the parks and in bars as a cultural thing. Dominoes are played in a lot of countries in Latin America and the West Indies. When I was in New York, many of my Latin friends played constantly with me, but I was always blanking them in games.

Sheila

Sometime in 2009, a group of people from my Paraíso school class of 1959 organized a celebration to commemorate the fiftieth

Part 2. Life After Life

anniversary of our graduation. The event was held at the Continental Hotel in Panama City. I was on the program to play a couple of songs with a little group of musicians hired for the event. Ana and I were at a table, and across from us were some young people. I suddenly saw a young lady walking straight toward me. She came over and asked whether I was Carlos Garnett. When I told her I was, she informed me that my daughter Sheila had been trying to reach me but couldn't. Sheila apparently told this lady (who happened to be her coworker back in the United States) to give me her phone number and have me call her, as she knew I was going to attend this particular event. Sheila and I had lost contact after I left the United States, and she couldn't get hold of me. I called her as soon as I could, and we began to keep in touch a lot more.

Her mother Lucille had made a stupid decision back when Sheila was born and kept her from really knowing who her father was. Since Lucille remarried as soon as we split, she decided with her new husband that they were not going to let Sheila know about her Garnett name, a decision I was not too happy about.

Sheila eventually found out about it all when she was already a grown woman. Lucille ultimately couldn't keep it from her. Sheila then married and had a family of her own. I remember at some point in the early 1990s, I even had the opportunity to meet my granddaughters after much insistence on my part. Sheila agreed to meet up at Prospect Park, so the next day my grandson Dawid and I went to the park to meet Sheila and her two daughters, Dawid's little cousins. We took a cab and waited at the park entrance. She had told me before what she and her two daughters would be wearing.

When they arrived, it was all hugs and kisses with my granddaughters. Both were beautiful little Black girls. Their names were Shaquanda and Sade, and it was Sade who brought a little guitar with her to play. Her mother told me she loved music, and luckily enough I had my flute. We sat down, and I told Sade to play anything she wanted and I would just follow. It was a fun time with my beautiful granddaughters, but Sheila had four children, and her two boys did not come to meet me. Her husband didn't allow it; he held them back, and because of him I never got to meet my two grandsons from my daughter Sheila.

If Joe Lovano Says So...

It had been a while since my last appearance at the Panama Jazz Festival back in 2007. Three years later, I finally got a call from Danilo Perez to perform at his festival once more, so I booked the event with my usual band of Panamanian musicians. At this point, the group was really cooking because they all had been studying with me for a long time.

Danilo Perez brought down very good musicians like New Orleans jazz pianist Ellis Marsalis, drummer Terry Lynn Carrington, and tenor saxophonist Joe Lovano. It was with Joe that I had a very fond exchange that still gives me motivation today. The day of the presentation with my group, the production team told me that we had a time limit of 45 minutes because of the tight schedule. The show started, and everything went well. People were jumping and screaming during the last song, so I kept going a little longer. Next thing I knew, Danilo Perez was not so happy, giving me the look of death from the side of the stage because I was over my time limit. I kept burning my solo and finished the song to a big standing ovation. Out of nowhere came Joe Lovano straight toward me, giving me a big hug. His face was full of excitement as he said, "Carlos, you have one of the best tones I have ever heard on the tenor saxophone." Now that made me feel good! First Randy Weston gave me the best of compliments a few years back, and now Joe Lovano. Those words have constantly resonated in my head ever since.

My friend Charley Anderson videotaped that night's show. I played "Somewhere Over the Rainbow," and Joe Lovano went crazy over my performance. Somewhere on my computer I must have that recording from my Akai recorder. Believe it or not, that comment from Joe Lovano pushed me to play even harder at almost 72 years of age.

To finish off that year and make matters even better, the day after my 72nd birthday, on December 2, 2010, I married my "Purum," Ana Maria Gaskin. We are still strong today, and I give thanks and praise to Yahweh for putting her in my life.

Part 2. Life After Life

From Continent to Continent

Trombonist, composer and arranger Phil Ranelin invited me to perform at a tribute concert for Eric Dolphy in Los Angeles, California. Dolphy was one of those greats who died way too soon. His passing shocked the music world in the 1960s. Phil was a big fan of Dolphy, so he put this thing together. Eric Dolphy had Panamanian roots because his mother was born in Panama, so I felt this strong connection, you know? Eric Dolphy had a Panamanian mother; I had a Panamanian mother. We both had West Indian descent as well.

During the concert, we performed classic songs by Eric Dolphy and a few composed by Phil, who had some great compositions and arrangements. I had met him earlier when he came to Panama to visit some of Dolphy's remaining distant family and to seek help from the Panamanian government to honor Dolphy. Unfortunately, that effort did not get anywhere. In Panama, culture, music, and art are not important anymore. Back in my days as a youth, public schools had good music programs. Teachers actually knew about music. Now they don't even have music classes anymore. Public schools barely have roofs and running water. It's really sad. Phil Ranelin, an important international musician, took time to come to Panama to try to promote awareness of the works by Eric Dolphy, a man with a Panamanian past, but the government didn't care. At least Danilo Perez was able to give Dolphy some sort of recognition in one of the Panama Jazz Festivals.

I enjoyed my stay in Los Angeles, hanging and playing with Phil, but soon enough I left for New York and performed at the twelfth Annual Central Brooklyn Jazz Festival with my real group. This event had over 100 artists, including very respected jazz musicians like Charles Tolliver and Arturo O'Farrill. The events were all over the city in venues, organizations and colleges like Medger Evers College, which was where my group performed. It was a lot of fun playing again with Carlton Holmes on piano, Brad Jones on bass, and Taru Alexander on drums. I also invited my spiritual brother Charles Pulliam as a guest percussionist. The Central Brooklyn Jazz Festival was organized by some guys whom I used to know from playing back at the East.

While in Brooklyn for the festival, I was reading the newspapers and saw an article about Stanley Wright (a.k.a. Suleiman-Marim Wright), who was found dead in the trunk of his car in front of his house. This happened around 2011. I had met Suleiman years earlier when I formed my first group in New York around 1965–1966. I was in Brooklyn looking for a bass player and hooked up with him for a "pick a side" gig. Stanley later changed his name to Suleiman, and he was at the forefront of the local Islamic movement.

I remember that Suleiman and his wife had a house where people would get together and sometimes jam. I went there a couple of times. Suleiman was the first one to tell me about writing my own music. I will never forget that. Thanks, Suleiman; may Yahweh bless your soul. His daughter N'Bushe Wright became famous years later, acting in the movie *Blade* with Wesley Snipes.

After performing at the twelfth Annual Central Brooklyn Jazz Festival, I headed back to Panama and then went straight to Austria to appear at the annual Inntone Jazz Festival. I was a busy musician even at my advanced age, flying from Panama to Los Angeles and then to New York and even as far as Austria. Over in Austria, I was booked to perform with the ensemble of promoter/producer Paul Zauner. This group included my friend from years past, Jerry Gonzalez on trumpet, as well as Kirk Lightsey on piano and Paul on trombone with two great Austrian musicians on bass and drums. The week before the festival, we performed at a concert in Linz, Austria. It was great to see Jerry after many years, and we got to remember the days in the 1970s when he played in my group. We had a lot of fun performing and hanging out after the gigs, Jerry, Kirk and me. During the festival, Paul had some guy interview me about my career. The video is somewhere on YouTube.

I remember that I was eating fish meals three times a day over there in Austria. Everything was pretty okay in life except for my eyesight, which was getting worse at this point.

A Panama Jazz Festival in My Name

Danilo Perez decided to honor me at the ninth Panama Jazz Festival in 2012. Every year, the festival is dedicated to a Panamanian figure in jazz, whether they be alive or dead—it doesn't matter. The event has shed light on some of the jazz greats in Panama, and that's a very positive thing. I must admit that and give Danilo all the credit in the world. This time around, it was my turn to get the honor, which gave me the chance to finally bring my group from New York to perform with me for the event. It was a great reunion for us, especially as my bandmates got to see my beautiful country. I had Carlton Holmes on piano, Brad Jones on bass and Taru Alexander on drums. I also invited one of my students, Aquiles Navarro, to play on trumpet, and my friend Miss Idania Dowman served as a vocalist. We did a great show and received standing ovations at both of our performances.

At the festival, Danilo presented me with an award for my musical achievements here in Panama, in the United States of America and around the world. Before and after the presentation, Cuba's great pianist Chucho Valdes performed, along with the great Cuban songstress Omara Portuondo. What an honor! It was a great night!

Even though Danilo and I had our differences, I must say that there is a lot of value to what he has achieved, especially with the Panama Jazz Festival, which allows many Panamanians to experience internationally acclaimed jazz acts that would otherwise be difficult to bring to the country. I am grateful to him for giving me the opportunity to bring my group to Panama and play at the beautiful Plaza Cathedral in the "Casco Viejo."

This happened to be the final festival held at the "Casco Viejo," a place where the city of Panama thrived during its colonial days. Later Danilo moved the festival to the "Clayton" area, now called "Ciudad del Saber," where a U.S. military base used to be located.

Unlimited Creative Imagination

My student Aquiles Navarro started with me as a student but then became a part of my group. When I met him as a "young buay," I gave him my number so that he could call me for classes, and a few days later he did. He was very enthusiastic, so I started teaching him about jazz. He went everywhere with me—I mean, *everywhere*. Later, he would even take me to the police and the "corregiduria" (a name for the municipality authority in Panama). I had to take care of some problems with a woman, let's put it that way.

When Aquiles began studying with me, I always knew he had what I like to call UCI—that is, unlimited creative imagination. It's a term I use to describe myself and a few others too. It's a concept that I developed. I haven't mentioned it yet in this book, but I will now. When I'm teaching students, I tell them about UCI and look to see whether they have it. You see, everything is a thought at first. Everything on this planet is or was a thought. The Almighty Creator made Earth in a thought. The universe was a thought. This book was a thought at first. When I think about myself, how I got here or where we are all going, it's because of my imagination, so UCI. It's limitless.

That's my motto, and I tell it to all my students. I coined those words, and it's time for the world to know the concept (ha ha). It's an insight into my creativity in music as well. Every time I write, it's UCI. My creations are unlimited—endless. It all comes from the Almighty Creator. I didn't go to music school, but that wasn't an impediment for unlimited expression, knowledge and ideas. All my songs came from my imagination. I have loved to create ever since I started to play the sax. That's why you're supposed to think and practice. The ideas come from different angles. Then you develop. Study on your own. How do you think I got my style? The melodies on my songs are unlimited.

Aquiles was one of those students to whom I tried to impart the principles of UCI, and he got them. The concept of UCI should be followed by anyone who makes creative stuff.

An Unforgettable Return to Japan

One day while sitting at home, I was contacted by a Japanese promoter, Mr. Shuya Okino, who wanted to organize a show in Japan. He called me out of the blue and started talking about bringing me to Japan. I told him, "Sure, man, I got this new CD ..." But no, he wanted my old music. The old vinyl stuff. *Black Love, Let This Melody Ring On*—you know, the far-out stuff. He talked about bringing me to this event called the "Tokyo Crossover Festival." Mr. Shuya wanted me there but without my group. I agreed, so he sent me a contract to perform. I really think the Japanese people loved my old music more than anyone else, especially what I recorded in the 1970s—music that was recorded more than 40 years before this show. With my vision getting worse, I had to listen to my old compositions and write the charts over again. It was quite a learning experience for me. I was able to dissect and analyze what I had done many years ago. It was interesting, to say the least.

In Japan, they treated me like royalty and put me in the best hotel in Tokyo. I was surprised at the rehearsal, for they had printed out all the charts and already rehearsed them before I got to Japan. Everything was sharp. I was pleased and impressed, which allowed me to relax, knowing that we were going to have a great show. The guest singer was from England, Bembé Segué. She did a fantastic job, and I was pleased with her renditions of my songs. She told me that my version of "Mother of the Future" with Norman Connors' group was a big hit in Europe, where everybody had T-shirts that said, "Mother of the Future." (I will have to make some myself.) The band consisted of great young Japanese musicians; I was very impressed with all of them! Sometimes after rehearsals, they would ask me a lot of questions about my career and music. I loved sharing stories with them.

Shingo Okudaira was also a part of this show. I had communicated with Shingo via e-mail telling him that I would be going to Japan and would love to see him. He showed up at the first rehearsal with his parents just to see me. Both of his parents attended Shingo's performances whenever and wherever they could. After our first show, Shingo's father shook my hand with a $100 bill inside and told me, "That's for you, Carlos." How nice is that? His father saw me live when I first went to Japan in 1970 with Art Blakey and had loved my style on the saxophone ever since. Life can take many turns. I never thought that the son of a Japanese fan from my tour in 1970 would eventually become my drummer and dear friend.

While in Japan, a beautiful young Japanese lady was assigned as my guide and interpreter. Her name was Yukari; she was always pleasant and nice. The promoter, Mr. Shuya Okino, made sure I was

An Unforgettable Return to Japan

comfortable and took me to the best seafood restaurants in Tokyo. Those dinners were always complemented with some of Japan's best wines. I had a wheelchair, and everyone treated me like royalty. What a great return and welcome to Japan for me.

The night of my concert at the Tokyo Crossover/Jazz Festival, the auditorium was packed, wall to wall, and it was standing room only. I was certainly surprised. My mind just said to me, "You are a big star." There was a great atmosphere all around. Imagine what it meant for me to perform five of my old tunes from the early 1970s. We played them in this order: "Mystery of Ages," "Mother of the Future," "Banks of the Nile," "Samba Serenade," and "Señor Coltrane," with my former drummer Shingo Okudaira as a guest on that final song. The audience was in a very good mood, and I had a lot of fun talking with them. The show was fantastic. I later felt really sorry we did not record it. Maybe somebody in Japan has it? (If so, please contact Mr. Jaime "Jota" Ortiz!)

Many of the musicians and fans had my old vinyl albums and had kept them in mint condition, mostly preserved in nice plastic

Sold-out show at the Tokyo Crossover/Jazz Festival in 2012 (photo by Maria Golomidova, used with permission).

sleeves. I was impressed and flattered when they asked me to sign them. I signed over 100 autographs that night. Mr. Shuya paid me well too, somewhere in the region of $5,000, which was the most I had received for a show on my own in my life. Now that's something to think about.

What a week I had in Tokyo, Japan. I'll never forget it. Thank you, Mr. Shuya!

Shekinah's Smile

Four months after I returned to Panama from Japan, I had a laser operation on my left eye. It went well; although the procedure was not as successful as I had hoped, it did improve my vision a little. I kept on playing because, you know, that's what I do.

My good friends Mr. and Mrs. Damani and Ife Keane had an annual jazz show especially for tourists whom they brought from the United States to Panama. As usual, my group performed for this special event. They organized the show yearly to coincide with the events of the Panama Jazz Festival. For this performance, I used two of my former students who happened to be in town: Aquiles Navarro on trumpet and Angie Obin on flute. The show turned out so great that I thought I needed to record the group.

Anibal De Leon, my drummer, told me about the PTY Studios, so I called and booked some time for that same weekend since Aquiles had to go back to the United States in a few days. We did most of the songs on a Saturday, and Aquiles left the following Sunday. A day after that, we recorded Idania Dowman on vocals. She sang a "bossa nova"–style composition that I had written over 10 years earlier while I was still living in Brooklyn. Later that week, I overdubbed and laid down two more songs on the saxophone. The session came out great. The title track was called "Shekinah's Smile," a song I wrote for my seventh daughter, who bears that beautiful name. Shekinah means "glory" in Hebrew. I ended up using that name for the album as well.

Because of my failing vision, I did not perform for quite some time. After more than a year, I formed a new band, and it sounded great. Juan Carlos De Leon stayed in the group, but now I added Chale Icaza on drums and Carlos Quiros on bass. My intention was to record a set of new songs for a new album with this group, but I wasn't able to for different reasons. At that point, I had a new manager/agent, but not much was happening. Danilo Perez was opening a new jazz club around that time, but I couldn't seem to get a gig there. I wonder why not? Whatever the reason, the fact that there is a prominent jazz club is a good thing for Panama. My group and I, though, found ourselves playing on and off at this place called Cafe Chic over in "Calle Uruguay," which had a very busy nightlife back then. But that place eventually shut down, as most bars do in Panama. Places don't seem to last that long. Danilo's club is still around, which, again, is nothing but a good thing.

A few months after doing *Shekinah's Smile*, I was driving around one day with a lawyer friend of mine, Herbert Harmann, and he decided to stop by the Alfaro Music Shop on a popular street in Panama named "Via Argentina." Herbert wanted to get some nice speakers. He was now acting as a sort of manager to help me get gigs and stuff like that. It so happens that I wasn't blowing as much as before, which made me feel a little sad. While hanging around the store, I checked out some ukuleles, and then this salesperson who knew me came over to talk. I started looking at the sax section and asked him whether I could check one of them, to which he agreed. The horn was selling for $3,000, but I did not have that kind of money. While looking at it, I noticed that the bell had a dent, but I still told Herbert how much I wished I could buy the horn. Two or three days later, he surprised me and brought the horn over! He had bought it for $2,000 because of the dent on the bell, and I gave him my word that I would pay back $250 a month until it was mine. And that surely happened. I got my brand-new Yamaha soprano YSS 475.

"Derrame Leve" (Mild Stroke)

As time went on, I was having more problems with my vision. Simple tasks turned very complicated. My music writing was affected immediately. I recall composing a song on my computer program

Part 2. Life After Life

in June 2014, which turned out to be the last one I could write for myself. I had been using new software to write music for quite some time. Computers were capable of great things nobody would have ever thought about in years gone by, especially musicians. Long gone were the days of cutting staff paper in half and writing notes so small that I, the composer, could barely read them.

I had a couple of gigs here and there, but it was getting hard to play. My eyes were hurting a lot, and I couldn't do much about it. I do remember being able to see a handful of lottery tickets that had my picture printed on them. It was a tribute to me from Panama's national lottery, but I was never notified about such a thing, nor was

Panamanian national lottery ticket in honor of Carlos Garnett (Jaime "Jota" Ortiz personal archive).

"Derrame Leve" (Mild Stroke)

I given any sort of payment or aid from them for using my image. My wife had to go and buy the tickets so I could keep a few for myself! They didn't even ask for my permission. They probably thought I was dead since they don't know or give a shit about us artists.

November is the "mes de la patria" in Panama, when everyone celebrates Independence Day, Flag Day, and so forth. In November 2015, I was on the "Cinta Costera," a sort of coastal road in the city with big parks on the side. Ana and I were watching the parades for patriotic festivities. I even had to tell some guy to move from in front of me because he wouldn't let me see the parades and the people dancing. After the parade, we went home and all was fine. This was on November 5, as I vividly recall. The next day, I suffered a mild stroke.

I was on 15th Street, "Rio Abajo," where I lived with Ana. That morning, I got up as usual and made myself some coffee; as I was walking to the kitchen, Ana saw me kind of strolling strangely. She asked me whether I was all right, and even though I told her I was okay, she could tell there was something wrong. Sure enough, I lost my balance and couldn't move.

My wife called for her nephew Eloy, and they put me in a car and carried me to the clinic down the road. Once I arrived, the people at the clinic told me they couldn't examine me there, so I called my brother Fernando in the United States, who then proceeded to call my other brother Wendell in Panama. In those days, I didn't keep in touch with Wendell as much as Fernando did, so I didn't even know how to reach him.

Wendell arrived shortly at the clinic with this other guy, Luther. I had been told that I needed to go to another place called the "Arcángel" hospital to get proper care. I wasn't sure of what was going on. Once we got to the hospital, they told me that I had to go to another hospital, the "Santo Tomás" hospital, this time for a brain scan. Turns out, they didn't have the necessary equipment at the "Arcángel" hospital. An ambulance came for me, and soon enough I was at "Santo Tomás." The doctors put me in and out of that scanning machine and told me that I had suffered a mild stroke. They also let me know that if they found a blood clot, I would have to stay; if not, I could go back to the "Arcángel" hospital for monitoring. Fortunately, they did not find any menacing issues, so I was able to go. I was tired of running all over the place. Can you imagine if it had been more serious? I would have died from everyone treating me like a ping pong ball jumping from one place to the other in my delicate condition.

Back at the "Arcángel" hospital, doctors kept me under supervision, making sure I was better, and eventually they let me leave. Back at home, I was taken care of by my loving family as well as my beautiful neighbor Magdalena, who helped me with foot, tongue and speech exercises (going "la la la la la" for minutes). I also recovered very well thanks to the kung fu exercises that I had learned while at the New York State Division for Youth.

Before my "derrame leve," or mild stroke incident, I was already kind of blind, but I could see a little. A few of my friends had big strokes, and now they are dead! I had been very lucky in a way, I guess, but now I was pretty much fully blind. The stroke didn't affect my blowing too much (thank Yahweh again!), because I could still play, but the tenor was getting more complicated, so I had to blow my soprano more and more.

The real problem for me was that the loss of my eyesight meant the days of writing music myself on staff paper, and later on my computer, were gone. I had written my fair share of compositions, over 300. I knew I must keep writing and playing, but now it was all going to be much more difficult for me. Nothing in life can prepare you for blindness.

The Salvation Army

A few years ago, my good friend Joe Fields passed away. I am so grateful to have worked with him because he allowed me to do the things I wanted to do musically. He didn't want anything to do with the ownership of my songs, and that was the most important thing for me. Joe had the money, so I got on his case about producing my albums. Ever since those Norman Connors days he had wanted to record me.

After Joe died, his son Barney Fields started running the record label. When I learned of his father's passing, the first thing I did was

The Salvation Army

call Barney to let him know how much his father meant to me. Joe ran some of the most original record labels in jazz history, and I was lucky enough to be a part of his legacy. He gave musicians complete artistic freedom, worrying only about what he had to do once the music was already on the tapes.

I wasn't feeling at all great after Joe's death; on top of that, my day-to-day life became more uncertain due to my blindness. Luckily, I started going to the Salvation Army every Friday right after my stroke. A friend of mine by the name of Everet Proverb—or DJ Everet, as I call him—told me about what was happening over at the Salvation Army, and he started to take me himself. It was a great meeting place for blind people like me. Turns out, Everet's father went to school with me in Paraíso, and his aunt Violeta Proverb used to sing with the Gay Crooners back in the day! Everet also became the sound engineer for the new group that I would soon establish, the Diggers Descendants Calypso Band.

I liked going to the Salvation Army because I could socialize, but it was also great just to get out of the house. At 8:30 in the morning, Everet picked me up, and he brought me back home by 3:00. It's nice getting up every Friday when you have a little plan, you know? When I got there, I always took my horn out and played a little. Then they would give us a nice "derretido" (grilled cheese sandwich) and a cup of coffee. I would eat my stuff and blow my horn. Time went by a little faster there than at my house.

In the main hall there were tables, and the one I usually sat at always had some nice acquaintances like Mateo Musa, Carlos Anderson and Lalo Chacon sitting with me—all blind men. Mateo I knew from before through Shekinah's mother. Carlos was a piano player from Bocas. Lalo was a guitar player, a very good one (and a good singer too). If I played a note, he could tell me what note it was. Lalo was born blind, as opposed to me, who enjoyed 77 years of my life blessed with vision. The other guys were West Indian, but they were always talking in Spanish because Lalo, who was from the "interior" (that is, rural Panama), couldn't speak English. I complained once in a while about it.

Sometimes we did some church singing in Spanish, and I just went along because they were not singing the truth. They didn't know it, but that's okay. I did my research on the Bible; they didn't.

After the stroke, I could really play only my soprano sax, and going to the Salvation Army helped me brush up my skills because I practiced as much as I could there. Slowly, I got my abilities back. No later than a month after my stroke, I was performing at this place called the "Teatro Amador," a renovated theater in the old part of Panama City. I had already played there a couple of years

Top: Carlos Garnett and his soprano sax at "Teatro Amador," Panama, 2015 (photo by Carlos Agrazal, used with permission). *Bottom:* Carlos Quiros (left), Carlos Garnett (center), and Aquiles Navarro (right) at "Teatro Amador," Panama, 2015 (photo by Carlos Agrazal, used with permission).

back, so I knew about the venue. I was barely fit to play but decided to follow through, so I called together some of the guys from my groups, including Chale Icaza, Carlos Quiros, Juan Carlos De Leon and Aquiles Navarro. Everyone liked the show, and I thought I played pretty well given the circumstances of my health.

The Diggers Descendants

Calypso music runs through my veins. I am always playing my ukulele, singing old songs or composing new ones on my own. That love for calypso never stopped, even after the stroke. The simplicity of the music allowed me to not go too hard on my soprano sax, so I kept on going. My motor skills were getting a little better every day, and so was my blowing. Enduring a mild stroke was too much for certain parts of my body and brain, but the mind is a powerful thing. Mine was prepared to battle for my music. I even got myself a new band that is still active to this day. It wasn't jazz this time, though. The group was called the "Diggers Descendants Calypso Band," a name that I came up with. There's a little story behind it.

I've mentioned the Johnny B previously in this book, and it's because this place used to be famous in Panama. A lot of West Indians from the United States used to go there. I played dominoes at the Johnny B all the time. Sometimes I would go only for a quick "basilon" (a good time) and have a drink or two. One day, I was hanging out there, and a couple of guys came up to me while messing around with a ukulele and a piano. We had a good time playing together. They were out of tune and sounded amateur, but it was fun singing Panamanian and other calypso songs. We never really got together again after that, but I knew one day we might see each other again.

A couple of years later, I was back again at the Johnny B, and I saw those same guys playing songs right next door at a restaurant owned by a guy called Barbicas. The band was in tune, to my surprise, so I went over with my ukulele and played a few songs. They all remembered me, and the next thing I knew, we started getting together for a weekly gig. The restaurant was packed sometimes, with people loving the music and eating stuff I don't eat (like pig's

Part 2. Life After Life

feet). Sadly, Barbicas died shortly thereafter, and a guy named Lucho bought the restaurant. Turns out that Lucho enjoyed playing calypso and soca for his customers, inviting us all the time to perform. At the beginning, we kept showing up with only a ukulele, a guitar and tumba drums, with all of us on singing duty. After a while, I started taking my horn, and everyone was happy because now I could solo something that wasn't happening before. My good friend Carlos Alfredo Brown also became the bass player in the band.

Everybody who came to the restaurant knew about my accomplishments around the world, so this gig started getting popular. My wife kept telling me it wasn't my band, but I didn't care because I was there having fun. During the rainy season, I even got wet while playing, but that's all right because it's Panama!

We had a commitment to stay together, and the band was getting more serious, so I started taking them to the place where I rehearsed with my jazz groups, which was called "Plug and Play." One time while rehearsing there, somebody asked us about the band name, and we didn't really have one, so I started thinking about it. My brain works quickly with creative thoughts. I felt myself making all these connections to come up with good names on the spot.

When I first joined the band, there were two guys who played ukulele; one was Skimba, and the other Carlos Arenas. (Ironically, there were actually three people named Carlos in the band.) As my head was thinking about all these names for the group, I said, "Skim Arenas," but Skimba didn't want to use his name. Everyone kept making suggestions until suddenly I thought about our ancestors from the West Indies who came to build the canal. When the United States started building the Panama Canal (in itself a big undertaking, one that the French couldn't finish), they brought in a large number of West Indian laborers to do the job. Even before that, when the interoceanic railroad was being built, there were thousands upon thousands of Black people from Cuba, Jamaica, Barbados, Trinidad and Martinique coming to Panama. These West Indians were called "diggers," so I mentioned that, and everyone liked it. Since we were the descendants of those diggers, the name of the band became "Diggers Descendants."

In the Latter Years...

The band rehearsed every Saturday at the Plug and Play rehearsal rooms, where they charged me a $10/hour special prize. I was happy with the group because when I first met them, they played only three or four chords. I told them we needed to get away from the same old thing and write new songs. I encouraged them to learn, and they improved. The band's sound and popularity grew so much that we were invited to play at the 2018 Panama Jazz Festival. We talked to one of the organizers, who said he was a big fan of calypso music. He didn't sound like he knew too much. The whole band was booked to play at "Ciudad del Saber" for the festival. The day of the show, we played our asses off, and when we got done, the crowd gave us a nice standing ovation, so we played another song. As soon as we finished, the crowd got up again! They wouldn't let us go, so we played another encore. Once we finished the second encore, they wanted more! Another standing ovation! So in total we played three encores thanks to three standing ovations. For that show, I got paid $19 after three standing ovations. Can you believe it?

In the Latter Years...

My life has led me to many favorable incidents that I can cherish in my memory forever, but some decisions have been really tough to make. Selling my Selmer tenor saxophone was one of them. My eye doctor kept telling me that blowing the tenor was putting too much pressure on my eyes, so things needed to change; otherwise, my eyesight would certainly worsen. You see, the stroke had left me pretty much blind, but I could still see shapes and shadows. That was something to hold on to, you know? Like the best of the worst. I certainly didn't want to lose that.

One day I got a call from one of my old students, Charles Dougherty, who said he was looking for a tenor sax. After a few discussions, I agreed to sell him my tenor. He was very happy, honored and excited about getting it, and we arranged a price. Charles had played with me in my Cosmos Nucleus big band, and he looked up to me. I spoke to him recently, and he still has my horn. At least it is in good hands.

Part 2. Life After Life

Being blind is a burden, but I give thanks and praise to Yahweh because I was able to see my whole life, not like my friend Lalo from the Salvation Army, who was born this way. I cannot see my hand; I cannot see my face in the mirror. The hardest part is that I will always need help, no matter the task, and I must resign myself to the fact that I will remain this way until I die.

My advice to whoever reads this book is that if you think your eyesight is deteriorating, go see a doctor right away—don't wait. Let me tell you a story about being blind: A few years after my stroke, I went with my oldest daughter to Florida. Being blind, I was required to travel with a wheelchair. At the airport, my daughter Chela and my granddaughter took me somewhere to sit down and wait for boarding. There was a guy assigned specifically to push the wheelchair for me, so the girls went to shop while the man conveyed me to the gate. After a little strolling around with my sax and ukulele in hand, we seemed to arrive at the gate, and the guy just left me there, telling me he would be back. A few minutes passed, which seemed like ages, and suddenly I had to pee, but I'm blind, so I kept calling for help to the point that I started yelling. The guy never showed up! He probably went to carry some other blind or crippled guy because that's how they make their money. I started to call out and yell, "Help, somebody, somebody!" but nobody came until a woman started talking to me out of nowhere. She was on her way to Jamaica and told me I was at the wrong gate! They were going to send me back to the island of my ancestors, I guess. Thanks to her, one of the guys at the boarding gate came and helped me go pee and everything. That's what being blind is like—helplessness.

My email address is colder than ice. Nobody goes there to check for mail anymore. Sometimes my wife looks, but only after I pressure her into doing so. Can I reply to whoever writes? Absolutely not! Ana has to help me with it. So don't email me. I even had trouble collecting money because of this problem, since some kind of tax issues did not allow me to collect certain funds available for me in Europe. Hugh Lawrence told me about it. He called BMI Europe, and they said I couldn't get the money because of tax problems they had notified me about. I had to call the Harry Fox Agency, and they put me through a bunch of bullshit only to not be able to collect anything at the end of the day.

A couple of years ago, Dwight Brewster called; we kept in touch all the time. While talking, I mentioned that it had been over 40 years since I got any money from royalties. He couldn't believe it, so he immediately gave me his lawyer's phone number. Soon enough, I was speaking to him on a three-way call. The lawyer was a guy by the name of Ellis Rich in the United Kingdom. He worked for a company called Supreme Songs and, after learning about my situation, offered me a contract to collect my royalties worldwide for a percentage. I told him that I had hundreds of songs registered around the world. Ellis then sent me the contract through the internet. My wife printed the document, and I signed it, had it scanned and sent it back to him. I negotiated 25 percent with them. Afterward I talked to my friend Ron Warwell, and he said it was a good decision. Ellis said he was going to collect some money for me right there in England.

Weeks later, Ellis Rich called me up to let me know that he was going to send me a check for $1,400. Turns out, in 2015 a label called Soul Brother Records purchased some of my catalog from Muse Records and rereleased some CDs. They even made a vinyl record compilation called *Mystery of Ages*. Barney Fields must have arranged that deal. Thanks to this release and to Ellis Rich, I got a royalty check for the first time in 52 years. The label must have made much more money. Let's hope they cough some up soon.

Being blind will make your days much more repetitive. I was no longer able to drive my white Mitsubishi Mirage. There was no more playing dominoes at Magnolia Bar or the Johnny B, no more going out with my wife to have fun and dance. Years earlier, I used to go constantly to the "Parque Omar," the nicest park in Panama City, where I would play for hours by myself. I rehearsed right there many times for shows. People would gather around to listen to me play, cheering after long solos. I became sort of an attraction at the park. One time, I met Samuel Dawson from Bocas del Toro, who became a good friend and would later drive me daily up to the park. He and I had debates on different stuff too. Samuel used to say a phrase to me

Part 2. Life After Life

all the time that I will never forget. He used to say "put it in your pipe and smoke it" whenever he wanted me to remember something.

There were a few things I did that kept my spirits high: playing my sax and writing new music. Since I was not able to write by myself anymore, I started to rely on a young guitarist from the Panamanian province of Chiriquí: Ricardo Pinzon. He had a great sound and could play his ass off. He was coming to my house to study my patterns of improvisation, and he also helped me write my new songs on staff paper. We would go over the melodies, chords and voicings for him to then write it all down. There's an electric piano at home, and I used it to play the chords for "Rickypin," which is what I call Ricardo.

From all the practicing at home, I felt my chops were good enough to start another jazz group. Why not? I was writing new material, and the "young buays" were very excited to play with me. I decided to form a new group with Rickypin on guitar, Carlos Quiros on bass, and Jordan Zimmerman on drums. Carlos studied in Puerto Rico and has a very good tone on the upright. Jordan is a more reserved drummer, but I like his sense of time and how he plays behind my solos.

My brain is faster than my body, and the musical ideas just come out of nowhere all the time, sometimes as I am lying in bed in the early morning. In my house, I have had to memorize precisely where everything is located. That is the only way for me to move around without having to rely on someone's help. When I go to the bathroom, I count the steps. I know the turns. I can feel the floor and touch furniture like the chair and sofa for reference. That's how I get to the piano sometimes to play around and compose new music. I can compose on the ukulele or the sax or the piano. It all starts as UCI (unlimited creative imagination, remember?). I am blind, but I can almost see a light in the darkness coming from the music.

It pains me to accept that my bad memory at this point led me to lose another of my horns. Yes, you probably guessed it, it happened in a taxi. I don't know what is wrong with me, losing a horn in a taxi again. And this wasn't Japan, where the taxi driver went all the way back to the hotel to return my horn. This time a blind man was taken advantage of by a taxi driver who could have found me if he had really wanted to. He probably pawned the damned horn for 20 dollars. It still pains me so much that I am not going to go into detail. Once again, here I was, depressed and crying with no saxophone.

One day, my wife Ana was talking to her daughter who lives in the States and told her about my situation. Like a blessing from Yahweh, she offered to lend me the money to get a new horn, as she was saving to buy a car. She sent $2,000 to me, and I called my friend Carlos Quiros, who worked at the Supro Music Store. Carlos got me a great price on another Yamaha YSS soprano saxophone. That's the horn I am using right now, always leaning on my right knee because it's too heavy for me at this age. You might wonder how a thin soprano can be too heavy for me, but let me tell you, you haven't lived through a "derrame leve" or mild stroke, or maybe you have but don't play saxophone. After the stroke, my physical abilities were reduced, and in order to blow the horn, I needed to rest it on my knee. I couldn't have cared less. I had a brand-new horn.

After many months, I finally finished paying Ana's daughter back, and it felt very good because I don't like owing money to anybody.

Mr. G at the Anita Villalaz Theater

While working in the New York State Division for Youth, all the kids would call me "Mr. G." Rickypin, my newest guitarist, also called me "Mr. G." One day, he told me that he had a good friend who was a fan of mine and that it would be a good idea for this guy to produce a jazz concert for my new group. We agreed to invite him over. A couple of days later, he showed up as we were rehearsing a new song with no name. That day, I met my great friend and biographer Mr. Jaime "Jota" Ortiz. He came over, and I immediately knew he was a big fan, because he was talking about all my albums and songs from my Muse Records days in the 1970s. He knew my music better than any of my other Panamanian fans.

Mr. Jota kept calling me "Mr. G" too, so I decided to use that title for the song I was working on with Rickypin. We spoke about his ideas for the show, agreeing on a date for the presentation. He already

Part 2. Life After Life

had in mind the "Anita Villalaz" theater in the historic old part of Panama and told me the best date would be November 19 of that year (2019), which was a month or so away. I told Rickypin that we needed to start rehearsing with the newly formed group as soon as possible. We rehearsed at Plug and Play a few times during that month. My blowing was coming along great. Mr. Jota came to the rehearsals, and he would tell me how good we sounded. I felt great about playing jazz again, as it had been quite some time. Mr. G was ready.

The day of the show, Jordan picked me up and we arrived at the Anita Villalaz theater for the soundcheck. I could sense the hall had great acoustics. My student Giulio Jimenez was kind enough to lend Mr. Jota a set of really nice microphones for the horn. Mr. Jota's brother Miguel was in charge of the sound for the night, and he did a very good job. For this show, I added a young percussionist named Oscarito Cruz, the son of a respected musician with the same name. He added the Latin percussion layers that I have always enjoyed in my music.

After the soundcheck, I waited backstage and drank a little Panama beer that Mr. Jota had for the band. Time went by, and I could hear the people coming in. I was getting excited because I could hear all my classic songs played on the sound system. Mr. Jota had his turntables set up and was reproducing my albums from the original vinyl. "Saxy" from my *Cosmos Nucleus* album was banging on the speakers. I hadn't heard some of my old music in so long. It was most certainly a night of Carlos Garnett's music. Finally, the time came to go onstage after Mr. Jota gave some really nice and encouraging words on my career and all my accomplishments. It felt good to hear those words coming from a fellow Panamanian.

As I approached the stage, I could hear a loud roar! Man, the place was packed! It felt like my days at the Pitt Inn in Japan, where people went crazy when I performed. The set started out with "Mr. G," and everyone clapped like mad when they heard it was a new composition. The show went on, and I could not have been happier with the result. Here I was being honored by young musicians and a crowd of young Panamanian fans. A lot of my old fans and friends also showed up. I must say, the night was a big success.

The Autobiography and the Pandemic

Carlos Garnett with his group at the Anita Villalaz theater, November 2019. From left: Oscar Cruz, Jr.; Carlos Quiros; Jordan Zimmerman; and Ricardo Pinzon; Carlos Garnett front center (photo by Milton Scantlebury, used with permission).

The Autobiography and the Pandemic

After the Anita Villalaz show, my dear friend Mr. Jota stayed in touch with me almost every week. He really gained my confidence

Part 2. Life After Life

because I could sense he was a good man, and he delivered on his word. He started asking me whether he could come over to the house to interview me. Mr. Jota had all these interesting questions no one had really asked me before. I told him how before I lost my sight, I was writing a sort of memoir, trying to put some thoughts and experiences on my computer. It was something I was doing every once in a while; the next thing I knew, I had some very interesting facts about my life on the word processor.

As soon as I told Mr. Jota about my writing, he started to pressure me into letting him read it. Honestly, at first, I was not too sure about giving that piece of my life history to him, but he was so persistent that I allowed him to get it out of my computer. The next day, he was calling me and telling me that he had a plan to turn the memoir into a real book. I really couldn't recall how much material I had laid out in my writing, but according to Mr. Jota the text was very short—only a few pages—and missing too much important information. He decided to start interviewing me and editing all those conversations into an autobiography. He and his brother Miguel came over to my apartment one time and recorded me for about three hours, with Mr. Jota asking me all sorts of questions about my life.

Mr. Jota and I agreed to be partners in the autobiographical project, getting to work right away. We had a few interview sessions arranged, but then the month of March 2020 rolled on by, and the coronavirus pandemic hit the entire world. Getting together for the interviews was now almost impossible because Panama was on lockdown. To make matters worse, I am an old man at high risk if I ever get the virus, so Mr. Jota decided to carry out the interviews by phone. He and I have spoken for hours upon hours for the last several months, and I am so grateful to him because it was one of the moments of my day that I looked forward to the most. Thinking about my past and digging in my brain for old memories kept me very entertained during lockdown.

Mr. Jota also prepares himself well and conducts a lot of research on my music and life. He has dug up recordings I didn't even remember existed. He played for me a record I made in the late 1970s with trumpeter Milt Ward. At first, I told him he was wrong and that it wasn't me in that record. He played the album for me a few times, and eventually I came around and realized it indeed was me! I couldn't remember anything about that session. Mr. Jota told me he plays bass, and one time he asked me whether I had played with Henry Franklin. As soon as he said the name, memories came into my head of jamming with him over in California. I believe I was there at a gig with Norman Connors. There were so many great musicians I was able to perform and play with; it's really a grace from Yahweh.

There was also an instance when Mr. Jota played recordings I had made at Rudy Van Gelder's studio with Andrew Hill, which weren't released until almost 40 years after being recorded. That session took place right after I had recorded *Lift Every Voice* with Andrew. I went back to Van Gelder and completely forgot about it! Mr. Jota brought to my attention the fact that he could hear a soprano sax as well as a tenor on the song "Mahogany," which can only mean I played both on the same song! That must have been the first recording I ever did on a soprano sax. If it weren't for Mr. Jota, I would never have remembered this stuff.

Mr. Jota also played for me bootleg recordings I did with Art Blakey in Japan that I had never heard, along with the recording of one of my most memorable concerts, the Ann Arbor Jazz and Blues Festival with Miles Davis. He would bring these bootleg recordings he found digging through the internet and play them for me.

Talking over the phone with Mr. Jota during the pandemic became a daily occurrence. He worked hard on a very detailed chronological timeline, which allowed him to come up with the material to paint a full picture of my life as best as he could. After all that work, he was able to put together my own "autobiography," which you are reading right now, so I owe a lot to Mr. Jaime "Jota" Ortiz! Bless him, with his enthusiasm and patience.

Let Us Go (To Higher Heights)

This coronavirus is a rare occurrence, so I wrote a song about the first responders. It's just a thought, you know, and I love to play around with words:

Part 2. Life After Life

The first responders,
They are great, and are human wonders,
We love them so much,
They are the first responders.

We owe so much to them right now, all the doctors, nurses and emergency responders. I hope they don't come for me anytime soon!

Besides all my talking with Mr. Jota, I also talk with many friends and family, usually over the "magicJack" telephone service provider on my computer. In addition, I recently talked to my student Aquiles Navarro. Mr. Jota has also gotten in touch with some of my old friends like Shingo Okudaira, Taru Alexander and Panamanian soul singer Ralph Weeks, and they have all called me recently to talk about life and recall our experiences together. It has been good for my state of mind.

During the pandemic, I also received a royalty check from an unexpected source: Andrew Hill. I don't recall ever receiving any royalties from him in the past. We never recorded any song of mine. I don't know how or why, but my ex-wife in New York called me to tell me that she had a check for me from Andrew Hill. She mailed it to me, so I could cash it. What do you know—a check from Andrew Hill in the middle of the coronavirus chaos. You all know I've had my fair share of problems getting royalties in the past. A few months ago, Mr. Jota helped me contact BMI to follow up on the situation, and a man called Paul Cook told him that I had indeed had some tax issues but that they were now resolved.

Mr. Jota—my great friend, interviewer and editor, the man who knows more about me than all the women in my life put together—has been trying to nudge me into listening to some new jazz guys, especially tenor players. He came to my house the other day and played some music by this guy called Kamasi Washington, a young tenor player. He is one of the most recognized musicians in the jazz scene these days, and I enjoyed listening to him. I can see the influence my style has had on him—maybe not directly, but perhaps indirectly. I can sense that he takes inspiration from Black culture and African themes. Mr. Jota tells me he wears these big African robes. I don't know, I can't see shit. Maybe one day he will come forward and say whether I was ever an influence on his playing, or maybe not. I know Mr. Jota tried to contact him to get an impression on my career. Regardless, I heard his music and liked some of it. Some other songs of his kind of put me to sleep, but that's just me; I am an old, difficult man sometimes.

One day, Mr. Jota called me up and told me that he had gotten two replies from very important people in my life whom he had contacted via email: Dee Dee Bridgewater and Ron Carter. They both had really nice things to say about me and shared some comments with Mr. Jota. Ron wrote:

> *I always admired how he would take famous jazz melodies like "Maiden Voyage" and "Giant Steps" and with his Panamanian/Latin rhythms make them his own. I look forward to reading his bio and finding out his secrets!*

Can you believe it? Reading those comments from Ron Carter and others from Dee Dee made me feel really good even after being confined to my apartment without being able to go out or receive any visits from family or friends. This is what Dee Dee Bridgewater shared with Mr. Jota about me:

> *Carlos Garnett was a musical visionary, an amazing musician who thought outside the box. My times with him were always culturally enriching as he traveled in international circles unknown to me at the time that we met in New York in the early 1970s. We socialized often at his Brooklyn apartment, and even rehearsed the background vocals for the track "Banks of the Nile" from his 1974 album* Black Love, *and in concert with his group Universal Black Force. Carlos was warm, open, engaging, always soft spoken ... he treated me, and all the women he interacted with, with the utmost respect. Carlos is a spiritual and nurturing soul and those characteristics were always reflected in his music.*

Words cannot describe how good I felt the day Mr. Jota shared those words from Ron and Dee Dee with me. Ron Warwell used to tell me all the time not to feel down and out, because I had achieved a lot in my career. I am certainly a very blessed man to have shared the best studios and stages with jazz greats like Ron Carter and Dee Dee Bridgewater.

Part 2. Life After Life

Another thing I enjoy a lot is listening to all my old recordings, which Mr. Jota was kind enough to put on a USB drive for me. I got this portable speaker that plays music directly from the USB. I've got all sorts of music in there, even some Black Majesty and other Panamanian calypsonians. Since I'm blind, I've had to memorize all the different button positions and functions. I did the same thing with my phone in order to make calls, memorizing the patterns in the buttons with the different sequences and the feel of each part of the phone so I can place a simple call. That's how you live when you are blind. Things speak to you through the language of touch.

One of the things I do at home to keep sharp is my exercise routine. In my days at the New York State Division for Youth, I learned a little bit of kung fu, and I still practice some of the exercises I learned then. Tuesdays, Thursdays and Saturdays are the days when I work out. I move my fingers for several minutes, bend my knees in repetitions of 50, and do foot, arm and neck exercises going all the way from the tips of my toes to my head. My eating habits are also well kept by my wife Ana and by my angel "Ma," my mother-in-law who lives with us and takes care of me. She cooks me all kinds of good food like "corvina" (bass), "pargo rojo" (snapper, another local fish) and tuna, as well as a lot of salmon. Usually, I eat with just a salad or "aguacate" (avocado), which I eat a lot of. My health is good; I feel great, except for my teeth, which give me a lot of pain. I'm guessing I will have to go to the dentist soon to get some teeth pulled out, and maybe I'll look handsome when this book comes out. See that wordplay right there?

I wrote five hymns the other day and played them at midnight while everyone was sleeping. My mother-in-law sleeps in a room next to the piano, so I can't make much noise when playing at night. I wrote a song for her telling her how much I love her. She doesn't like it. "Ma" is five years older than me, and she's always looking out for Carlos Garnett. I thank Yahweh for her. I have a urinal, and sometimes it fills up! The other day I went to the bathroom to dump it and missed! It was a disaster. She told me she would take care of it. What an angel.

After what seemed like an eternity (eight months, to be exact), I went outside for the first time to play with the Diggers Descendants in a major event hosted by the Ministry of Culture, which is a big institution in charge of cultural development. Mr. Jota was kind enough to pick me up and escort me to the show. Since the country was still on lockdown, we played live at the historic Balboa Theater in the old Canal Zone, and the show was transmitted for all the country to see. It was fairly obvious that the presenters at the event didn't know anything about music. They seemed like a pair of clowns, to be honest. That's the sort of people we've got promoting cultural events?

One thing that is worth mentioning is the disappointment I have felt toward the different government and cultural institutions of Panama. I know first-hand that Mr. Jota tried in every way possible to get support for this book from people at all different levels over at the Ministry of Culture and beyond, but to no avail. This is a new institution set up precisely to support important Panamanian projects like this book, but that support never materialized. They even have an editorial! It's shameful!

Mr. Jota and I spoke many times about his frustration at the fact that people in positions of power who could actually make a difference were not doing anything at all to help this project. Many would falsely say they were willing to help, even asking for more information or recommending that we apply for some sort of aid, but when the time came to really deliver, they just went silent. We all know we are still in the middle of a pandemic, but that is no excuse for turning their backs on me, as they did throughout my life. I never got any financial support from the government as an internationally respected artist. If it weren't for the retirement checks I got from working for decades at the New York State Division for Youth, I would have really struggled! This book presented an opportunity for the government to set things right and help us commemorate an important part of Panamanian history. We needed a small contribution, just a hand, but they were too greedy, thinking about their own corrupt selves.

In the end, everything happens for a reason. The fact that this book was not picked up by the Panamanian Ministry of Culture gave us the opportunity to go further and further until Mr. Jota finally reached McFarland and Co., which didn't even think twice about

Part 2. Life After Life

releasing my life story, and we must thank them for that vision. At one point, we almost gave up on this project, but Mr. Jota's persistence got us to where we are now—an incredible achievement, I must admit. Everybody in Panama whom Mr. Jota contacted for support only to have them turn their backs on us should be ashamed.

These days I'm wondering whether that great show at the Anita Villalaz theater in November 2019 is going to be my last jazz performance, because this pandemic doesn't seem to be going anywhere.

The Diggers band was going to record, but this coronavirus messed that plan up. We were going to do a song I wrote called "Rumble in the Jungle," just like Muhammad Ali and George Foreman—a rumble in the jungle down in Panama. It's about problems between a man and a woman:

And when the news got out in the street,
how she bust up his mouth and knock out his two front teeth.

Another song the Diggers band was going to do was "Daddy's Maybe":

Momma's baby, daddy's may-be.
You better take a DNA test to be sure that the baby is yours.
Right now, it's still a mystery,
because momma don't know who her baby Dad-dy.

Ideally by the time this book is out, and the virus is gone, these songs can be recorded. I have many other ones too! I'm writing a song called "Black Lives Matter" because of all that happened with George Floyd. I lived through shit like that. Racism in Panama, racism in the United States—racism everywhere. That's why I created the Universal Black Force. That's why I wrote *Black Love* almost 50 years ago.

I live in this beautiful country called Panama, with all its problems and virtues. But I am a product of this land, so I always write music with Panama in mind. Just a few days ago, I wrote another one for my country:

Panama, my beloved Panama, a beautiful country in Central America,
Panama, my beloved Panama is between Costa Rica and Colombia.

You gotta hear me sing it with the ukulele. Reading it ain't doing it justice.

Let Us Go (To Higher Heights)

I'm still trying to teach the newer generations that it's not all about music. My philosophy when I worked at the New York State Division for Youth was to go to the teenagers and tell them about my past. I started using drugs in the early 1960s and stopped using them in 1979. I changed; I'm a different person. I live in righteousness. When I was with those kids, I would make it clear that I used drugs. I told them about how I thought I needed them. I would say these things because I thought it was good for them to hear. Man, I did all kinds of stuff until 1979! I later gave the same message to Aquiles, Giulio and all my students throughout my entire career. "Los Nietos Del Jazz," the young "likibuays," also got my word on it. Because I'm not ashamed. I want them to learn from the mistakes I made. I told my great friend and biographer Mr. Jota the other day, "I'm blessed to be alive talking to you, Brother Jota. I should be dead."

These days I have been waking up in the morning inspired by a particular lullaby. I'm going to have to sit down at the piano and maybe record it....

Carlos Garnett (left) with Jaime "Jota" Ortiz at the Anita Villalaz theater, Panama, November 2019 (photo by Milton Scantlebury, used with permission).

Index

Abdul-Jabbar, Kareem 60
"Abide with Me" (song by Henry Francis Lyte) 11
Accra, Ghana 148
Acoustic Sound Studios, Brooklyn, New York 134
African-American Teachers Association 70
African Art International Festival 148
African House, Queens, New York 133
"African Lament" (song by Carlos Garnett) 152
Agrazal, Carlos 184
Alexander, Roland 29, 37, 130
Alexander, Sheryl 103
Alexander, Taru 130, 133, 172, 174, 196
Alfaro Music Shop, Panama City, Panama 179
Ali, Rashied 28, 68
Alisema (album by Shingo Okudaira) 147, 149
Alkebu-lan: Land of the Blacks (album by Mtume Umoja Ensemble) 73
Allen, George 169; *see also* Lord Panama
Alphonso, Roland 113, 162
Al-Rouf, Khaliq 65
Amen-Ra, Akum Ra 95, 103, 105, 107, 127
Amherst College 74
Aming, Choy 43
Anderson, Carlos 183
Anderson, Charley 154, 161, 171
Anderson, Clif 168
Anderson, Wes 37
Anita Villalaz Theater, Panama City, Panama 191–193, 200
Ann Arbor Jazz and Blues Festival, Michigan 78, 195
The Apache Restaurant, New York 113
Aramaki, Shigeo 147
Archibald, Rex 155

Arenas, Carlos 186
Arlington Inn, New York 29, 70
Armstrong, Herbert 104
Arnet, Jan 51, 55
Art Blakey and the Jazz Messengers 51
Atlantic Records 50
Avenida Central, Panama City, Panama 64

The Baby Grand, New York 28, 70
Badoo 129
Balakrishna, Khalil 77
Balboa, Panama City, Panama 157
Baltimore, Maryland 62, 74
Bandy, Greg 148
"Banks of the Nile" (song by Carlos Garnett) 86, 177, 197
Baptist Church 7
Barretto, Ray 67
Barron, Kenny 47, 155
Bartee, Claude 35
Bartlett Contemporaries Band 42
Bartz, Gary 70, 72, 73, 77, 78, 83, 130
Bass, Mickey 51
Bauza, Mario 106
The Beatles 77
Beccabunco, Mario 154
"Bed Stuy Blues" (song by Carlos Garnett) 104
Bedford-Stuyvesant, New York 60, 104
"Bedroom Eyes" (song by Carlos Garnett) 40
Benbow, Warren 103
Benjamin, James "Fish" 84
Bennett, William 28
Berger, Andy 161
Berna, Juan 154
Beverly, Frankie 124
Big Fun (album by Miles Davis) 82
Birdland, New York 48
Birdsong, Edwin 87

Index

Black Christ of Portobelo Festival, Portobelo, Panama 129
The Black Eagles 117, 118, 123, 124
Black Lives Matter 200
Black Love (album by Carlos Garnett) 86–95, 109, 127, 141, 160, 175, 200
Black Majesty and the Mighty Bamboo Band 19
Black Saint, Narashino Japan 136
Black Unity (album by Pharoah Sanders) 70
Blackwell, Ed 68
Blades, Rubén 67, 163
Blake, Alex 85, 86, 159
Blakey, Art 18, 51, 76, 85, 110, 115, 122, 127, 132, 156, 157, 162, 176, 195
Blue Coronet, New York 41
Blue Note Jazz Club, Tokyo 56
The Blue Note, New York 48, 110, 131
Blue Note Records 53, 54, 138
"Blues for Mr. C" (song by Carlos Garnett) 141
Boa, Victor 15, 107, 153, 154, 157, 158, 160, 161
Bobo, Willie 45
Bohio Florencia, Panama City, Panama 151
"Bolerock" (song by Carlos Garnett) 110
Bonner, Joe 70, 109
Booth, Juni 47
Boquete, Chiriqui, Panama 161, 168
Boquete Jazz Festival 161
Bourne, Melvin 23
Boyce, Reggie 156
Brackeen, Joanne 55
Bradshaw, Sonny 142
Brecker, Randy 51
The Breevort Theatre, New York 45
Brewster, Dwight 99, 100, 112, 189
Briceno, Rolando 107
Bridgewater, Dee Dee 66, 86, 197
Brodie, Hugh 29
Brodie, Scott 37
Brooklyn, New York 27, 96, 104, 107, 111, 113, 117, 125, 129, 138, 148, 150, 155, 162, 166, 169, 172, 178
Brooklyn All Stars Jazz Band 148
Brooklyn Jazz Emporium 148
Brooklyn Jazz Festival 172
Brooks, Roy 62
Brown, Al 104
Brown, Carlos Alfredo 64, 186
Brown, Maurice 37
Brown, Sam 37

Brubeck, Dave 51
B.T. Express 68
Buddah Records 78
Burton, Ron 70
Byard, Jaki 60

Cables, George 51
Café Chic, Panama City, Panama 179
Calle Uruguay, Panama City, Panama 179
Camden University 74
Caragar Music 49
"Caribbean Sun" (song by Carlos Garnett) 92
"Carlos II" (song by Carlos Garnett) 85
Carne, Jean 84
Carrington, Terry Lynn 171
Carter, Betty 87, 88, 93
Carter, Regina 156
Carter, Ron 83, 150, 197
Cary, Mark 147
Casco Viejo Cathedral, Panama City, Panama 159, 174
Catalyst Records 58
"Catch Me If You Can" (song by Carlos Garnett) 134
CBS/April Blackwood Publishing 99, 100
CBS Records 78
Celebrity Club, New York 33
Central Park, New York 98
Cezannes, Houston, Texas 151
Chacon, Lalo 183
Chambers, Carlos 66, 86, 117, 125
"Chana" (song by Carlos Garnett) 92
Chandler, Leon "Ndugu" 73
Charles, Rudolph "Lefty" 15
Cherry, Don 68
Cheyney State University, Pennsylvania 74
Chief Bay 89
Chitlin' Circuit 32
Ciudad del Saber, Panama City, Panama 174, 187
Civic Theater, San Diego 81
Clarke, Natalia 137, 159
Clarke, Neil 66, 74, 85, 94, 103, 130, 135
Clarke, Stanley 70
Clayton, Panama Canal Zone 162
Clovis, Danny 153
Club Baron, New York 18, 48, 52
Club Bombardy, Panama City, Panama 153
Club La Boheme, New York 47

Index

Club Lo Que El Viento Se Llevo, Panama City, Panama 20
Club Maxim, Panama City, Panama 16, 26
Club Michelle, Brooklyn, New York 129, 132
Club 24, Panama City, Panama 16; *see also* Encanto Theater; The Elks
Cobham, Billy 104, 160
Cobham, Wayne 103, 104
Coleman, George 63
Coleman, Ornette 63
Collective Black Artist Band 89
Colón, Willie 99
Colón City, Panama 17, 18, 155, 169
Coltrane, John 35, 63, 111, 132, 141
Columbia Records 76, 77
The Commodores 114
Conley, Terry 129, 130
Connors, Norman 65, 70, 78, 83, 86, 90, 98–99, 130, 175, 195
Constance, Harry 65
Copa Airlines 163
Cosmos Nucleus (album by Carlos Garnett) 100–106, 193
Cosmos Nucleus Big Band 101, 109, 155, 168, 187
Count Basie 100
The Country 99, Isahaya, Japan 149
Cowell, Stanley 73
Cox, Ray 24
Cox, Stanley Bryan 154
Crocamo, Eduardo 159, 163
Crown Heights Affair 68
Crumby, Skip 37, 41
Cruz, Oscar, Jr. 192
Cruz, Will 151
Cunningham, Bob 130
Cuscuna, Michael 85

Dance of Magic (album by Norman Connors) 78, 99
"Dance of the Virgins" (song by Carlos Garnett) 110
"Dancing Daffodils" (song by Carlos Garnett) 141
Daniels, Lenny 65
Dara, Olu 65, 97
Dark of Light (album by Norman Connors) 83, 99
Davis, Betty 85
Davis, Miles 51, 74–83, 115, 122, 156, 157, 195
Davis, Richard 53–55

Dean Street Café & Jazz Club, New York 131, 133
Debreano, Santi 24, 160, 165
Dehjonette, Jack 76
De Leon, Anibal 159, 163, 178
De Leon, Juan Carlos 159, 165, 179, 185
"Delilah" (song by Victor Young) 150
The Democratic Republic of the Congo 66
Denis, Rodrigo 159
Diana Ross and the Supremes 33
Diggers Descendants Calypso Band 183, 185, 199, 200
Dimensional Sound Studios, New York 110
Dinza, Eusebio 165
The Disciples 89
Dollar Brand 68
Dolphy, Eric 104, 172
Don Alias 76
Dooly, Jim 148
Dorham, Kenny 34
Dorsey, Leon 139
Doudy, Jim 91
Dougherty, Charles 103, 187
Dowman, Idania 16, 174, 178
Downbeat Magazine 69, 71, 104, 167
Drinkwater, Skip 78, 83
Duchin, Eddie 19
Duchin, Peter 19
Dudley, Bepo 24
Duran, Roberto 76
Durham, Mark 69

Earland, Charles 138
The East 49, 70, 73, 87–90, 148, 172
Eastman, Clarence 90
Eastman, Gerry 148
Eaves, Hubert 84, 94, 95
"Ebonesque" (song by Carlos Garnett) 86
Edgehill, Guillermo 74, 107
El Chorrillo, Panama City, Panama 19, 22
El Dorado, Panama City, Panama 154
El Marañon, Panama City, Panama 5, 14
The Elks, Panama City, Panama 16; *see also* Club 24; The Elks
Ellington, Duke 100
Elmina's Slave Castle, Ghana 148, 152
Encanto Theater, Panama City, Panama 16; *see also* Club 24; The Elks
"Epitapher Zackerism" (song by Carlos Garnett) 142

205

Index

Ervin, Booker 54
Esquire Club, Colón City, Panama 18
"Eternal Justice" (song by Carlton Holmes) 134
"Everybody Plays the Fool" (song by The Main Ingredient) 99
The Exciters 64

Fania Records 99
Fantasy Lounge, New York 34, 45
Farrah, Shamek 129
Farrell, Joe 54
Fernandez, Angel 103
Fields, Barney 182, 189
Fields, Joe 78, 84, 92, 94, 95, 97, 98, 106, 110, 130, 132, 133, 134, 138, 141, 182
"Fifthology" (song by Carlos Garnett) 147
The Five Spot, New York 48
Floyd, George 200
Ford, Vincent 13, 21, 69
Foster, Al 77
Fowlkes, Curtis 103
Francis, Carlos 14, 15
Franco, Guilherme 86, 104
Franklin, Henry 194
Freeport, New York 38
Fuego en Mi Alma (Fire in My Soul) (album by Carlos Garnett) 133
Fuller, Curtin 51
"The Future Is Ours" (song by Carlos Garnett) 66

Gaithers, New York 45
Gale, Eric 49
Gamboa, Panama Canal Zone 12, 15
Gardner, Derrick 150
Garvey, Marcus 155
Gary Bartz NTU Troop 72
The Gay Crooners 14, 69, 183
Gaye, Marvin 33, 100
Gentle Benjamin 152
George, Roderick 43
Get Up with It (album by Miles Davis) 82
Ghetto Child (album by Charley Anderson) 163
"Ghetto Jungle" (song by Carlos Garnett) 96
"Giant Steps" (song by John Coltrane) 132, 150, 197
The Gig, New York 45
Gillespie, Dizzy 158
Gittens, Leroy 16

gold roll 8
Golden Gate Club, Panama City, Panama 16
The Golden Key, Panama City, Panama 16
Golomidova, Maria 177
Golson, Benny 59
Gonzalez, Jerry 173
Gooding, Cuba, Sr. 99
Gordon, Gladstone "Bat" 24
Grand Hotel, Kingston Jamaica 146
Grecha Record Label 20, 21
Green, Bunky 52, 127
Greene, Cyril 103
Grillo, Frank "Machito" 106
Gumbs, Onaje Allan 86, 148
Gunn, Russell 141, 142
Gutierrez, Graciela Perez 107

Hancock, Herbie 78, 83
"Hang 'Em Up" (song by Carlos Garnett) 49
"Happy Children Song" (song by Carlos Garnett) 142
The Happy Landing, New York 45
Hardman, Bill 55
Harlem, New York 27, 52, 75
Harley, Rufus 72
Hart, Billy 70, 76, 86
Hayes, Gerald 37, 46
Hayes, Louis 46
Haynes, Roy 55
Henderson, Eddie 78, 83
Henderson, Joe 19, 48, 72
Henderson, Michael "Mike" 77, 81
Herrera, Guillermo 153, 154
Heyward, Jimmy 29, 37
Hicks, Al 37, 129, 130
Hicks, George 37, 44
High Note Records 133, 138, 150
Hill, Andrew 53–55, 132, 195, 196
Hino, Motohiko 56, 110
Hino, Terumasa 56, 109
HOG Radio Station, Panama City, Panama 20
Holmes, Carlton 130, 131, 133, 140, 142, 172, 174
Holt, Scotty 51
Houston International Jazz Festival 151, 165
Howard, Mike 148
Hubbard, Freddie 35, 42, 46, 88, 115, 141, 155, 156

206

Index

"I Want to Talk About You" (song by Billy Eckstine) 66
Icaza, Chale 179, 185
"I'll Do Anything for You" (song by Denroy Morgan; uncredited composer Carlos Garnett) 123
The Imperials 100
"Impressions" (song by John Coltrane) 144
Impulse Records 70
In Concert (album by Miles Davis) 79, 80, 82
Inntone Jazz Festival 173
Inoue, Yosuke 147, 149
Irish Jazz Resort, Houston Texas 151
"It's Summertime" (song by Carlos Garnett) 123

Jackson, Anthony 93, 95
James, Stafford 65
James, Wendell "Papito" 142
Jami, Hakim 37, 65, 130
Jarrett, Keith 77
Jarvis, Earl 17
Jarvis, Raul 17
Jazz Crusaders 151
The Jazz Messengers '70 (album by Art Blakey and the Jazz Messengers) 60
The Jazz Passengers 150
Jenkins, Cora 66, 86
Jenkins, Evelyn "Ayodele" 61, 86, 93, 95, 101, 109
Jimenez, Giulio 163, 192, 201
Joe Franklin TV Show 114
Johnny and the Hot Rods 19
Johnny B, Panama City, Panama 185, 189
Johnson, Gus 34
Johnson, Reggie 14, 17
Jones, Brad 129, 130, 131, 133, 142, 150, 172–174
Jones, Elvin 65, 130, 147, 157
Jones, Etta 57
Jordan, Carlos 65, 66, 96
Jordan, Clifford 55
Jordan, Louis 10, 167
Journey to Enlightenment (album by Carlos Garnett) 92–97, 135
The Jungle Rat 99

"Kafira" (song by Carlos Garnett) 104
Kalyan 100, 112
Karashima, Fumio 136, 147, 157
Katy, Texas 150

The Kay Gees 100
Keane, Damani 178
Keane, Ife 178
The Keg, New York 45
Kemah Boardwalk Jazz Festival 151
Kenny G 138
Kenyatta, Robin 85
The Keyboard, Toyota Japan 149
King, Howard 94
King, Martin Luther 46, 62
The Kingston Lounge, New York 45, 131
Kirkland, Kenny 101, 103
Knitting Factory, New York 70
Kool & the Gang 100
Kullhammer, Jonas 153, 165, 168

La Boca, Panama Canal Zone 11, 22
La Magnolia, Panama City, Panama 169, 189
"La Primera Vez Que te Vi" (song by Carlos Garnett) 137
"Last Day of Carnival" (song by Black Majesty) 20
The Last Poets 72
Lateef, Yusef 62
The Latin Jazztet 151
Laurence, Trevor 34
Lawrence, Hugh 162, 188
Lawrence, Jeff 129
Lawson, Cedric 77, 79
Leacock, Cecil 15
Lee, John 109
Left Bank Jazz Society, Maryland 62, 74
Legends of Tambo Jazz (album by Carlos Garnett and Victor Boa) 154, 161
Lennon, John 77
Lesesne, Harvey 99, 100
Let This Melody Ring On (album by Carlos Garnett) 95–100, 175
"Let This Melody Ring On" (song by Carlos Garnett) 95
"Let Us Go (Into Higher Heights)" (song by Carlos Garnett) 92
Lewis, Tiger 151
Liebman, Dave 81
Lift Every Voice (album by Andrew Hill) 53, 195
Lightsey, Kirk 173
Lincoln Center, New York 79; *see also* Philharmonic Hall
Lincoln Terrace, New York 61
Lincoln University 74
Linz, Austria 173

Index

"Little Dear" (song by Carlos Garnett) 110
"Little Sunflower" (song by Freddie Hubbard) 134, 141
Live at the East (album by Pharoah Sanders) 69
Live! on Soul 55
Lodge Hall, Brooklyn, New York 155
Lopez, Wichy 154, 159, 165
Lord Byron 16
Lord Cobra 22, 152
Lord Delicious 22
Lord Kitty 152
Lord Kontiki 22
Lord Panama 22; *see also* Allen, George
Lord Wymba 22
Los Nietos del Jazz 201
Lovano, Joe 171
"Love Flower" (song by Carlos Garnett) 93
Love from the Sun (album by Norman Connors) 83, 99
"Love Thy Neighbor" (song by Carlos Garnett) 134
Love Warmth and Affection Band 65
"Lover Man" (song by Davis, Ramirez & Sherman) 49, 50, 144
Lucas, Reggie 66, 77, 81, 86, 93, 95
Lucas, Stan 99

Mabern, Harold 59, 63
Macero, Teo 76, 77
Macias, Chachi 17, 107
"Mahogany" (song by Andrew Hill) 55, 195
"Maiden Voyage" (song by Herbie Hancock) 133, 197
The Main Ingredient 99
"Manha de Carnaval" (song by Luis Bonfa) 150
Mariette, Roberto 26
Mario Bauza's Afro Cuban Jazz Orchestra 106
Marsalis, Ellis 171
Martin, Mike 44
Marvelous Marv 52
Masekela, Hugh 53
Massey, Zane 103
McBee, Cecil 63, 70, 101
McBee, Cecil, Jr. 101, 103
McCartney, Torrie 148, 151
McCleary, Albert 16
McCleary, Otis "Junior" 109

"McCoy Next Block" (song by Shingo Okudaira) 150
McDonald, Ralph 85
McDuff, Jack 68
McFarland & Company, Inc., Publishers 199
McKindo, "Rubber Legs" 24
McLaughlin, John 76
McPherson, Charles 60
Medgar Evers College 172
"Meet Me at the Parkway" (song by Carlos Garnett) 137
"Memories of Coltrane" (song by Carlos Garnett) 111
Mighty Sparrow 151, 152
Mingus, Charles 60, 76, 115, 122, 142, 156
Ministry of Culture of Panama 199
Minot Sound Studios, New York 94, 95
Miraflores Locks, Panama City, Panama 6
"Miriam" (song by Black Majesty) 20
"Mr. G" (song by Carlos Garnett) 191
Misty (song by Erroll Garner) 66
Mitchel, Blue 48
Mitchell, George 150
Mito Art Hall, Japan 136
Mixon, Daniel 37, 41
"Mon Cherie" (song by Black Majesty) 20
Mona 86
Monday, Paul 31
Monk Club, Matsuyama, Japan 149
"Monkash" (song by Andrew Hill) 55
Montego Bay, Jamaica 145
Montego Joe 151, 152
Moody, James 10, 167
Moon Shadow (album by Carlos Garnett) 149
"Moon Shadow" (song by Carlos Garnett) 150
Morant, Claude "Black Majesty" 19, 69, 93, 198
Moreira, Airto 78
Morgan, Denroy 113, 117, 118, 123–125, 127
Morgan, Lee 48, 122
"Mother of the Future" (song by Carlos Garnett) 66, 86, 99, 175, 177
Mouzon, Alphonse 109, 110
Mtume, James 73, 74, 76, 77, 86
Musa, Mateo 183
Muse Records 84, 91, 94, 96, 98–99, 109, 112, 138, 189, 190

208

Index

"My Commanding Wife" (song by Oscar Reid) 16
"My One and Only Love" (song by Guy Wood and Robert Mellin) 141
Mystery of Ages (Carlos Garnett compilation album) 189
"Mystery of Ages" (song by Carlos Garnett) 103, 104, 177
"Mystic Moon" (song by Carlos Garnett) 134

Nakamoto, Mari 136
Nakamura Hotel, Japan 56
Nassau County, New York 38
Navarro, Aquiles 174, 175, 178, 184, 196, 201
Navarro, Juan Carlos 157, 159
Neil, Steve 131, 132, 139
New England Conservatory of Music 51, 159
The New Love (album by Carlos Garnett) 109–114, 127
The New World Club, New York 53
Newport Jazz Festival 51
"No Time to Lose" (song by Carlos Garnett) 49
Nueva Alegria Big Band 16, 17, 107
Nueva Gloria, Panama City, Panama 17
Nugent, Dino 154, 165

Obin, Angie 178
O'Farrill, Arturo 172
Okino, Shuya 175, 176
Okudaira, Shingo 131, 132, 133, 135, 147, 157, 176, 196
On the Corner (album by Miles Davis) 76, 79, 82, 85
"Organyk Groove" (song by Carlos Garnett) 138
Ortiz, Jaime "Jota" 21, 113, 157, 177, 180, 191, 192–201
Ortiz, Miguel 192
Over Jazz Club, New York 45

Palo Alto, California 80
The Paltia, Niigata, Japan 136
Pan-African Cultural and Jazz Festival 148, 151
The Panama Big Band 156
Panama Canal Company 5, 186
Panama Canal Zone 1, 2, 5, 7, 8, 11, 12, 15, 17, 19, 22, 26, 69, 150, 157
Panama Jazz All Stars 160

Panama Jazz Festival 155–159, 171–174, 178, 187
"Panama La Patria Mia" (song by Carlos Garnett) 137
Panama Red 64
"Panama Roots" (song by Carlos Garnett) 96
"Panamoon" (song by Carlos Garnett) 133
Paraíso, Panama Canal Zone 5, 8, 96, 138, 150, 160, 162, 169
Parker, Charlie "Bird" 36, 111
Parque Omar, Panama City, Panama 96, 189
Patton, John 138
Paul's Mall, Boston 79
Payne, Alfredo 23, 137
Paz, Vitin 107, 158
Pearce, Jerry 24
Pearce, Terry 24
Pedro Miguel locks, Panama City, Panama 6
peppermint bush 31
Perez, Danilo 24, 155, 156, 160, 165, 171–174, 179
Perez, Gilberto 10, 11
Perez, Luis Carlos 159
Philharmonic Hall, New York 79; see also Lincoln Center
Pinzon, Ricardo "Rickypin" 189, 190
The Pitt Inn, Japan 136, 147
Platea, Panama City, Panama 165; see also Take Five Bar
Plug and Play, Panama City, Panama 186
Polar Music Prize 165
"Pony" (song by Black Majesty) 20
Portuondo, Omara 174
Poughkeepsie, New York 30
Prema 95, 96
Prescott, Roy 19
Price, Leo 32, 39, 70
Price, Lloyd 32
Prince 100
The Professional Arranger Composer (book by Russell Garcia) 101
Professor Bright 24
Prospect Park, New York 102, 108, 119, 122, 129, 131
Proverb, Everet 183
Proverbs, Violet 15, 183
PTY Studios, Panama City, Panama 178
Pulliam, Charles 66, 74, 84, 94, 95, 135, 172
Purdie, Bernard 49, 138

Index

Queens, New York 67
Quiros, Carlos 179, 184, 189, 190

Rag, Kyoto, Japan 136
Rainbow City, Panama Canal Zone 12
Rancho Grande, Panama City, Panama 65
Ranelin, Phil 172
Ranglin, Ernest 144
The Red Barn, Texas 151
Red Cat Jazz Café, Houston, Texas 151
Red Tank, Panama Canal Zone 6
Reich, Steve 168
Reid, Bert 123
Reid, Oscar 16
Resurgence (album by Carlos Garnett) 130–133, 141
Riba Smith Studios, Panama City, Panama 154
Rice University 151
Rich, Ellis 189
Richards, Ricardo 154, 161
Richmond, Danny 60
Ridley, Larry 35
Ridley, Mike 34, 40, 43
Riis Beach, Brooklyn, New York 96
Rio Abajo, Panama City, Panama 65, 164
Rivera, Ismael 23
Roach, Max 87
Robinson, Justin 147
Rollins, Sonny 69, 105, 165, 166–168
Rosicrucianism 92
Ross, Raymond 63, 84
Roy, Badal 77
Ruggles, Houston, Texas 151
Rutgers University 74

Sabeb Lounge, Colón City, Panama 16
Sakurai, Ikuo 136
Salam, Abdul 127
"Salsa Blue" (song by Carlos Garnett) 150
Salvation Army 182–184
Sam Ash 77
Sam Rivers Trio 87
"Samba Serenade" (song by Carlos Garnett) 95, 177
Sample, Joe 151
San Diego, California 81
San Miguel, Panama City, Panama 17
Sanchez, David 160
Sanders, Pharoah 69, 139, 155
Saturday Night Special, Norman Connors 98–99

Savant Records 138, 150
Savoy Lounge, Philadelphia 47
Saxton, Bill 130
"Saxy" (song by Carlos Garnett) 103, 192
Scantlebury, Milton 193, 201
Scott, Bill 30
Scott, Shirley 18
Segue, Bembe 176
Selective Service Board 27
The Selecter 162
"Senor Coltrane" (song by Carlos Garnett) 177
"Shalome" (song by Carlos Garnett) 134
Shaw, Woody 47, 53, 62, 122
Shekinah's Smile (album by Carlos Garnett) 178
"Shekinah's Smile" (song by Carlos Garnett) 178
Shina, Yutaka 149
Shorter, Wayne 156
Silver, Horace 62
Silvester, Tony "Champagne" 99–100, 112
Singh, Antonio 161
Sir Jablonski 22
Sistas' Place, New York 129
The Skatalites 113
Skimba 186
Slammin' & Jammin' (album by Charles Earland) 138
Slewfoot (album by Norman Connors) 99
Slonimsky, Nicholas 36
Slugs, New York 48
Smith, Mauricio 24, 85, 137, 155, 160
Snipes, Wesley 173
"Softly as in the Morning Sunrise" (song by Hammerstein & Romberg) 66
"Song in my Head" (song by Carlos Garnett) 133
Sorolo 23, 129
Soul Brother Records 189
A Soul Experiment (album by Freddie Hubbard) 49
Sparks, Melvin 138
Spectrum, Philadelphia 79
Sproles, Victor 55
Stanford University 80
Stanley Wright 41; *see also* Suleiman-Marim Wright
Station Bar, Colón City, Panama 18
Stern, Mike 156
Stitt, Sonny 18, 52
Stone, Sly 51

Index

Stoute, Ed 37
Stowe, James 103
Strata-East Records 73
Strickland, Marcus 168
Strickland Lumber Company 145
Suleiman-Marim Wright 173; *see also* Stanley Wright
Sullivan, Charles 84, 85, 86
Sun Ra 55
Supreme Songs 189
Supro Music Store, Panama City, Panama 190
Swing Papa 22
Sylvester, Jorge 160
Systems Two Studios, New York 147

Take Five Bar, Panama City, Panama 165; *see also* Platea
"Take the Coltrane" (song by Carlos Garnett) 10, 133
Tambo Jazz 154, 160
Tamborito 154
"Taurus Woman" (song by Carlos Garnett) 60, 63, 85
Teatro Amador, Panama City, Panama 184
Teatro Balboa, Panama City, Panama 157, 199
Teatro Rio Abajo, Panama City, Panama 16
Tedesco Recording Studio, New Jersey 141
"Terra Nova" (song by Robin Kenyatta) 85
Texas International Jazz Festival 151
The Thesaurus of Scales and Melodic Patterns (book by Nicolas Slonimsky) 36
The Third World 124
Thomas, Leon 70
Thoms, Renato 160
Thorne, Chico 17
Tijuana, Mexico 81
Timana 109
Tokyo, Japan 56, 176, 177, 178
Tokyo Cross Over Festival 175, 176
Tolliver, Charles 172
Top Flight Records 124
Torrijos, Martin 160
Toussaint, Johnny 29
Toussaint, Mari 147
Tropelco Record Label 20
Tropical Club, Colón City, Panama 18
Trowers, Robert 150
Turner, Jim "Slow" 16

Turre, Steve 70, 155
Turrentine, Stanley 18, 103
Turrentine, Tommy 60
Two Gun Smokey 22

Ubarte, Carlos 165
"Uncle Ben and Aunt Jemima" (song by Carlos Garnett) 111
Under Nubian Skies (album by Carlos Garnett) 141
Universal Black Force "UBF" 46, 62, 65, 66, 67, 70, 71, 73, 74, 81, 85, 87–92, 135, 159, 163, 197
University of Houston 151
The Up, New York 45
"URD14ME" (song by Carlos Garnett) 134

Valdes, Chucho 174
Van Gelder, Rudy 55, 132, 137, 138, 195
Van Gelder Studio, New York 55, 132, 137, 138
Victor One Studio, Tokyo 59
Vietnam War 86
Village Gate, New York 60, 66, 122, 163
The Village Vanguard, New York 48

Waits, Freddie 53–55
Walker, Junior 16
Walker, Newton, Jr. 16
Ward, Carlos 67, 194
Ward, Milt 112
Ware, Bill 129
The Warehouse Disco 106
Warfield, Jerry 111
Warwell, Ron 41, 65, 67, 72, 82, 87–93, 96, 98, 101, 105, 111, 112, 125, 129, 130, 133, 138, 189, 197
Washington, Andrew 103
W.E.B. Du Bois Cultural Center, Ghana 148
Webb, Art 78, 83
Wee Rockin' Willie and His Band 29
Weeks, Ralph 65, 137, 196
West Indians 5, 8
West 77th Street, New York 75
Weston, Randy 159, 160
Weusi, Jitu 70, 148
"What" (song by Carlos Garnett) 142
"What the World Needs Now Is Peace and Love" (song by Carlos Garnett) 59
White, Gene 24
White, Russell 65

Index

"Who's Gonna Love Me" (song by The Imperials) 100
Wilkins, Felix 45, 137
Williams, Buster 73, 86
Williams, Richard Rafique 28
Wilson, Alonso 24
Wilson, Barbara 157, 158
Wilson, Jackie 33
Wilson, Marcos 24
Windsor Lounge (Club W), Panama City, Panama 20
"Wise Old Man" (song by Carlos Garnett) 103
Wonsey, Anthony 129, 138
Workman, Reggie 129
Wright, N'Bushe 173

The Young Black Poets 89
The Young Bloods 89
Yusef, Lumumba 89

Zaggy 24
Zappa, Frank 51
Zauner, Paul 173
Zawadi, Kiane 37, 65, 97
Zimmerman, Jordan 190, 193

www.ingramcontent.com/pod-product-compliance
Lightning Source LLC
Chambersburg PA
CBHW032042300426
44117CB00009B/1164